ETHNOGRAPHIC PRACTICE IN THE PRESENT

EASA Series
Published in Association with the European Association of Social Anthropologists (EASA)
Series Editor: **James G. Carrier**, Senior Research Associate, Oxford Brookes University

Social anthropology in Europe is growing, and the variety of work being done is expanding. This series is intended to present the best of the work produced by members of the EASA, both in monographs and in edited collections. The studies in this series describe societies, processes, and institutions around the world and are intended for both scholarly and student readership.

ETHNOGRAPHIC PRACTICE IN THE PRESENT

Edited by

Marit Melhuus, Jon P. Mitchell
and Helena Wulff

Berghahn Books
New York • Oxford

Published in 2010 by
Berghahn Books
www.berghahnbooks.com

©2010, 2012 Marit Melhuus, Jon P. Mitchell and Helena Wulff
First paperback edition published in 2012

Library of Congress Cataloging-in-Publication Data
Ethnographic practice in the present / edited by Marit Melhuus, Jon P. Mitchell
 and Helena Wulff.
   p. cm. -- (EASA series)
Includes bibliographical references and index.
ISBN 978-1-84545-616-0 (hbk) -- ISBN 978-0-85745-159-0 (pbk)
1. Ethnology--Research. 2. Ethnology--Authorship. 3. Ethnology--Fieldwork. I.
 Melhuus, Marit. II. Mitchell, Jon P. III. Wulff, Helena.
GN345.E64 2010
305.80072--dc22
                              2009045265

British Library Cataloguing in Publication Data
A catalogue record for this book is available from the British Library.

Printed in the United States on acid-free paper

ISBN 978-0-85745-159-0 (paperback)
ISBN 978-0-85745-452-2 (ebook)

*This book is dedicated
to the memory of Eduardo Archetti*

Contents

Acknowledgements

The Introduction is an amended and expanded version of a chapter written for *The Sage Handbook of Social Science Methodology*. A full reference is included here, and I am grateful for their grant of copyright to use this material:

Mitchell, J.P. 2007. 'Ethnography', in W. Outhwaite and S.P. Turner (eds), *The Sage Handbook of Social Science Methodology*. London: Sage, pp. 55–66.

Chapter 1, 'Ethnography and Memory', is an amended version of a chapter written by Johannes Fabian for his book *Memory Against Culture* (Duke University Press, 2007) We are grateful to Duke University Press for their grant of copyright to use this material here.

List of Contributors

Cristiana Bastos is Associate Professor of Anthropology at the Institute of Social Sciences, University of Lisbon.

Simon Coleman is Professor of Anthropology at the University of Sussex.

Alexei Elfimov is Professor of Anthropology at the Institute of Ethnology and Anthropology, Russian Academy of Science, Moscow.

Johannes Fabian is Professor of Anthropology at the University of Amsterdam.

Christina Garsten is Professor of Social Anthropology at the University of Stockholm.

Dimitra Gefou-Madianou is Professor of Social Anthropology at Panteion University, Athens.

Douglas R. Holmes is Professor of Anthropology at the State University of New York, Binghamton.

Sharon Macdonald is Professor of Social Anthropology at the University of Manchester.

George E. Marcus is Professor of Anthropology at the University of Californa, Irvine. Before 2005, he was longtime chair of the Department of Anthropology at Rice University.

Marit Melhuus is Professor of Social Anthropology at the University of Oslo.

Jon P. Mitchell is Reader in Anthropology at the University of Sussex.

Judith Okely is Emeritus Professor, University of Hull and Deputy Director, IGS, Queen Elizabeth House, Oxford University.

Ute Röschenthaler is Research Fellow in the Cluster of Excellence 'The Formation of Normatice Orders' at the Goethe University, Frankfurt am Main.

Aud Talle is Professor of Social Anthropology at the University of Oslo.

Thomas Widlok is Professor of Anthropology at the University of Nijmegen.

Helena Wulff is Professor of Social Anthropology at the University of Stockholm.

Introduction

Jon P. Mitchell

Origins

This volume brings together the results of two workshops held at the eighth biennial conference of the European Association of Social Anthropologists (EASA), in Vienna 2004.[1] Each sought to assess the position of 'ethnography' within the discipline of sociocultural anthropology, focusing less on the well-developed critique of anthropology 'as a kind of writing' (Spencer 1986) than on the methodological implications of ethnographic practice in fieldwork. Ethnographic fieldwork is often hailed as the distinguishing feature of anthropology as a discipline, and anthropologists defend it as a method that generates theoretical insights that could not have been generated in any other way. However, in recent years, the 'classic' tradition of ethnographic fieldwork has been questioned. As the grounds of social life are shifting, so is ethnographic practice, provoking more mobile and multi-locale fieldwork with more flexible forms of methodological pluralism (Wulff 2002, 2008; Lien and Melhuus 2007; Mitchell 2007). Simultaneously, 'ethnography' has become increasingly popular outside anthropology, across the social and human sciences, as a term to describe relatively long-term qualitative research. This methodological exportation and modification led us to reflect on the current 'state of play' within ethnographic practice – what is 'ethnographic practice in the present'?

The chapters that make up this volume are written by scholars representing sociocultural anthropology in a broad sense – from a range of different European and North American traditions. They deal with contemporary ethnography in a variety of interdisciplinary contexts – anthropology with history, linguistics, psychoanalysis, ethnology – and 'mobile' fields – corporate social responsibility, transnational refugees, trans-regional 'associations', AIDS responses, international airports. Authors reflect on the ethics of the 'new' ethnography, on the role of memory in 'retrospective' or 'post-fieldwork fieldwork' (Cohen 1992), on the practical challenges of mobility to a discipline classically premised on stasis.

History

'Ethnography', of course, means, literally, 'writing people' and is therefore rooted in the notion of description – of a particular society, culture, group or social context: 'The most common conception of the descriptive character of ethnographic accounts is that they map the morphology of some area of the social world.' (Hammersley 1992: 23). This description is, for Hammersley, based on three central features: induction; context; unfamiliarity (ibid.: 22–23). The inductive process within ethnographic work sees general statements about human society and culture – what one might call 'theory' – emerging out of the description of particular events. Ethnography is for this reason – explicitly or implicitly – wedded to the notion of the case study, which describes in detail a particular event or series of events, to derive from it broader inferences about social process or the human condition (Gluckman 1940). A major part of the legitimacy for this inductive process is careful attention within ethnographic work to the context of events. Events seen out of context might be misunderstood, it is assumed. Indeed, so central is context that it is not merely a precondition for the development of general theory out of particular events; rather, context well described is the development of theory: 'description *is* explanation' (Hammersley 1992: 23; see also Dilley 1999; Melhuus 2002). The description of events in context is particularly poignant – indeed necessary – when dealing with situations unfamiliar to the general readership. Such work allows us to see the world from 'the native's point of view' (Malinowski 1922: 25), to better understand the motivation and meaning of social action.

The methodology that has developed alongside – and to deliver – these descriptive goals is what Clammer (1984) has called the 'fieldwork concept'. This involves a long-term period of social immersion in a particular setting, from which is generated the totalising and holistic descriptive account – the 'ethnography of' the group being researched. Within this fieldwork, the dominant method is 'participant observation', although, like 'ethnography', this label is used to gloss over the variety of methods actually used by ethnographers – from simple observation, to the collection of stories/ life histories, interviewing, household surveys, archival research, and so on. Indeed, in practice, ethnographers tend to let context drive not only their descriptions but also their research questions and methodological practice.

According to legend, this 'method' was invented by Bronislaw Malinowski. A Polish ex-patriate at the London School of Economics, he was researching in Australia in 1914 when war broke out. As a Pole, he was technically an enemy citizen, but, rather than being incarcerated, was allowed to spend the war years in the Trobriand Islands conducting first-hand empirical fieldwork among the people of the islands, and through that developing the classical method of ethnographic fieldwork.

From his work in the Trobriands, Malinowski produced a number of influential monographs that were the first works of anthropology to emerge from the long-term personal engagement of a scholar with the people being studied. Until then, anthropology had been a synthetic discipline, generating general theories of human-kind based on the relatively thin and certainly partial evidence of missionaries, travellers and colonial officials. This 'armchair' anthropology was mainly geared towards the *post hoc* justification – 'proving' – of existing theories of human social evolution, which placed different societies on a hierarchical axis of development, from the 'primitive' societies of aboriginal groups to the 'civilised' nation states of Enlightenment Europe.

Malinowski's ethnographic method – and with it his Functional school of anthropology – emerged as a critique of this evolutionary perspective. It offered a humanistic redemption of peoples previously condemned as 'primitive', and an empirical method for explaining the inherent logic of their apparently backward social practices. At the heart of this was a focus on social function – which democratised social analysis by demonstrating that even the most apparently irrational activities nevertheless 'make sense' from a functional point of view. The demonstration of function was dependent on an approach to holism that the new field methodology enabled, and an attention to context.

Malinowski railed against the often implicit but sometimes explicit racism of nineteenth-century evolutionism. In his account of the Trobriand economy, for example, in *Argonauts of the Western Pacific* (1922), Malinowski set out to critique the prevalent argument that the backwardness of 'primitive society' was the consequence of a lack of organised and passionate striving for economic gain. What he showed, in his account of *kula,* was that Trobrianders were every bit as rigorous and devoted as the most go-getting entrepreneur, in the planning and execution of *kula* exchanges: 'After reading *Argonauts,* some commentators might impugn Trobrianders for putting their faith in bangles, but they could not fault them on their work ethic to get those bangles. A tacit criticism was that natives would labour for themselves, not their colonizers' (Reyna 2001: 17).

His relativising argument about economy struck directly at the staged evolutionary model. The key components of Malinowski's approach were the pursuit of context – that sociocultural phenomena, no matter how apparently backward, strange or irrational, could be explained if seen from within their own context – of function, and of the social whole. Holism was permitted by the new methodological discipline of ethnographic fieldwork, which enabled the anthropologist to view different aspects of social life in relation to one another, and as they operated in practice: 'the so-called functional method in modern anthropology consists in the parallel study of mutually dependent phenomena or aspects of tribal life. The functional principle teaches that if you want to understand magic, you must go outside magic, and study economic ritual within the context of those practical activities in which it is really embedded' (Malinowski 1922: 324).

The focus on practice heralded a new empiricism that favoured an inductive process in which theoretical models and classificatory schemas were derived from direct, on-the-ground observations rather than preordained evolutionary models: 'The most important thing for the student … is never to forget the living, palpitating flesh and blood organism of man which remains somewhere in the heart of every institution' (Malinowski 1934: xxxi).

This 'bedrock reality' (Stocking 1984: 174) was met during ethnographic fieldwork, which involved three interlocking techniques (Young 1979: 8–9): first, 'the statistical documentation of concrete evidence' (Malinowski 1922: 24) to generate an overall picture of the culture or society as a whole; through spatial mapping, drawing up genealogies and consulting censuses, documenting legal and normative frameworks, etc; Secondly, documenting 'the imponderabilia of everyday life' (ibid.), to account for the ways in which the structural frameworks are inhabited; and thirdly, collecting a corpus of characteristic narratives, common phrases and sayings, folk tales and mythologies, seen as 'documents of native mentality' (ibid.) with which to build up a picture of life as seen through the eyes of the 'native'.

Reflections

What emerged from this was less a methodology than a set of guidelines for ethnographic practice. The generation of ethnographers that followed Malinowski were given little in the way of practical guidance, and what they were told was famously obtuse. As an eager pre-fieldwork graduate student in the 1920s, Evans-Pritchard was famously told little more than 'take ten grams of quinine every night and keep off the women', before embarking on fieldwork in Sudan. Malinowski himself told him 'not to be a bloody fool' (Eriksen 1995: 16).

By the 1960s, however, there was a recognition that ethnographers should be rather more explicit about what happens during fieldwork, partly to instruct neophyte ethnographers, and partly in acknowledgement of the place of the ethnographer themselves in the constitution of ethnographic knowledge. Evans-Pritchard himself had written in 1950 that anthropology – and the work of the ethnographer – should be seen as an active process of knowledge construction, more akin to the construction of historical narrative than to the more impassive or neutral 'discovery' of facts:

> we have ... to observe what the anthropologist does. He goes to live for some months or years among a primitive people. He lives among them as intimately as he can, and learns to speak their language, to think in their concepts and to feel in their values. He then lives the experiences over again critically and interpretatively in the conceptual categories and values of his own culture and in terms of the general body of knowledge of his discipline. In other words, he translates from one culture into another. At this level social anthropology remains a literary and impressionistic art. (Evans-Pritchard 1962: 22)

These remarks prefigured the post-Geertzian emphasis on anthropological representation, but also signalled a new concern to reflect upon the contexts of ethnographic practice. The 1967 publication of Malinowski's personal fieldwork diary provoked much soul-searching within anthropological circles about the realities of ethnographic practice. It raised questions about the true nature of 'participant observation' and the levels of rapport Malinowski was able to develop with local Trobrianders, revealing his sexual fantasies about and apparently pejorative attitude towards the 'natives' with whom he was at such pains to empathise in his published work (see Rapport 1990). What became clear was that where Malinowski's predecessors had conducted anthropology from their armchairs, he moved it only to the veranda, from which he could survey local life from a comfortable distance (see Singer 1985).

It was in a reflective atmosphere, then, that the 1970 publication *Being an Anthropologist* (Spindler 1970) emerged, as a collection of essays on ethnographic fieldwork by contributors to the Holt, Rinehart and Winston series Case Studies in Cultural Anthropology. This series had been created to provide ethnographic case study material for anthropology students, but in a slightly different format from the usual ethnographic text. As Spindler, one of the editors of the series, explained, 'the term "case study" was originally selected rather than "ethnography" to avoid the connotations of formality and completeness usually evoked by the latter term' (1970: xiii). This signals an awareness of the literary conventions and structures that shaped the writing of ethnographic work – a theme that was to emerge more strongly in the 1980s.

More than anything, the contributions to *Being an Anthropologist* testify to the particularity of different pieces of ethnographic fieldwork. Each 'field' is different, presenting unique problems and challenges; and each 'fieldworker' is different, responding to those problems and challenges in different ways. Rather than a set methodological framework for identikit research, transferable from one context to another, the fieldwork concept describes a flexibility of approach and a willingness to respond to the constraints and possibilities of the field, rather than imposing a version of fieldwork upon it. The volume therefore demonstrates the range of activities that the 'fieldwork concept' includes.

Jeremy Boissevain conducted fieldwork in Malta from 1960 to 1961, which contributed to his ethnography of Maltese village politics (1965). His chapter for *Being an Anthropologist* (Boissevain 1970) traces the development of this fieldwork and the various methods it involved. His interest in politics at a time of political tension determined that direct questioning of informants was problematic (ibid.: 78). Like many ethnographers, the inquisitive Boissevain was assumed to be a spy by at least one intrigued informant (ibid.: 72). Participant observation was necessary both to establish rapport and to ensure invitations to key events in the village. He reports long hours of what he terms 'informant servicing' (ibid.: 71) to establish trust, and rounds of visits to church, coffee shop, and grocery store to catch up on village gossip. Boissevain was accompanied during fieldwork by his wife and young family, and emphasises that just as he saw his informants 'in the round' – in the variety of different social roles they adopted – so too they saw him in his various social roles. To this extent he was 'participating' in village life as much as 'observing' it, and much of that participation involved what one might term 'social learning' – learning and adopting local expectations of correct social behaviour in order both to 'fit in' and to better understand how those expectations operate. He describes what he calls a 'typical day' of participant observing:

Monday, September 19, 1960, started as usual. On the way to pick up the car I learned from Pietru that a number of Requiem Masses were to be held that day in memory of a nineteen-year-old boy electrocuted a year before in one of the quarries surrounding the village ... [later] I went first to the little bazar of Pietru's sister, where I spent forty-five minutes talking to Pietru's two sisters, his mother, and three customers who came to the shop. I then crossed the street to talk to a farmer, who had come to get a drink in Pietru's cousin's bar. We spent the best part of an hour discussing his farming problems and, of particular importance to me, his reactions to the discussion of the parish priest in church the day before about the financial situation of the Saint Rocco Confraternity … [I then] worked intensively with the parish priest on my household card system …

After lunch, I reviewed the household cards I had prepared with Dun Gorg in the morning, and wrote up the case histories and other information he had provided. (Much later I compared his data to the door-to-door census of my own, and found his to be amazingly accurate.) After my wife and daughter returned home at 3:45 I took the car to the garage to wash it. Carmelo Abela came home at about 4:30. After his tea he came and gave me a hand with the car. When he started to tell me how he had met his fiancée, I began to wax the car to have an excuse to stay with him. As soon as Carmelo left me for his fiancée, I returned home and wrote up the story of his courtship while the details were still fresh …

That evening at 8:00, I met Pietru accidentally in front of the parish priest's house. We decided to go for a walk outside the village to find some cool air. At about 9:00 we returned and sat in front of the school chatting. Pietru told me the story of his own courtship and the difficult time he had deciding to break his engagement. We also discussed at great length the evil eye; it had given him a fever the day before. At about 10:30 Pietru went home, and I stopped by his aunt's wine shop … I left after fifteen minutes. Although I intended to write up my notes fully, when I got home I found that I was too tired. I simply filled in my diary for the day and outlined the topics to write up the following day. I went to bed at about midnight. (ibid.: 75)

This lengthy excerpt gives a sense of the rhythm of fieldwork, and its dependence on chance encounters. It also demonstrates the extent to which many of the data gained during ethnographic fieldwork are determined by the concerns of the informants, rather than the researcher. The stories of courtship did not form part of Boissevain's initial (1965) ethnography, but did feature in subsequent work, which not only described courtship as an important aspect of village life (Boissevain 1969), but also contributed towards the development of a theory of social networks and connectedness (Boissevain 1974). Many of these chance snippets of ethnographic data are furnished by key informants – with whom the ethnographer establishes a particularly strong rapport. These are sometimes deliberately chosen, as official or unofficial research assistants, sometimes delivered to the ethnographer by a higher local authority – chief, administrator, priest – and sometimes self-selected, presenting themselves to the ethnographer in ways that are impossible to refuse.

Details of ethnography were recorded 'on the move' in a field notebook – sometimes in note form, and sometimes in more detail – and were later written up and indexed as field notes proper. During more formal interviews, he might have his notebook open, when a contemporary ethnographer might use a tape or digital recorder. He also recorded ethnographic data using photography – subsequently asking informants to explain what was going on in particular photographs, or to name those shown on a photograph (Boissevain 1970: 77). His system of keeping household record cards with key demographic information contributed to the collection of genealogies, and was supplemented by Boissevain's own survey. What emerged, as with all ethnographic projects, was a huge corpus of field notes – undigested or semi-digested 'data' – that fed into the production of his ethnographic texts.

Critique

It is against the backdrop of this 'classic' tradition of 'village ethnography' that this volume is written. The 1980s saw the emergence of interest in ethnography as a kind of writing, and a critique of the politics of ethnographic representation (see Marcus and Clifford 1986). This went alongside a critique of the notion of 'the field' as a location for ethnographic research (Gupta and Ferguson 1997; Marcus 1998; Amit 2000; Coleman and Collins 2006). The representation of cultures and societies as bounded, homogeneous and static units was bound up with the assumption that 'the field' was a particular kind of place: local, often isolated, spatially demarcated; a view that contributed to the other part of the 'fieldwork concept' – the 'village study'. Gupta and Ferguson argued that this notion of the field had been fetishised by ethnographers, both intellectually and institutionally (1997: 2–5), creating expectations about ethnographic fieldwork and ethnographic careers that reinforced the essentialist 'othering' of the cultures and societies ethnographers researched. They point towards the emergence of newer fields, which 'decenter and defetishize the concept of "the field"' (ibid: 5), incorporating a reflexive focus on 'own' rather than 'other' society, and breaking down the spatialised metaphor of the field.

The most influential argument in favour of a reconfigured 'field' is George Marcus's (1998) call for a 'multi-sited ethnography'. This ethnography 'moves out from the single sites and local situations of conventional ethnographic research designs to examine the circulation of cultural meanings, objects, and identities in diffuse time-space. This mode defines for itself an object of study that cannot be accounted for ethnographically by remaining focused on a single site of intensive investigation' (Marcus 1998: 79–80). Rather, it involves a more fragmented and comparative approach to examining varied instantiations of a particular phenomenon, brought together in unity by the creative constructivism of the ethnographer, who establishes links and commonalities, often through extended metaphor (ibid.: 89–90). In more practical terms, multi-sited ethnography involves following processes in motion, rather than units *in situ*. It also involves a reconsideration of the politics of ethnography, away from an investigation of 'subaltern' peoples, seen in the context of an exploitative world system, towards an investigation of the system itself. This is achieved through 'following' various processes in motion. Marcus thus suggests we 'follow the person' in pilgrimage, migration or even life-cycle; 'follow the thing' through commodity and exchange chains; 'follow the metaphor' as key concepts of contemporary life – 'immunity' (Martin 1994), 'performance' (Rapport 1997), 'participation' (Stirrat and Henkel 2001) – emerge and circulate in public culture; 'follow the plot, story or allegory' in mythology, popular history or social memory; 'follow the life or biography' of particular individual research subjects; or 'follow the conflict' as it links adversaries, combatants, observers and conciliators (Marcus 1998: 90–95).

With this more fragmented and plural approach to ethnography, the stock-in-trade of more 'traditional' ethnographic research – long-term ethnographic immersion by participant observation – is substituted by shorter-term research methods; interviews, focus groups, life histories etc. Marcus acknowledges the potential loss of quality of ethnography inherent in this move, but argues that the key feature of ethnographic work that is preserved in multi-sited fieldwork is that of 'translation' (ibid.: 84) of meaning from one culture to another. Indeed the key components of ethnography as outlined by Hammersley – induction, context and unfamiliarity – are – at least potentially – maintained in multi-sited fieldwork, but what disappears is the ambition of holism.

For Marcus, this is a virtue, as the older commitment to holism is revealed in contemporary critical ethnography to be a fiction (Marcus 1998: 33–34). However, it does raise questions about the distinctive character of ethnography in relation to other qualitative methodologies, and about the integrity of anthropology as a discipline that has come to define itself in terms of its ethnographic practice. It is these questions that the chapters of this volume address.

Chapters

Much contemporary ethnographic practice involves not a single period of fieldwork, which is then written up before moving on to another field, but much longer-term engagement with the same field – through repeated, often shorter, field trips and/ or periodic return to original field notes to reanalyse or reconsider key elements of the analysis. It is this latter process that Johannes Fabian addresses in the opening chapter, arguing that of all the human faculties it is memory that lies at the centre of ethnographic practice. During fieldwork we are often dependent on the memories of our informants, and certainly on our own, as the example of Boissevain demonstrates. Moreover, when we enter into the kind of 'post-fieldwork fieldwork' (Cohen 1992) that concerns Fabian, memory becomes increasingly significant. He raises questions about the status of field notes as independent 'data', suggesting that, without the ethnographer's memories within which they can be contextualised, they are meaningless. These contextualising memories might be semantic, but more commonly are more inchoate memories of emotion, music, smell, food etc. His is a manifesto, then, for an enduringly humanised ethnographic process, firmly located in the ethnographer themselves.

Judith Okely's focus is also memory, though, where Fabian draws inspiration from the humanities, broadly conceived, she explores the possibilities offered by Freudian psychoanalysis for understanding the ethnographic process. She focuses particularly on the concept of free association as a method whereby unconscious memories are drawn into the mind of the analysand as random ideas or images, and subsequently become ordered by the psychoanalyst, who observes hidden patterns and themes within them. This process of inchoate memory becoming ordered, she argues, is central to ethnographic practice. Not only does she cite the truism that ethnographers arrive in the field with their own autobiographical 'baggage', she also demonstrates the ways in which this can influence both the development of ethnographic practice in the field and its analysis in the office. She gives three examples from her own research that can be understood through free association – where biographical elements contributed to the orientation of the ethnography. Her fieldwork among Gypsies in England and in farming communities in Normandy were certainly influenced by her past, but it is her 'retrospective fieldwork', of a return to her English boarding school, that takes us most clearly back to the theme of memory. Here, Okely's engagement with the space of 'terror' in what she clearly regards as a repressive institution moves her to re-enact a lesson on the slave trade, which confirms the detached and disinterested attitude of empire. Memory is thereby mobilised not only in the analytical process, but also in the process of political critique.

If Okely is concerned with an interdisciplinary engagement between anthropology and psychoanalysis, Thomas Widlok explores the possibilities opened up for anthropology by new methods of linguistic documentation. He moves ethnography from the accounting for 'peoples' or 'cultures' to languages, focusing on the practice of compiling a linguistic 'corpus' – a compilation of linguistic data derived from as many 'sessions' as possible, which, although comprehensive, does not necessarily claim to be encyclopedic. The sessions are recorded and stored electronically, using contemporary digital technology to provide a searchable resource. Widlok highlights the implications of this model of data collection and storage for the ethnographic understanding of context. Although the contextualisation of social action is often regarded as the strength of ethnography, in practice contextualisation is frequently foreclosed, as ethnographers seek interpretation through the foregrounding of particular contexts over others. What the corpus permits is a multiplicity of modes of contextualisation for the linguistic practices that are being documented, enabling a plurality of contexts to endure as part and parcel of the ethnographic record.

Christina Garsten develops the notion of interface, or the metaphor of the crossroads in her reflections on ethnography in the field of corporate social responsibility (CSR). Placing the ethnographer, rather than the data themselves, at the centre of the network of analysis, she sees CSR as a lingua franca through which a distinctive community is produced, generating forms of social practice and forms of 'locality' – conferences, electronic message boards. That these localities are translocal raises questions for Garsten as to whether the extended intimacy and 'depth' offered by more traditional forms of ethnography are compromised by such research. Her answer comes in part from George Marcus and his conviction that the newer multi-sited ethnography obviates depth as it utilises the ethnographer's existing awareness of the contexts of social practice.

George Marcus himself offers further examples of the promise of multi-sited approaches to ethnographic fieldwork, as exemplified by the work of his research students, and particularly two who, like Garsten, examine the production of knowledge – of risk among South Korean fanciers, and of freedom of information in Poland. Also like Garsten, the research involved 'ethnography by appointment,'[2] with time taken up less by the kind of serendipitous 'hanging out' exemplified by the Boissevain example than in planning and arranging interviews, attending events and scouring the Internet. Marcus suggests a technique of 'nested dialogues' – involving repeated encounters between ethnographers and their subjects in both individual and collective contexts – to generate ethnographic depth, but also concedes that ethnographic projects of the variety conducted by his students should be seen as provisional rather than definitive. To this extent, he echoes Widlok's definition of the provisional linguistic corpus with its multiple contextualisations (achieved by Marcus through nested dialogues). He also repeats Fabian's and Okely's observations on the value of long-term engagement with particular ethnographic fields. Doctoral projects, he concludes, are a first stab at analysing processes that are broader and deeper than a single 'ethnography' can capture.

If the 'newer' ethnography generates methodological problems, it has also been affected by ethics and accountability, as discussed by Sharon Macdonald. She charts the rise of not only ethical guidelines within the discipline of sociocultural anthropology, but also research ethics committees – which are often university faculty-level institutions and modelled on the ethics committees of medical research. If ethics are defined this narrowly, Sharon Macdonald asks, what are the implications for ethnography? Do the regulations even work against ethical ethnography? Like those of Okely and Fabian, her chapter is based on 'retrospective fieldwork' – her recollections of the emergent research ethics framework at the University of Sheffield. She describes the position she adopted within the research ethics committee, partly acting as an advocate of ethnographic practice, inserting key phrases into the wording of the final policy that she hoped would enable more flexible and informal research methodologies to pass through the ethics governance process. She notes, however, that even with these concessions much relies on the way in which particular committees choose to interpret the policy, and that there is a danger that, as in various cases elsewhere, the move will be towards ever more stringent and restrictive implementation. One of the self-illustrating points that Macdonald's chapter also raises is its own status as research and ethical practice, in relation to both of which – like so much ethnography – it does not fit the narrow medical model of a predefined project involving prior informed consent.

Alexei Elfimov takes the debate about ethnography outside the confines of Anglo-American-influenced sociocultural anthropology to offer a different interdisciplinary engagement – between 'Western' and 'Soviet' anthropologies. He contrasts the 'glory years' of the former in the 1920s Malinowskian revolution with contemporaneous developments in the latter, arguing that, while Western ethnography emerged in a context of a highly individualised intellectual environment, Soviet ethnography was characterised by a 'polyphonic collectivism'. Rather than the work of the lone heroic fieldworker, ethnography involved larger teams conducting multiple interdisciplinary case studies, which combined social and physical anthropology, linguistics and psychology. What emerged for a moment was a multi-perspectival, multi-contextual documentation of a particular community that arguably resembles the linguistic corpus. Elfimov describes contemporary Russian anthropology in something of a methodological crisis and increasingly turning towards the 'Western', Malinowskian model of ethnographic practice. However, he suggests that it is perhaps the earlier Soviet model of multiple case studies that has a potential for new research designs suited to the conditions of contemporary society under globalisation.

Globalisation is at the centre of Aud Talle's chapter on female circumcision among Somali refugees in London. Rather than a more generalised description of the Somali refugee collectivity, Talle focuses on a particular woman, Sadiya, and the changes she has experienced as she moved from Somalia to London – loss of status, being defined as an immigrant 'other' and lack of local comprehension of the context and meaning of female circumcision. Following Hastrup (1995), Talle distinguishes an 'older' realist ethnography from a 'newer' reflexive mode, within which 'context' is seen as a property not of social relations viewed objectively but of the encounter between the ethnographer and her subject. In narrating not only Sadiya's story but also that of the relationship between Sadiya and herself, Talle is able to offer an account of the multifaceted and multidimensional contexts of female circumcision in exile.

Ute Röschenthaler returns us to questions of the past, focusing less on the methodological implications of memory – that of either ethnographer or ethnographic subject – than on the implications for ethnography of reconstructing the past. She examines the dissemination of 'associations' or secret societies across parts of Cameroon and Nigeria, taking an approach that is best characterised as translocal than multi-sited. She suggests that these associations, which are conceptual entities despite often being associated with a particular material culture, might legitimately be approached as material 'things' with a 'social life' (Appadurai 1986). Her approach saw her travelling throughout the region, taking oral accounts of the movements of the associations to piece together a reliable account of their dissemination. Here, again, we see ethnography striving for a multi-perspectival, multi-contextual account of a particular social process.

Like many anthropologists, Cristiana Bastos found herself catapulted into particular types of research through her engagement with not only a particular social group but also a particular social issue – in her case the AIDS pandemic in Brazil. She argues that, despite its apparent novelty, anthropologists have conducted multi-sited fieldwork since before the term was coined, and indeed that at the very centre of ethnography itself is the critical juxtaposition of 'the field' and 'home' that has built within it inherent multisitedness. Bastos describes herself gaining access to AIDS non-governmental organisation (NGO) circles in a manner similar to that of Garsten in the CSR world – through conferences, workshops, interviews etc. The ethnography placed her at the interface of local and global responses to AIDS, and enabled her to chart the emergence of a distinctively 'Brazilian' AIDS intervention, locally framed but interlinked with new transnational processes that involve India and Southern Africa, among other places.

Finally, Dimitra Gefou-Madianou returns us to the concept of free association and the significance of memory – both for the ethnographer and for her subjects. Again a reflection on long-term fieldwork association with a particular social group, Gefou-Madianou argues that mutual free association generates a relationship wherein the ethnographer becomes an empathetic identifier with the subject of research. The context is a social group – the Arvanites – who have been displaced by the building of the new Athens airport in advance of the 2004 Olympic Games. Where one would have expected a picture of a demoralised and disillusioned Arvanite community, Gefou-Madianou demonstrates how the airport has generated a new space of liberation, revealed through the ethnographic practice of mutual free association. She also shows how transformations of space and locale in the airport recast assumptions about the literal field of enquiry and demonstrates how these subversions alter the communicative space of ethnography.

Structure

The volume might be divided into two sections. The first five chapters – by Fabian, Okely, Widlok, Garsten and Marcus – deal with conceptualising ethnography: thinking through the process of ethnography as practice and assessing where newer forms of ethnography might take us. The last five chapters – by Elfimov, Talle, Röschenthaler, Bastos and Gefou-Madianou – deal more explicitly with the practice of ethnography in particular contexts. Thus, whilst the first half of the volume starts from more general, thematic and theoretical concerns, considering how they might be brought to bear on particular, practical contexts, the second half works the other way round – starting from particular examples of ethnographic practice and working outwards from that to the more theoretical level. As a pivot between these two complementary approaches lies the chapter by Macdonald, who considers the conditions of possibility of ethnographic practice in the present– in the context of audit culture and increased sensitivity to ethical procedures. The volume then closes with two short contributions – the first by Coleman, who presents a synthesising round-up of the themes that emerged in his reading of the chapters. This complements, but is inevitably different from, the thematic synthesis attempted in the final section of this introduction, and brings the volume full circle. The second, by Holmes and Marcus, reaches outwards from the volume towards a new conceptualisation of the relationship between ethnographers and their research interlocutors, and a new understanding of ethnographic practice.

Themes

A number of interlocking themes emerge from this collection, raising critical questions about the state of present ethnography and its position within contemporary anthropology. It is clear, for example, that ethnographic practice places anthropology on the fringes of the social sciences, or at least with important links to the humanities. Contributors advocate a method sensitive to the interpretive and intuitive, emphasising the importance of empathy – even friendship – with research subjects, which differs from the more detached and scientist approach of many other social science methodologies. This raises issues not only for research ethics – as Macdonald demonstrates – but also for the legitimacy of ethnography across the social sciences.

As a primarily interpretive practice, ethnography is also characterised in this volume by the provisionality of its results. To this end, a number of contributors emphasise the importance of multiple contexts. Indeed, both Widlok and Elfimov suggest models for enabling multiple contextualities to build themselves into the ethnographic process – through the linguistic corpus and Soviet multiple case studies. Rather than generating definitive statements about the nature of particular groups or processes, present ethnography's power seems to be to highlight multiple perspectives and contexts.

Multiple perspectives are also drawn from multiple field sites, and a number of contributors highlight the value and difficulties of multi-sited fieldwork. What they strive for is a means of generating, through this 'fieldwork by appointment', the same 'depth' that is claimed for more traditional fieldwork. Bastos, Garsten and Talle, in their different ways, argue that the ethnographer can succeed by placing herself at the intersection of a number of different processes – again generating multiple perspectives on a given issue. Marcus, on the other hand, and again citing provisionality, effectively argues that this depth is unattainable in a single ethnographic project, which should not be seen as an end in itself, but as a first step in the development of a broader thematic project.

To this extent, Marcus echoes what a number of other contributors emphasise: the importance of long-term, repeated, contact with a particular field – which can involve repeated trips to the same location or contact with the same research subjects; but might just as often involve 'post-fieldwork fieldwork', in which an ethnographer returns to her field notes to reconsider and reanalyse. This brings into focus the significance of memory and the past – either as a specific object of ethnographic enquiry – as with Röschenthaler – or as an inherent part of the ethnographic process, as emphasised by Fabian, Okely and Gefou-Madianou. Memory is also significant for Talle, whose shared memories with her Somali informants enable both the development of fieldwork rapport and an understanding of the broader context of her London research.

It is on the issue of context that I wish to conclude. If, for Hammersley (1992: 22–23), ethnography is rooted in induction, context and unfamiliarity, it is context that perhaps poses the biggest challenge for present ethnographic practice (see Dilley 1999, Melhuus 2002). If ethnography is to maintain its integrity, then its 'newer' manifestations must find new ways of generating context. In a sense, all the chapters we present in this volume have this key issue at their centre. Although there is little in the way of explicit and sustained discussion of 'context', it is nevertheless itself a context within which the volume can be read.

Clearly, ethnographic practice has evolved, and so has anthropologists' willingness to discuss ethnographic practice. This volume attempts to trace some of the contents, contexts and implications of present ethnography as practised within sociocultural anthropology. Maintaining one of the key messages from the volume – provisionality – we do not wish to present this collection as definitive. Neither do we wish to overdetermine an interpretation of its various themes. As shown in the contributions by Coleman and Holmes and Marcus, different readers will find different resonance and inspiration in the various contributions. Hence, the volume is to be read as a provisional statement about the 'state of play' within contemporary ethnographic practice.

Notes

1. The workshops were 'Ethnographic Practice in the Present', organised by Helena Wulff and George E. Marcus, and 'Ethnography: the costs of success?', organized by Marit Melhuus and Jon P. Mitchell.
2. A phrase coined by Inger Sjoerslev in her paper prepared for the workshop 'Ethnography: the Costs of Success?', one of the two workshops that led to the publication of this volume.

References

Amit, V. 2000. *Constructing the Field.* London: Routledge.

Appadurai, A. 1986. *The Social Life of Things: Commodities in Cultural Perspective.* Cambridge: Cambridge University Press.

Boissevain, J. 1965. *Saints and Fireworks.* London: Athlone.

———. 1969. *Hal-Farrug: a Village in Malta.* New York: Holt, Rinehart and Winston.

———. 1970. 'Fieldwork in Malta', in G.D. Spindler (ed.), *Being an Anthropologist.* New York: Holt, Rinehart and Winston, pp. 58–84.

———. 1974. *Friends of Friends: Networks, Manipulators and Coalitions.* Oxford: Blackwell.

Clammer, J. 1984. 'Approaches to Ethnographic Research', in R. Ellen (ed.), *Ethnographic Research.* London: Academic Press, pp. 63–85.

Cohen, A.P. 1992. 'Post-fieldwork Fieldwork', *Journal of Anthropological Research* 48 (4): 339–54.

Coleman, S. and P. Collins (eds). 2006. *Locating the Field: Space, Place and Context in Anthropology.* Oxford: Berg.

Dilley, R (ed.). 1999. *The Problem of Context.* Oxford: Berghahn.

Eriksen, T.H. 1995. *Small Places, Large Issues.* London: Pluto.

Evans-Pritchard, E.E. 1962. *Essays in Social Anthropology.* London: Faber.

Gluckman, M. 1940. 'Analysis of a Social Situation in Modern Zululand', *Bantu Studies* 14: 1–30.

Gupta, A. and J. Ferguson (eds). 1997. *Anthropological Locations.* Berkeley: University of California Press.

Hammersley, M. 1992. *What's Wrong with Ethnography?* London: Routledge.

Hastrup, K. 1995. *A Passage to Anthropology: Between Experience and Theory.* London: Routledge.

Lien, M.E. and M. Melhuus (eds). 2007. *Holding Worlds Together. Ethnographies of Knowing and Belonging.* New York and Oxford: Berghahn Books.

Malinowski, B. 1922. *Argonauts of the Western Pacific.* London: Routledge and Kegan Paul.

———. 1934. *Coral Gardens and their Magic.* London: Allen and Unwin.

———. 1967. *A Diary in the Strict Sense of the Term.* London: Routledge.

Marcus, G. 1998. *Ethnography Through Thick and Thin.* Princeton: Princeton University Press.

Marcus, G. and J. Clifford (eds). 1986. *Writing Culture.* Berkeley: University of California Press.

Martin, E. 1994. *Flexible Bodies: the Role of Immunity in American Culture from the Days of Polio to the Age of AIDS.* Boston: Beacon Press.

Melhuus, M. 2002. 'Issues of Relevance: Anthropology and the Challenges of Cross-cultural Comparison', in A. Gingrich and R. Fox (eds), *Anthropology, By Comparison.* London and New York: Routledge, pp. 70–92.

Mitchell, J.P. 2007. 'Ethnography', in W. Outhwaite and S.P. Turner (eds), *The Sage Handbook of Social Science Methodology.* London: Sage, pp. 55–66.

Rapport, N. 1990. 'Surely Everything has Already Been Said about Malinowski's Diary!', *Anthropology Today* 6(1): 5–9.

———. 1997. 'Hard Sell: Commercial Performance and the Narration of the Self', in F. Hughes-Freeland (ed.), *Ritual, Performance, Media.* London: Routledge: 177–93.

Reyna, S. 2001. 'Theory Counts: (Discounting) Discourse to the Contrary by Adopting a Confrontational Stance', *Anthropological Theory* 1: 9–31.

Singer, A. 1985. *Broniwslaw Malinowski: Off the Verandah.* Part of the 'Strangers Abroad' series for Central Television. 52 minutes.

Spencer, J. 1986. 'Ethnography as a Kind of Writing', *Man* (ns) 24 (1): 145–64.

Spindler, G.D. (ed.). 1970. *Being an Anthropologist: Fieldwork in Eleven Cultures.* New York: Holt, Rinehart and Winston.

Stirrat, R.L. and H. Henkel. 2001. 'Participation as Spiritual Duty; Empowerment as Secular Subjection', in B. Cooke and U. Kothari (eds), *Participation: the New Tyranny?* London: Zed Books, pp.168–84.

Stocking, G. 1984. *Functionalism Historicized: Essays on British Social Anthropology.* Madison: University of Wisconsin Press.

Wulff, H. 2002. 'Yo-yo Fieldwork: Mobility and Time in a Multi-local Study of Dance in Ireland', *Anthropological Journal on European Cultures*, issue on Shifting Grounds: Experiments in Doing Ethnography, 11: 117–36.

———. 2008. 'To Know the Dancer: Formations of Fieldwork in the Ballet World', in N. Halstead, E. Hirsch and J. Okely (eds), *Knowing How to Know.* Oxford: Berghahn Books, pp. 75–91.

Young, M. 1979. *The Ethnography of Malinowski: the Trobriand Islands 1915–1918.* London: Routledge.

1

Ethnography and Memory

Johannes Fabian

This chapter will primarily address the writing of 'ethnography'; little will be said about fieldwork. The reasons are personal. It will soon be twenty years ago that I carried out my last field research, whereas I am as busy as ever producing ethnography. My excuse is that, to my knowledge, we still don't quite understand how it came about that 'ethnography' (lit. ethno-writing) could become a synonym for fieldwork and hardly anyone seems to be bothered by the fact that 'ethnographic writing' is a clumsy pleonasm. One may suspect that this has to do with anthropologists' desire to be recognised as scientists and with the fervour we put into keeping empiry and theory apart (signalled by distinguishing between ethnography and ethnology). Professionalisation made us methodologise presence in the field (by declaring 'participant observation' a method) and blot out the constitutive, not merely instrumental, role of writing in our research practice. Nowadays most anthropologists realise that the presence we establish in the field (when we 'do fieldwork') is of interest and import only inasmuch as it is re-presentable, an insight that I believe should inform the kind of reappraisal of 'fieldwork under changed circumstances' that we are presently engaged in.

Why Memory?

When one no longer works at a university and looks back at a professional past that now seems longer than one ever imagined, this can be disconcerting; but retirement has certain unexpected advantages as well as new challenges. The way I experience this predicament does not for a moment tempt me to settle down in wisdom. On the contrary, making critical sense of our work as ethnographers and anthropologists turns out to be as unsettling as ever – and more daunting than ever because there is so much more to make sense of. This chapter builds on what I begin to recognise as a lifelong struggle to understand what present and presence mean and to follow the many ramifications these concepts have in our work. Because this will have a bearing on my main argument let me recall briefly the steps that preceded it.

The first one was a critique of conceptions of social science that had us assume that the object, or objects, of enquiry were unproblematically present in the sense of being given (and therefore called 'data') or – a somewhat less naive version of the same – could only be investigated inasmuch as they were given. Next came the insight that, just as the presence of the object of research was problematic, so was the presence of the ethnographer.[1] This is the case not only in its now generally accepted political or perhaps ethical sense but also with regard to the epistemological conditions that must be met by ethnography as a practice, that is, as action and interaction based, not exclusively but fundamentally, on communication between researcher and researched.

That insight made me daring or foolhardy enough to take on my discipline as a whole by confronting it with a glaring contradiction (Fabian 2002, orig. 1983): We maintain that anthropology rests on ethnography, that is, on communication, which is possible only when we acknowledge what I called the coevalness, the co-presence of researchers and researched, in turn made possible by the sharing of time, without which communication cannot occur. But we produce – the present tense applies to the time of writing the book – a discourse that consistently, not just incidentally, places those about whom we talk and write in a time other than ours, usually in an evolutionary or historical past.

Of course, this could not have been the end of a story. Contradictions call for resolution. We may be able to state them clearly and simply but we don't seem to have a clear or simple solution for the problem. The theme of this volume shows that present anthropology is in the midst of grappling for answers. Progress in this endeavour depends on our ability to reformulate general insights in terms of specific questions and to transform questions into tasks.

One more specific, yet still fairly general, way to face our predicament has been to examine critically the one activity without which the most intensive and extended fieldwork could not become ethnography: writing. The result was a debate that, I believe, was crucial for the survival of anthropology, though perhaps not in all the directions it took. Its core was and is the tension between presence and re-presentation. I have tried to approach this question from several angles. During recent work on what one may call a prehistory of ethnography, I explored one of them under the heading of memory and alterity – remembering the other (Fabian 2000, 2001a: chapter 9). Producing ethnographic knowledge, I argued, requires not just cognition but recognition, and thinking about re-cognition inevitably brings up the role of remembering in our work.

Memory in the Field

Observing, participating, communicating, (co-)performing, noting, collecting, recording, perhaps even measuring and surveying – these are the activities we associate with fieldwork. But remembering? What, if anything at all, do field manuals say about memory and research? When one stops to think about it, remembering/memory turns out to be involved in almost every imaginable aspect of ethnographic research, to the point (but this is something to worry about later) that one may begin to doubt the critical usefulness of such a focus. In a general way it could be said that much of ethnographic enquiry is getting people to remember. Let us for a moment grant that field research consists of collecting information about a society/culture, information that comes as answers to theory- and method-driven questions. It seems clear that, from questionnaire responses to elicited narratives, the information an ethnographer may gather needs to be recalled by 'informants' in order to be retrieved from some kind of shared cultural archive.[2] One may consider an alternative model: cultural competence vs. cultural performance. But this may not be so much an alternative to but a mode of envisaging the way in which information is articulated.

Cultural knowledge, once articulated, is memory-mediated. 'Mediated' means two things: memory makes articulation possible; and memory 'comes between' the presumed archive and the 'collectable' statement. In other words, apart from all the other epistemological conditions and problems that have been acknowledged, we need to consider the role of memory in ethnographic fieldwork in making that which is to be investigated present.

Presence is problematic not only on the side of the object. It is also involved in the ways the researcher establishes his or her presence among the people and in his or her 'field'. In this respect, I think, it makes little difference, though little differences may be worth exploring, whether ethnography is one- or multi-sited or whether its object is stationary or moving.[3] That memory must be involved in establishing an ethnographer's presence in the field is obvious when we see fieldwork as a learning process, perhaps analogous (and often homologous) to learning to speak a language. It makes some sense to imagine such learning as goal-directed and accumulative, but, as everyone who has learned another language ought to know, progress comes in halts and leaps, competence must be faked or pretended before it is mastered. All this gets even more complicated (and problematic) when we stop to think about the role of memory in learning, a role that is by no means limited to memory as a cognitive operation or capacity because remembering becomes memory, in a meaning that is relevant to what we are after, when it is represented and communicated. That is why passing off fieldwork as 'collecting material' is such an inadequate description of our activities.

Here is a reminder apt to make these necessarily abstract reflections about memory and presence a bit more concrete. Among the experiences a field researcher has, even during a first stint but perhaps more so in projects that make us return to people and places we had visited earlier, is a kind of quantum leap that our efforts can make after a period of absence. Our interlocutors are more willing and eager to help us, they are more talkative and tell us things they held back earlier, meetings become more productive and enjoyable when they are reunions, even short visits make us feel more at home than an extended stay when we started out. As I realised long ago, co-presence, to be experienced consciously, needs a shared past and it is during absence from each other that we find the time to make pasts that can be remembered.

As has been the case with other kinds of mediations involved in ethnographic practice (language in verbal communication, nonverbal communication, the senses and the body, gender and age, relations of power), the insight that memory mediates will be productive – likely to produce better understandings and interpretations – only to the extent that we are able to pin down what it means specifically. This is what I would like to do in the following when I look at various aspects of the ethnographer's work with the question of memory in mind.

Memory and the Making of Ethnographic Texts

No matter how far we care to go when we insist that anthropological writing is a literary activity, we distinguish ourselves from literary theorists and critics in that, as ethnographers, we work with texts most of which we do not find but have to make. There are at least three kinds of such texts: field notes, field diaries and records of conversations and other verbal performances.[4] In order to simplify matters and to stay within the limits of my competence, I shall consider only verbal (and aural) 'records' and 'texts' and leave visual documentation aside without in any way either negating its importance or overlooking the problems of relationship between aural and visual records.

Field Notes and Diaries

Much has been written about field notes, historically and methodologically but, as far as I am aware, the question of how memory may be involved has seldom figured prominently in this literature.[5] One exception is the thoughtful collection of essays edited by Sanjek (1990), where he also talks of the importance of ´head notes´, meaning that which springs to mind during the writing process but was never written down. One could say of field notes that they are memos, short for memoranda, a genre of writing (and a practice of communication) so current and prevailing that we tend to forget its literal meaning: memoranda are things to be remembered. But memoranda are also always *memorata,* things remembered. We take field notes not only in order to remember but also because we remember. Remembering, however, does not come in isolated acts: it is a practice and as such remembering is always memory work, an activity that includes forgetting whereby forgetting is no more natural or automatic than remembering.[6]

Furthermore, memory work is a social and cultural practice and, in the form that interests us here, a disciplinary practice. At the very least, we must acknowledge that field research is still informed by the kind of mnemonics that were laid down in *Notes and Queries*, a guide that was but one document in a long history (Stocking 1992; Stagl 1995). In subtle ways, theoretical positions and interests within our field tell us what we should remember and, when deeply internalised, they may determine what we can remember or must forget when we take notes.

Though a distinction between field notes and diary entries cannot always be made neatly, our professional habits of note-taking follow a method analogous to double bookkeeping. They include, apart from descriptive, topical texts, often consigned to index cards (or laptop databases), 'journals', which ethnographers keep much like their predecessors, the travellers and explorers (Fabian 2000, 2001a).[7] The connection between remembering and keeping a field journal may be too obvious to deserve much comment, except that it is an occasion to remind ourselves of the crucial role that memory plays in creating and maintaining a researcher's 'identity'. An experience common among fieldworkers is one that is often described as a loss of purpose and orientation ('What am I doing here?' 'What is all this about?'). To maintain purpose and orientation is work of the kind I have in mind when I speak of memory work.

Transcribing and Translating Ethnographic Texts

If recordings were made only for their content, that is, the information they provide, transcribing and translating them could be left, as it is often done, to helpers and, when the language is foreign and exotic, to native speakers. For an ethnographer to invest thousands of hours in these labours makes sense only if he or she has aims that require attention to communicative context, linguistic features and textual form. I happen to think that all ethnography should pursue such goals, but, between making minimal and maximal demands on the quality of ethnographic texts, there are, of course, many shades; we must all make compromises and we should all be wary of 'tape fetishism', a common temptation, discussed recently by Malcolm Ashmore, Katie MacMillan and Steven D. Brown (2004).

The authors make their points with the help of material from therapy and court sessions, taking a strictly outsider view of published or otherwise available transcripts not made by them. Much of what they have to say kept me nodding with recognition (especially something that is a minor issue in their presentation: transcribing vs. glossing; how does one transcribe 'screaming' or 'laughter'?). They are right when they insist that a tape (recording) is never simply an object, hence never simply given, and that every (recorded) text can have an infinite number of interpretations. Their solution for this conundrum is something they call 'professional hearing' which sounds reasonable but is in fact analogous to declaring that ethnography is an art. They don't pretend that there is a 'methodological' solution to their problems, and that is good. But their disclaimers (not an object, no one single interpretation) tend to avoid epistemological questions that must be asked. A tape is a material object containing material 'information', a recording is a record of an event.

Difficulties of transcription and translation make this record fragmentary, and this may be aggravated when a given recording documents speech that was unusually fragmentary 'in the event'. Perhaps this train of thought comes to me because I recently spent about two months on transcribing and translating a conversation with a healer and practitioner of magic. What makes this text more difficult than any I remember is this: though the issues related and discussed are serious and grave, there is something light and fleeting about this interlocutor's speech (which at times seems even to rub off on me; usually I have no trouble transcribing my own questions, but here I do). This goes for his articulation (pronunciation/ enunciation) as well as for his syntax and narration. And all that comes, as it were, on top of constant jumping between possible variants, switching dialects or simply resorting to gestures (see Fabian 2008).

Making knowledge out of such a record by finding and presenting understanding involves something that Ashmore et al. (2004) do not really see or acknowledge: taking myriads of decisions. To think of transcribing/translating as decision-making presupposes that problems posed by alternatives are to be resolved. But this is tricky ground. Is decision not already involved in recognising alternatives? Even at that stage, transcription does not 'come naturally'. Solving this kind of problem is not like answering a question because it is not questions that are posed or pose themselves but conflicts between competing answers that need to be 'settled'. In linguistic terms, transcription amounts to segmentation, cutting the sound of recorded utterances into words and sentences. To 'cut words', *kukata maneno,* means in Katanga Swahili 'to adjudicate a palaver', which is never simply sorting out right from wrong. Similarly, the decision process that interests us here is not a matter of sorting out correct from incorrect transcriptions or, taking this one step further, true from false meaning in translation.

To make decisions you need criteria and motives. It takes knowledge to make decisions that are to produce knowledge. Is pursuing a goal (transcribe and translate a recording) enough to make you go on taking decisions? Or must we postulate a kind of epistemological voluntarism, a *Wille zum Wissen,* a will to know, to paraphrase Nietzsche? And could it not be said that endurance (or stubbornness) is a prerequisite of such toil? I think that memory, the remembering that is required and triggered by the activities of text-making, contributes importantly to this part of the ethnographer's work. Two kinds of reasons lead me to assert this. One is practical and personal, the other theoretical.

The practical and personal are involved in what I said about transcription and translation as decision-making. This is not the place even to attempt to show this in detail. In a summary fashion, I just want to report what I can generalise from my own experience with texts recorded in Katanga Swahili. Transcribing and translating not only need remembering in the sense that the one who does it must have phonetic, lexical and grammatical competences – a repertoire learned in the past and capable of being mobilised in the present. Such remembering, which is of course required whenever we speak or write, no matter in what language, remains, as it were, in the background; it is more like a condition than an activity. But there are countless moments, especially those that make us stop with incomprehension or because we see alternatives that must be weighed, when we resolve problems because the recording makes us remember what we hear and what we understand. Such memory may be created text-internally, that is, in the course of working on a given text (how did I transcribe/translate a given utterance earlier?). It may also come as remembering a speaker's attitudes (including bodily postures, changes in directions of gazes, signs of excitement or lagging attention, and so forth) or as realising the significance of indexical and non-linguistic information, which all sound recordings are full of but which can be re-cognised (understood once again) only by the ethnographer who was present when the recording was made. Again, this would seem to be relevant to what has been said earlier about present and presence as a condition of ethnography.

One would have to figure out how exactly this works, for instance, when it turns out that translating a transcript requires listening to the recording again. Also, this brings home what I believe all practitioners of ethnographic text production would agree to: that the distinction between transcribing and translating is a very tenuous one (though it did figure prominently in the premises of structural approaches when linguists prided themselves on being able to establish the phonetic system, the morphology and the syntax of a language from texts whose meaning they did not need to understand).

Theoretical reasons that lead us to consider the role of remembering in the work of making ethnographic texts come into play when we combine our observations on toil and endurance with those on memory and identity. Without subscribing to notions of a static or single identity, it would seem obvious that the sustained efforts needed to carry out such a limited task as making a text, even more so those of carrying out research projects during our careers as ethnographers, would be impossible if we were unable or unwilling to remember.

'Ethnographic Writing' – and Reading Ethnography

It is now time to take what I said about memory and speaking one step further: Orality and literacy have in common that they depend on memory; they mobilise remembering in different media, but I belong to those who have found arguments that writing requires, or is indicative of, cognitive abilities higher than those required for speaking (or, for that matter, singing, dancing, carving, painting …) unconvincing. Certain connections between remembering and the kind of writing that interests us here, the crafting of 'ethnographies', are as obvious as they are deep-seated, historically, culturally and ideologically.[8] What we have learned from literary theory and criticism has made us aware, for instance, that even the genre we associate with (some may say: buried together with) modernist anthropology, the 'ethnographic monograph', had its roots in ancient arts of memory. The standard themes (the 'queries' in *Notes and Queries*) of a monograph were never only classificatory categories; as topoi, they were places we visited and revisited, and monographs were evaluated on our ability to do this and do it convincingly. To realise this has been our contribution to the debate on the rhetorical nature of scientific writing.[9]

It is one thing to acknowledge rhetoric in science; it is another to draw the stultifying conclusion that rationality is a futile pursuit. In unexpected ways, thought about memory can help us to avoid such a short cut. In my work on popular culture in Zaire/Congo I had many occasions to ponder the semantic proximity of *kuwaza*, to think, and *kukumbuka*, to remember.[10]

What this may teach us is that we need to relativise the bias towards reason as future-oriented, which leads to excluding past-oriented remembering from rationality. Conventional wisdom tells us that thinking belongs with 'truth', remembering with 'story'; and we all know that stories are lies (remember Carl Popper's tirades against history). What we know about memory and ethnography should make it impossible to hold such a view.

My comments here on memory and the writing of ethnographies are brief, but I want to conclude this section with an even briefer and somewhat anecdotal self-observation on reading ethnographies.[11] Recently, I read (much of) *Like People You See in a Dream* edited by Schieffelin and Crittenden (1991). This is an impressive multi-perspective ethno-historical account of a 1935 exploratory 'patrol' (by Hides and O'Malley) through Papua territory. I knew of the book but had forgotten that I owned it until I discovered it by accident while rummaging through my library – at the right moment, as it turns out (serendipity works). What I noticed immediately were amazing convergences with my *Out of Our Minds* (2000), a book on the exploration of Central Africa. The reason I did not consult this work 'on first encounters' when I wrote mine was that I had filed it away wrongly in my mind. I had misremembered it as being about first contact with missions (who play no role at all in this story). What made me pick it up eventually was a suspicion that it had a bearing on a paper about 'encounter and the making of anthropological knowledge' I had to prepare. I recall this now because the anecdote contains an important meta-lesson, one that is relevant to these reflections on ethnography and memory: in my experience, the main use of reading 'ethnographies' (including many that seem to have little to do with my Africa-centred interests) is not so much to accumulate or widen knowledge. One gets more re-cognition than cognition/knowledge from such readings. In other words, this sort of reading is really part of the ethnographer's memory-work.

Memory and Critique, Critique of Memory

As I continue to think about memory, I feel pulled, or driven, in two directions. One is to keep a critical distance from memory. It is a matter of not falling into an intellectual black hole. Memory can be an omnivorous, insatiable concept. Hence the need to remind myself and others of what we forget when we get fixed on memory. At the same time, I keep discovering new angles from which to think about memory. 'Ethnography and memory' has been one; another just occurred to me: could it not be said that 'critique' – in its concrete meaning of a practical/political attitude and a discursive strategy – is nothing but a way of remembering and reminding? Being the exercise of an intellectual capacity, it is not something one does or advocates 'above and beyond', 'outside', or 'against' whatever the critique is applied to. Critique, like memory, is therefore not optional. On the other hand (a third hand by now and probably not the last), critique, like remembering, is not a steady activity or state (compared with what we do routinely and could not do otherwise when we do research, think and write). It occurs in 'moments' and does not lead to 'conclusions' in the sense of endings. If thinking is like breathing, critique, as I said long ago, is a breathless activity. Perhaps remembering is like catching our breath.

But let me get back, for a moment, to rhetoric and the arts of memory in ethnographic writing. While we could not practise ethnography as a 'discipline' without submitting to a common regime of memory, it is also true that remembering in practices of ethnography can only be done by the individual practitioner. This opens up yet another perspective on much-debated 'autobiography' in ethnographic writing. At stake is not autobiography as a genre of writing (sometimes denounced as 'confessional') but autobiography as we use it in an imprecise sense (analogous to calling field research ethnography) when we really mean subjectivity and individuality as epistemological conditions of ethnography. Paying attention to remembering can help us understand better why and how ethnographers should face autobiography.

At this point I cannot refrain from noting a connection that may not be as lateral as at first appears. It is commonly agreed that anthropology found its modern theoretical conception somewhere in the intellectual climate created by Enlightenment thought and the critical reaction to the Enlightenment, Romantic thought. A key figure was Jean-Jacques Rousseau, theoretician of the social contract and a thinker who, as it were, straddled Enlightenment and Romanticism. In histories of anthropology we usually cite his essay on the origin of language and, of course, his Discourses. But Rousseau was also the author of *Les confessions*, a book at least as influential as his other writings. This is how it begins: 'Je forme une entreprise qui n'eut jamais d'example, et qui n'aura point d'imitateur. Je veux montrer à mes semblables un homme dans toute la vérité de la nature; et cet homme, ce sera moi' (Rousseau 1865: 1).[12] Rousseau was one of the first to express an insight that was later lost under the influence of positivism and its rather naive utopia of a social science conceived as a sort of physics of society. This was the discovery that the subject as the locus and agent of knowledge about 'la vérité de la nature' was the condition of an objective science of society/culture.

Prior to the conference upon which this volume is based, I discussed the topic of this chapter with H. Sonneveld, the administrative director of the research institute that sponsored my participation. He reacted with interest and even excitement. He had just finished reading Proust's *A la recherche du temps perdu*. It was in the course of our conversation that I began to see a significant aspect. If the central thesis holds – that memory plays a crucial part in the making of ethnographic knowledge at all levels, from 're-cognising' what constitutes a relevant or interesting object of enquiry to transcribing/translating recordings to writing ethnography – and if one irreducible aspect of individual remembering (but not of shared 'memory') is its involuntary nature, then it follows that an important part of ethnographic enquiry is out of control: which is, of course, antithetical to the run-of-the-mill 'theory of science'. And it is yet another reason for putting 'methodology' in place: only that which is controlled and can be kept safe from un-controllable factors can be methodology. Strictly speaking, this is the case only of techniques that need to be mind-less – not bothered by minding and remembering – while they are being operated, or of skills and operations that no longer need reflection. But even that is always only relative; the mind cannot be switched off except in operations carried out mechanically (not metaphorically, but literally: carried out by machines, computers) and reflection cannot be set aside except temporarily.[13]

I cannot resist adding arguments to the critique of naive scientism, which is also the point of a final observation, that concludes this chapter. Not enough would have been said about memory and ethnographic practice if I did not at least mention a kind of remembering that is as likely to ring bells of recognition for ethnographers as it is difficult to grasp theoretically. Here is some anecdotal evidence. Ever since I started fieldwork in the 1960s, I have brought along tapes on which I had recorded some of my favourite music, classical as well as rock and pop. Rather than listening to local radio (I became a fan of Congolese music somewhat later), I played the music again and again until the tapes got used up, as it were, by recording ethnographic texts. Even now, after almost forty years, certain pieces and tunes bring up memories of place and time, of situations and moods, which have in common that they seem to be ineffable. They have, to borrow a term from semantics, no referential meaning; but that does not make them less powerful and, I would argue, less productive. Such remembering, to which one should add memories of tastes, smell, sounds other than music and bodily experiences, is not 'stuff' we write about as ethnographers but it is a source of the energy we need for doing our work.

Let me end with rehearsing the same insight one more time by treating you to a bit of autobiography in the literal sense of the term. I had begun pondering the theme of this chapter when, after driving through the country and town in Germany where I lived during my school years, I noted down the following in my diary (on 11 October 2003):

> As always, I was touched, assailed, by what I call memories though I could not say what I remember. Usually neither events nor persons or situations. Smells, moods, and something ineffable of which I know that it is different from what other places can cause in me; but that is all. I could not name it. It feels like small charges, pleasant but kind of sad at the same time. Altogether, these memories make you want to take off. Perhaps that is what they are: rebounds – they presuppose bounds, of course. Another way I put it to myself: in these 'memories' you get back from a place (maybe also a person) what you once put into it. Often I have said that this town was the kind of place I have spent my life getting out of or away from. I could say the same of my family and the friends I grew up with. This does not mean that I ever felt I had to renounce or completely abandon that part of my youth. Just get away from it, don't let what you love eat you up.

Then I thought about the significance of memories that don't really remember a thing and seem to exist – as Humboldt asserted of language – primarily as *energeia*, energy, rather than *ergon*, reference/content. Could my autobiographical memories (and now I would include memories of events, persons, situations, etc.) serve to take off from, to jump off from, to bounce off from and thereby provide the energy that generates, what else, ethnography? One should try it out: take a powerful memory and confront it with a task at hand and then write about it in such a way that the memory that gives the impetus never shows up in the writing. That would be autobiography without autobiographical narrative/content.

It does not take long to see problems with this train of thought. Is it possible, important, useful to single out non-referential memories that take us back to a time before we became ethnographers? What about similar memories of places where we did fieldwork? Is what came later less powerful than what we experienced earlier, and if it is, why should it be so?

Notes

1. I should like to note, without being able to pursue this now, yet another relation that has become productively problematic, that between 'objects'. This, I believe, is behind the spectacular rehabilitation of material culture studies in social and cultural anthropology.

2. This view assigns to memory a role that is more encompassing than the one that, for instance, Stocking has in mind when he contrasts 'memory ethnography' (1992: 365) – eliciting from informants what they remember about a culture that has vanished or is about to – as typical of a Boasian approach in contrast to Malinowskian 'synchronic' observation of current behaviour.

3. 'Stationary or moving' consists of qualifications in a manner of speaking. No object of ethnographic enquiry, not even the limiting-case of a physical object, is strictly stationary or moving. Neither 'being' as such nor 'process' as such is in the domain of empirical research. That is why it is important to reflect on our ways of keeping what we investigate in a kind of middle state.

4. When I say that there are 'at least' three kinds of text we make, I have left an opening for written texts produced by those among whom we do research (often prior to, or after, and often without any direct connection to our research projects).

5. I found no entries for memory or remembering in the indexes of Atkinson (1990) and Stocking (1992). It was briefly discussed (put aside, as it were) as belonging to intuitive knowledge in Ellen (1984: 304); Van Maanen's (1988) index lists 'memory of fieldwork' with half a dozen references, but when I checked I discovered that he associates this kind of remembering with the telling of tales only; memory is not discussed explicitly.

6. If forgetting is part of memory work, then my concentrating in this chapter on remembering may pose a problem. As the saying goes, one can only do one thing at a time but there are omissions that may vitiate the entire argument. The best I can do at the moment is to affirm that I hold a dialectical concept of memory, something that I have tried to apply in a recent ethnographic paper (Fabian 2004; on memory work see also Fabian 2001a: chapter 10 and 2001b).

7. Not to forget 'letters from the field' to colleagues, friends and relatives, which may occasionally become part of ethnographies or be published as such.

8. Observations on the disembodiment of writing and writing as disembodiment (my favourite reference is Schön 1987) could therefore make us think about writing as disembodiment of remembering.

9. A similar observation may apply to practices discussed earlier: is transcribing a recorded text not done for someone, for a project or an audience, hence a form of arguing, a rhetorical activity, even leaving aside the value we ascribe to texts and documents in establishing an ethnographer's 'authority'?

10. Such proximity also exists in other languages, for instance, in German *denken* and *gedenken*, or in English with 'to think of' as a synonym of 'to remember'.

11. As far as I know, the sophistication we acquired as critics of anthropological writing has yet to be matched by a comprehensive critique of anthropological reading. Probably this reflects the neglect of reading in recent debates about literacy. Only recently have we begun to make reading an object of ethnographic enquiry (Boyarin 1993).

12. My translation: 'I am about to start an undertaking never tried before and never to be imitated. I want to show to the likes of me a human being in the whole truth of nature; and this human being will be me.'

13. Being at least in part 'out of control', remembering belongs to the conditions of enquiry that I called ecstatic in *Out of Our Minds* (2000).

References

Ashmore, M., K. MacMillan and S.D. Brown. 2004. 'It's a Scream: Professional Hearing and Tape Fetishism', *Journal of Pragmatics* 36: 349–74.
Atkinson, P. 1990. *The Ethnographic Imagination. Textual Constructions of Reality.* London: Routledge.
Boyarin, J. (ed.). 1993. *The Ethnography of Reading.* Berkeley: University of California Press.
Ellen, R.F. 1984. *Ethnographic Research. A Guide to General Conduct.* London: Academic Press.
Fabian, J. 2000. *Out of Our Minds: Reason and Madness in the Exploration of Central Africa.* Berkeley: University of California Press.
———. 2001a. *Anthropology with an Attitude. Critical Essays.* Stanford: Stanford University Press.
———. 2001b. 'Forgetting Africa', *Journal of Romance Studies* 3: 9–20.
———. 2002. *Time and the Other.* New York: Columbia University Press.
———. 2004. 'Forgetful Remembering: A Colonial Life in the Congo', *Africa* 73(4): 489–504.
———. 2008. *Ethnography as Commentary: Writing from the Virtual Archive.* Durham, NC: Duke University Press.
Notes and Queries on Anthropology, published in various imprints 1874–1951. London: Edward Stanford; Harrison; Routledge and Kegan Paul.
Rousseau, J.J. 1865. *Les confessions,* new edn. Paris: Garnier Frères.
Sanjek, R. (ed.). 1990. *Fieldnotes. The Makings of Anthropology.* Ithaca: Cornell University Press.
Schieffelin, E.L., and R. Crittenden. 1991. *Like People You See in a Dream. First Contact in Six Papuan Societies.* Stanford: Stanford University Press.
Schön, E. 1987. *Der Verlust der Sinnlichkeit/ oder Die Verwandlungen des Lesers. Mentalitätswandel um 1800.* [The Loss of Sensuality or The Transformation of the Reader. Change of Mentality around 1800]. Stuttgart: Klett-Cotta.
Stagl, J. 1995. *A History of Curiosity. Theory of Travel 1550–1800.* Chur: Harwood Academic Publishers.
Stocking, G.W. Jr. 1992. *The Ethnographer's Magic and Other Essays in the History of Anthropology.* Madison: University of Wisconsin Press.
Van Maanen, J. 1988. *Tales of the Field. On Writing Ethnography.* Chicago: University of Chicago Press.

2

Fieldwork as Free Association and Free Passage

Judith Okely

Introduction: the Concept of Free Association as a Counter to Positivism

Without consciously realising it at the time of proposing this paper for the EASA conference in Vienna in 2004 upon which this chapter is based, I drew on ideas from Sigmund Freud and psychoanalysis. Now I realise that this can be seen as a tribute to the great writer who moved to Vienna aged four and who studied and graduated in that city and lived there until 1938.

Psychoanalysis has been explored in relation to cross-cultural interpretation and experience, especially in Freud's *The Interpretation of Dreams* (1900/1954). Here I examine the process of fieldwork, the interaction between the anthropologist and those with whom she lives and whom she encounters in the field, and again the process of interpretation and writing up.

Despite the pronouncements about the death of positivism, there is nevertheless a continuing presence of such approaches in the social sciences. Information technology has been used to elaborate ever more quantitative routes to knowledge at the expense of others. So-called qualitative methods have been subjected to increasing routinisation and formulaic strictures. Discourse analysis is reduced to word searches in transcribed interviews, and often the so-called analysis is conducted by individuals who never actually conversed with, let alone met the individuals whose texts are being processed.

Instead, I wish to return to an open-ended approach to fieldwork and one that I suggest has always been conducted by the most convincing anthropologists. In preparation for my forthcoming book *Anthropological Practice* (Okely 2010), I have had extensive dialogues with some twenty anthropologists whose fieldwork around the world has shown remarkable common patterns of which they were not always fully aware and which are consistent with much of this chapter. I was interested in what they did in practice rather than what methods books suggest should be done. However, there are aspects that I did not pursue at the time or that the anthropologists could not have volunteered in the context of such dialogues, however informal. I shall therefore draw mainly on my own fieldworks and suggest that anthropologists reconsider their own fieldworks in the light of my proposals.

Free association, as a psychoanalytical practice, entails being open to whatever comes into the person's mind, namely, random ideas and images, through a non-directed process for constructive analysis. The analysand/patient is expected to lie down on the couch and say whatever comes into his or her head. Then the psychoanalyst has to make sense of hidden patterns and themes. Deliberately engineered thoughts and tactics by the analysand are often dismissed as rationalisations.

Freud wrote that free association:

> involves some psychological preparation of the patient. In the attention he pays to his psychical perceptions and the elimination of the criticism by which he normally sifts the thoughts that occur to him. ... It is necessary to insist explicitly on his renouncing all criticism of the thoughts that he perceives ... .the success of the psychoanalysis depends on his noticing and reporting whatever comes into his head and not being misled, for instance, into suppressing an idea because it strikes him as unimportant or irrelevant or because it seems to him meaningless. He must adopt a completely impartial attitude to what occurs to him, since it is precisely his critical attitude which is responsible for his being unable, in the ordinary course of things, to achieve the desired unraveling of his dream or obsessional idea ... the self observer ... need only take the trouble to suppress his critical faculty ... innumerable ideas come into his consciousness of which he could otherwise never have got hold. (Freud 1954: 101–2)

Freud suggested that:

> If we trust that great poet and philosopher Friedrich Schiller, poetic creation must demand an exactly similar attitude. In a passage in his correspondence with Korner ... Schiller (writing on December 1, 1788): It seems a bad thing and detrimental to the creative work of the mind if Reason makes too close an examination of the ideas as they come pouring in ... Looked at in isolation, a thought may seem very trivial or very fantastic; but it may be made important by another thought that comes after it ... where there is a creative mind, Reason ... relaxes its watch upon the gates, and the ideas rush in pell-mell, and only then does it look them through and examine them in a mass. (Schiller in Freud 1954: 102–3)

Entering the Field: No Innocent Arrival

There can be similar processes in approaching anthropological fieldwork, with adaptation for its mobility. Here the anthropologist is both the analysand and the analyst. The anthropologist does not arrive as innocent. S/he brings the flotsam of prior representations and alternative knowledge which affect his/her initial experiential understanding. I argue that this prior baggage should be used creatively. The classical psychoanalyst retains distance. The latter does not engage in self-disclosure, but, by retaining distance and anonymity, frees the analysand to project on to the analyst feelings and experiences from early primary relationships. This is not therefore the identical context for the use of free association in anthropological fieldwork. Matters develop in complex ways as the fieldwork and the encounters continue.

The anthropologist in a post-positivist era does not and cannot remain distant and anonymised (Okely 1992). Rosaldo and others pursued the notion of the positioned subject who 'observes with a particular angle of vision … the notion of subject position also refers to how life experiences both enable and inhibit particular kinds of insight' (Rosaldo 1989: 19).

Agar succinctly described how he brought into the field all his past knowledge and experience, however random and seemingly irrelevant to the project. These may include 'a previous ethnography, two novels, your general idea of the human condition, childhood experiences with your parents, and who knows what else' (Agar 1980: 6). Note here that he included both imaginative literature or non-fiction and what also interested Freud, namely pre-adult experience. When Agar worked as an anthropologist in the US rather than overseas, other social scientists and researchers would continually ask him what hypothesis he was testing and what method he was using. Exasperated, he eventually informed them he was using what he called the 'funnel method', that is, he considered the material from fieldwork would first have to be poured into the wider opening of a funnel-shaped vessel, which, in moving down to the narrower base, would be refined. This mechanical image or 'tool' silenced his interlocutors. More importantly, it pointed to an approach that does not decide in advance what is relevant. I have also found that the term has impressed research grant committees sceptical of ethnography.

In this chapter I concentrate on what the anthropologist brings with her or him. Mary Louise Pratt has pointed to the literary tropes and especially the arrival scenes that inadvertently draw on past literary and narrative texts and conventions (Pratt 1986). I suggest that the anthropologist is bringing more than literary resonances of style, but also content. This extends beyond literature to art and indeed total experience: both the individual and the historical/cultural contexts the anthropologist has inhabited.

I explore especially visual associations, memory and knowledge, which become embodied (Okely 2007). I examine the process of fieldwork from the early beginnings to the experience and through to thinking and analysing it, culminating in the final texts, which may take different forms over time. When I interviewed the numerous anthropologists, I did not pursue in depth their prior intellectual or experiential baggage. I therefore lean primarily on my own practices to explore issues related to free association. I draw on several research projects: in Normandy, the Gypsies in England and my boarding-school 'field experience' (Okely 1996: chapters 7 and 8) reconstructed from nine years' participation to anthropologist as observer and free-associating witness.

It was the rural inhabitants of Upper Normandy who drew me towards the visual in anthropology. I returned to the field with a camcorder. I have focused also on the memory of the visual through films or performative arts, which were rattling around in my subconscious and on which I drew almost unknowingly for comparisons, resonance and interpretations. It may be relevant that the films and performances are from within Western culture and that I have done all my anthropological research in the West and in Europe.

The films include *Les Enfants du Paradis* (1945), Anderson's *If* (1968) and Claude Lanzmann's *Shoah* (1985). Then there is Bizet's opera *Carmen*. I had seen all before fieldwork in the relevant location. Then there are the art images, namely the paintings of Cezanne, Monet, Pissarro and Millet, all of whom painted Normandy a century earlier. This affected my research focus in combination with that of the Normandy residents. I produced my own film footage. My ensuing publications also carried a visual load (Okely 2001).

There were no films of my fieldwork among the Gypsies. But I have nonetheless been fixated on specific visual images. I gained access to the local newspaper photo archive and was able to reproduce many photographs from my field area without having to take any intrusive pictures myself (Okely 2006). Many were of people I had known and lived with. Some, like the photos of a funeral, were of an event I attended. My very choice of photos, especially those linked to a funeral of a young father and witnessed by his children, revealed how I had, through initially unconscious puzzlement, come to be one of the first anthropologists to analyse the symbolic meaning of Gypsy death rituals (Okely 1983, 2003a: 160–62, Williams 2002).

A preliminary analysis was made of the rushes of the three days' filming by Anna Grimshaw of my return to my boarding school in 1998 (Okely 2003b). This filmic record goes beyond what I have already characterised as performance. The individual returns to the location of the past experience, including terror. The place acts as a memory trigger and evokes the culture and institutional formation. The place evokes the memories but the speaking persons convey the interpretations of their remembered pasts.

Normandy: Art and Poetry

When I arrived in Normandy, the funding organisation had originally specified a comparative study of the rural aged. I did indeed spend most of the time with the aged. But soon there were other themes and aspects that drew me in, compatible with the specific focus. Here was the countryside that had been celebrated by the great French Impressionists. I had what have become global icons in my head and imagination as I drove through, walked in, worked in and gazed at the landscapes. I allowed my free association full reign. I was at first seeing the landscape as a Monet or Pissarro, just as earlier anthropologists drew on literary genres in their arrival narratives.

Instead of suppressing this visual sensitivity and the recurrent images welling from memory, I enjoyed them with full *jouissance* and began to look for ways in which the painters had confronted the landscape. Some had laundered it of many inhabitants. Millet had celebrated the physical labour of peasants. Monet had shown trains passing through rural scenes. Pissarro was torn between the materiality of the everyday and a rural idyll. Such debates and conflicts about the rural were also moving through my head.

This awareness of the visual, I contend, made me unexpectedly and extra alert to the residents' *own* visual concerns, namely their suggestions that I could not fully appreciate and understand their locality until I had seen it in May with the apple trees in blossom. These rural agricultural residents and workers, some of whom were semi-literate and most of whom had never entered an art gallery, emphasised the visual in a specific way.

I subsequently elaborated on the importance of the visual in the inhabitants' experience of rural Normandy (Okely 2001). The difference between an overarching and distant gaze and that of seeing through the entire being was unexpectedly clarified for me by a long lost phrase from a film, the famous *Les Enfants du Paradis,* which I had seen at the age of eighteen when studying in Paris. Here free association brought to my recollection the words of the actor Jean-Louis Barrault, who is talking about Garence, played by Arletty. He says 'Everyone looked at her but I was the only one to *see* her'. This difference between looking (*regarder*) and seeing (*voir*), in the script by the poet Prévert, had hung around in my subconscious for over twenty years. It re-emerged as relevant when I was participating in the lives of the Normandy residents. I recognised the contrast between the bourgeois owners or town dwellers who gazed at the landscape and those who worked and laboured in it. The sight of apple trees in blossom would have a special significance to those who tended the apple trees and who would later pick the fruits and make their own cider for home consumption (Okely 2001).

Thus, like Agar, I brought past baggage and, by letting go through free association, I was open to matching or comparable resonances among those with whom I mingled in the field. The psychoanalyst must also be made aware of inner responses to the words of the analysand and confront them to see where they resonate with or sometimes impede interpretation. Freud's recommendation that the psychoanalyst should let things emerge was developed by Bion (1977) who suggested that the analyst should be just floating or suspended (Okely 1996: 106–7).

Free Passage: Anthropologists' Change of Focus

Alongside the notion of free association, I also consider that of free passage, consistent with anthropologists being open to what occurs, rather than sticking relentlessly to pre-planned and rationalised controls. In my dialogues with the anthropologists I found a recurrent practice that many may consider obvious, but which goes against the grain of ready-made research grant proposals and the lurking hypothesis that 'true' positivist social scientists are expected to have set up in advance for 'operationalisation'.

The vast majority of the anthropologists I interviewed revealed that they had changed their research focus or even locality after arriving in the field. Joanna Overing had hoped to study large ritual gatherings but found herself with a people who lived most of the time in small groups. For technical reasons, at the last moment she was obliged to change her field location from New Guinea to the Piraoa in tropical-forest Venezuala (Overing 1996). Although she had not wanted to study kinship, she found that it was essential for making sense of the society.

Johnny Parry had done all the preparatory reading for a study of politics when he embarked on fieldwork in northern India. But he soon realised that no one was interested in politics. Instead, they were obsessed with the practice of women marrying into a higher caste. So he changed his focus entirely. His first post-fieldwork seminar paper was on that topic and, at the end, a lecturer said that what he was really talking about was 'hypergamy'. In all innocence Parry asked what the term meant (Parry 1997).

In the *Psychopathology of Everyday Life* (1914), Freud attaches supreme significance to slips of the tongue and mishearings which expose the surfacing of the unconscious. Here is an example of mishearing from anthropology: Malcolm Mcleod had been the research assistant of Evans-Pritchard at Oxford and happened to ask an eminent visiting French anthropologist where he might study witchcraft. The answer to his question that Mcleod received was 'the Asante'. He spent two years on a library thesis on the Asante and then went to Ghana. When he arrived, he hardly accessed witchcraft but was drawn to the wealth of material culture. Such was his passion for this, that in the long run he was to become the first Curator of the Museum of Mankind, attached to the British Museum, and organised international exhibitions of Asante art.

Five years after he first went to Ghana, Mcleod returned to Oxford and by chance met the same French anthropologist on another visit. Mcleod questioned him about his original advice. To his astonishment, the Frenchman replied, 'I did not say the Asante, I said the Azande!' Mcleod had misheard the original advice because, as someone already working with Evans-Pritchard, he would not have believed the recommendation that he merely retread in the great master's footsteps. He had travelled to Ghana through a mishearing but once there, responded to what engaged him most vividly (Mcleod 1996).

Nancy Lindisfarne (1997) described how, by absolute chance, she and Richard Tapper encountered music making in cafes in Afghanistan. Instead of turning away from this, they found it led them to unexpected corners and political rivalries. 'It was actually a thread that created a lot more spaces for us to meet people, unexpectedly and indirectly; beyond asking the question about music, we weren't directing what happened.' She and her partner did not cut themselves off by saying they were not trained musicologists and that music was not their research focus. Instead they, like other anthropologists, were open to what came their way and they seized the chance in creative, unexpected ways.

The free passage from preconceptions to the unpredicted is another form of free association: being open to events and persons and topics as they drift your way. A comparison can be made with the *flaneur* or *flaneuse*. The term *disponible* from André Breton (1937), the celebrated surrealist, is also apt. The surrealists were open to *objets trouvés*, or found objects, to which they gave meaning. But, in anthropological fieldwork, it is for the anthropologist to learn the meaning that others give to objects and practices. The similarity to the surrealist is the wandering, inquisitive and open quest for what is found on the way or round the corner. The openness is comparable to the state of mind the psychoanalyst expects of the analysand when free-associating. But, in fieldwork, the openness applies to events, persons and themes that may come in everyday action and encounters, not just when in a motionless and contemplative state.

Free Association in Past Locations

Anthropology and other social sciences have recently focused on memory. Fieldwork may thus also increasingly entail calling upon people to remember. The return to the exact locations may trigger hitherto buried detail and *post facto* commentary. This may regrettably be increasingly relevant for anthropologists studying past conflicts and even genocide, as in Rwanda and former Yugoslavia. The 'informants' may be most articulate when free-associating, especially in the highly charged locations of specific past events. Similarly, such approaches may be drawn upon in joyful events and ceremonies, as well as in a familiar place of everyday routines.

The performance of being filmed provides another example from my fieldwork where free association was a central part of the experience. Again, I did not fully realise in advance that this was what I was doing. Once an anthropologist, always so. We are open to ethnographic analysis wherever we go. A seemingly brief return to the location of my English elitist boarding school turned into fieldwork. Here I had been incarcerated from the age of nine to eighteen (Okely 1996: chapters 7 and 8). Anna Grimshaw, as the anthropologist film-maker, filmed both my and another former inmate's return over some four days as we were allowed to wander freely through the buildings and grounds of our school weeks before it was to be partly bulldozed and transformed into a hotel complex, alongside private residential houses.

My article on this experience explores our spontaneous reactions as we entered different spaces and spoke and performed to camera: 'The Filmed Return of the Natives to a Colonising Territory of Terror' (Okely 2003b).

Before embarking on this adventure, a psychotherapist told me of her excitement. 'We spend our time encouraging people to go back to their childhood in their minds and memory. Now you are going to do just that in the very location of your childhood. What will it throw up?' Here I select just one incident from the many hours of footage. As my companion Susan, another former inmate, and I wandered through the buildings, including dining room, chapel, gymnasium, dormitories, library and classrooms, we free-associated to camera and multiple memories welled up in stark detail.

For all the fact that this was primarily a place of pedagogy, where I had learned Latin, French, English literature, biology, geography, history, art history, art, chemistry, theology and civics, I recalled only *one* class-room lesson out of those nine years. I re-enacted it to camera, taking up the chalk and holding it with limp wrist as I re-visualised the teacher in front of the blackboard. I imitated her detached voice as she scratched rough shapes for Britain, Africa and the American South. She joined them up as a crude triangle. This is how in the 1950s we, mainly Brits, were taught about the slave trade, which was called the triangular trade. There was no hint of the cruelty, the near genocide involved; it was described like some simple trade exchange from England to West Africa to the southern US and back to England. The slaves were mere objects, comparable to the glittering things brought by the traders to Africa or the raw cotton then shipped from the US to England.

Unconsciously and resorting to free association in the exact location where I had long ago witnessed this lesson, I had resurrected what was an epiphany of the colonial, imperial lessons we were supposed to imbibe. Yet the film of this performed enactment also reveals that the presentation of this single recalled lesson is imbued with years of later knowledge and reflections on injustice. The anthropologist performer is free-associating, but also adding implicitly for the viewer her bitter critique in part disguised as irony. It is framed by later life. Free association from the past and the unconscious are blended with later knowledge and political awareness, indeed with an anthropological sensitivity to ethnographic detail, as well as anti-racism.

Here also is another form of fieldwork, where the anthropologist was a long-term participant, over a period of nine years of childhood, but who only became an observer retrospectively (Okely 1996: chapters 7 and 8). Traditionally, the anthropologist has arrived as a stranger, but I suggest that the practice of free association is relevant, whatever the context.

The place of terror provoked specific memories and for my part was fuelled by revenge. There must have been other experiences that were joyful and creative, but these rarely surfaced. There are implications for fieldwork in general. Usually anthropologists do the most rewarding fieldwork with those they admire or respect, rather than with those they despise. Susan Caffery, also a former inmate and my companion on this return, tended to remember moments of subversive happiness, when the children took control or celebrated rare party-like events that went against the impoverished, grim routine.

Stereotypes Interlocking

My next example is indeed of the anthropologist as stranger, namely my fieldwork among the Gypsies. Again, I did not arrive innocent and looking merely for the 'real facts' as laid out for collection. The images and stereotypes of the Gypsies are part of Western, if not global, culture. I was acquainted with literary and operatic images, especially Bizet's *Carmen*. I had heard of the nursery rhyme about children being told not to play in the wood with the Gypsies. Ironically, I was not prepared in advance to recognise that the clusters of caravans on the edge of motorways were in fact the Gypsies' encampments. These I had naively presumed were temporary places for road workers. The initial appearance was unromantic. I could have repressed all those fantasies and images in the search for 'real empirical facts'. But, instead, I allowed them to float somewhere in my imagination, especially since most outsiders reacted so emotionally when they learned what I was doing. They near-vomited their own free associations on to me, a theme I have developed elsewhere (Okely 2008). Eventually, I realised that the contrast between myth and reality was highly relevant. The Gypsies had to negotiate these very stereotypes on a daily basis. They had to respond to and manipulate others' free association of fantasies for their own protection or advantage. The Gypsy women had sometimes to perform as exotic persons, especially in the role of fortune-tellers (Okely 1996: chapter 5). At other times, men or women would perform as beggars or illiterate victims if that was what the non-Gypsy expected and preferred. Thus the baggage concerning images of the Gypsies that I brought with me was vital to the analysis and understanding of the Gypsies' own positioning. There was an interconnection between what my free association and seemingly random memories of stereotypes offered and the experience of the people who had become the objects of such non-Gypsy fantasies (Okely 1996: chapter 3, 2008).

A Reader's Free Association

A final example is the writing of a reappraisal of Simone de Beauvoir (Okely 1986). This could have been a straight chronological reading of her key texts with biographical interventions. I embarked initially on an opening and highly ambitious chapter that aimed to give the post-war European political and historical context when de Beauvoir wrote *Le Deuxieme Sexe* (1949). It did not work. I am not a historian. It would have taken an entirely new study. Instead, I found myself free-associating, recalling the significance of de Beauvoir's celebrated text for young women in the early 1960s, using myself as one example. This had an added significance as, although the book, when first published, received largely hostile reviews from the mainly male literary establishment, de Beauvoir described how her book lived through the hundreds of young women readers who sent letters of appreciation. I could therefore recapture some of that euphoria by recalling my own youthful responses some time before the Women's Movement. As archival source I had my 1960s Paris diaries and the record of my underlinings and comments in the original French editions. Toril Moi later (personal communication) suggested the parallels between my approach and that of Stanley Fish's 'reader response' (1980), i.e. the reader does not come innocent to a text but with prior baggage. The intention was not to reduce the meaning of any text to a mere personal and idiosyncratic reading. There are always broader cultural and historical contexts. I was using my evidence as a case study and found echoes in the reactions and comments of my generation (Okely 1996: chapter 9).

In my book I was able to contrast the earlier near-naive reading before the second wave of feminism and a later reading informed by a mass of feminist literature and debates. What was once novel and 'natural' in de Beauvoir was subject to later scrutiny for ethnocentricism and covert universalisms founded on biologisms, despite herself. This use of the two readings may be compared to the first arrival in the field and the deeper knowledge gained from long-term critical interaction.

Individual Encounters

Today there is more awareness of unmapped movements between places, with the effects of globalisation and transmigration, so the anthropologist may follow the people, not just the money, as 'Deep Throat' once advised in the Watergate case. Another interpretation of 'free association' could embrace chance encounters with specific individuals and potential associates, rather than the specialised psychoanalytical practice. Here, even when the anthropologist may be staying in a specific locality for an extended period of time, there are choices to be made. Chance plays a key role, if the anthropologist is ready to seize it.

I recall years ago a government social scientist arguing that I had to find a 'typical' set of 'informants' as if only these would provide access to the core of the culture being studied. In fact, from my own and others' material, it is often the hybrid individual or the person who has lived across cultural divides who is the most articulate about differences between systems (Okely 2000). Such individuals may well seek out the outsider, but that is not guaranteed.

England

In my fieldwork among the Gypsies, the very first week of living in a camp, I encountered a young woman who had lost a child in a driving accident some months before. She was in her late twenties and roughly my age. Our friendship grew from such chance events and both differences and similarities. She had lived part of her childhood in a house and was schooled and literate. Having lived on both sides of an ethnic divide, this young woman was not the 'typical' representative that positivists might seek. Her father a Gypsy and her mother a non-Gypsy, she pointed out the contrasts between her housed upbringing and her life on the road when she married.

We sat night after night in the shell of an old van, with a coal fire, until 2a.m., long after everyone was asleep. She went over and over the tragic details of her loss. She broke the rules by displaying a photograph of the dead child in her trailer. This was taboo, as it was supposed to summon up the ghost of the dead. However, the Gypsy woman said she wanted to see her son again. As the stranger listener, I acted as amateur therapist and was honoured to listen. She free associated in her narrative of the tragedy with repetitions that had exhausted other camp members through the preceding months. I, as a stranger, could listen anew and simultaneously benefit from insights into the Traveller world, which she was willing to give me in that highly charged atmosphere. Here was a chance encounter strengthened by the anthropologist being open to what the individual needed to free-associate and unburden.

This same woman defended me when I made mistakes and we became close friends. All this was thanks to chance and a biographical moment to which I could choose to respond.

Normandy

Often the anthropologist may be 'adopted' in a familial role. The relationship has to work on both sides and where there may be some reciprocity of unpredictable kinds. I found myself treated like a daughter in my later fieldwork in Normandy. There my closest associate was an older woman, Jacqueline Grégoire. Again, I met her by chance or through free association in the less psychoanalytical sense rather than through any advance planning. Granted, I had approached her as president of one of the many village clubs for the elderly. But soon she drew me into her world view. I learned to hand-milk one of her cows and she came to treat me as an honorary daughter. It was that encounter and all subsequent ones that presented me with a very different research focus. Her perspective on non-industrial farming was to influence the entire focus of my fieldwork (Okely 1994b, 1996: chapter 10, 2001) and this was something that never featured in the original research proposal. Retrospectively, I recognise that I had found the equivalent of a similar rural woman whom I had encountered during fieldwork in the west of Ireland: namely Kate Nee, who had inspired me when accompanying my then partner before we became fully fledged anthropologists (Brody 1973; Okely 2002). Through free association, the unconscious resonances with a wonderful experience from the past gave me the confidence to reach out to another powerful woman from another world.

Location Through Accident and the Seizure of this Chance

Sometimes it is through a chance encounter with an individual that a field location is found. The original focus may remain the same but the choice of exact location is often through accident and the mutual openness of both the anthropologist and the local individual.

Chance dictated the location of Michael Herzfeld's fieldwork in Crete. After being directed by someone to a specific place, he nevertheless went to the wrong bus stop and the bus driver led him to his own village:

> My wife and I went to Crete for a few days prospecting for a good field site, and I had in mind a village that was very much like the one that I had left in Rhodes … Well, we went to the wrong bus stop, and as a result of a conversation we had with a man there, I said, 'My wife's interested in local weaving, I'm looking for a place to study practices that have to do with where people marry, and how they decide where to marry, and so on' … I made it sound rather like folklore, and he seemed to understand pretty clearly what I wanted, what we both wanted. And … then he bellowed across at somebody walking by, to come over. This turned out to be the bus conductor, who said, 'Well, I go to a village called … And if you want to come and see it come along!'
>
> What he *didn't* tell us, and what we discovered at the end of the bus line … that we were actually going to *his* village. We stopped in front of a coffee house, which turned out to be *his* coffee house … he ushered us in, and there was his father-in-law and his father-in-law's brother, two wonderful elderly men, both dressed to the nines in full Cretan costume, and they made us feel very welcome, and they asked us what we wanted, and I very quickly explained …
>
> And he started to talk at great length about their marriage rules. After listening for a while … I asked him if I could write all this down. And he said 'Go right ahead' … And I must say that in the next hour or so I must have collected more information than I could normally get in a Rhodian village in the course of a week … Anyway … we came back. (Herzfeld 1999)

Free-ranging Discussion with Latent Structure

As already suggested in my rapport with the young Traveller woman, free association can also be applied to interview or dialogue format. I first 'interviewed' Jacqueline

Grégoire, partly to establish my research identity. But it was days and weeks of participant observation that led me to the main themes. It was only after I had known her for over a year that I finally approached her with a tape recorder. I already knew most of the answers to the broad-brush questions I posed. It was important to record her ideas in her own words. It became a free-ranging discussion where, although I did direct her to some of the main topics that interested her, I also encouraged digressions, revealing new perspectives that even then I had not predicted. Sometimes the very presence of the tape recorder galvanises the speaker, who recognises the chance to record a personal and materially lasting testimony. Such had been my early pre-anthropological experience with Harold Busby, a Deserter from the First World War and a man whom I had befriended (Okely: 1996 chapter 10).

Such 'interviews' are often dubbed unstructured or semi-structured. On the surface this is the case, if one takes the positivist interventionist stance. However, there are hidden structures, as in psychoanalysis. It is up to the anthropologist to detect the latent as well as overt themes after the action. The same applies to my free-ranging dialogues with anthropologists, whose answers to open-ended questions have revealed patterns of commonalities or differences of which they may not have been fully aware in our relaxed one-to-one exchanges. This format is very different from performative seminar papers or formal lectures with an audience of many and where 'talking off the top of one's head' is to be shunned.

In such exchanges, both in the field and with colleague anthropologists, the distance of the detached interviewer is inappropriate. There is mutual exchange and sometimes shared disclosure, 'thus promoting dialogue rather than interrogations' (Bristow and Esper 1988). 'In this interactive context, interviewees become narrators who improvise stories in response to researchers' questions, probes, and stories' (Ellis at al. 1997: 123). The engaged anthropologist, rather than the necessarily anonymised psychoanalyst, stimulates revealing dialogue through mutual trust and shared participation, even when vicarious (Okely 1994b).

Writing Up Long After Writing Down

Writing up, to return to Freud, is also a form of dreaming, of contemplation and letting go. Field notes, however detailed, can act as triggers. There is the evidence on paper or transcripts, the facts, the direct quotes and ideally a stream of narrative. But the interpretation comes also from the whole person; body, mind, emotion through memory and re-enactment (Okely 2007). Stray remarks, incidents or asides, either on the physical record or inscribed in the remembering brain, may suddenly crystallise and unwrap the confusions and mysteries. There are retrospective epiphanies. Here again is the uniqueness in research of long-term participant observation. Vast areas and nuances are lost if the research is written up by someone who has not been there. The research cannot be so easily delegated. The free association from past experience in the field is an added and vital element. This is not to underestimate the painstaking organisation and tabulation of the field material (Okely 1994a), in conjunction with previous published material and new varieties of sources, such as the internet and telephone.

I have sat in the studies of numerous anthropologists and seen their field notes and diaries. These are their core resources. But already anthropologists have discussed 'head notes' (Jackson 1990): those that were never written. I would broaden that to heart and body notes, which may only rise to the surface through free association.

To conclude: free association is often what anthropologists have practised, often in opposition to the formulaic and positivist directives increasingly found in methods books advocated by other social scientists. It has been used knowingly or, more often unwittingly in the approach to fieldwork, confronting lost or seemingly random ideas and images. Anthopologists have creatively responded to what the people themselves find significant and there may be a subtle interweaving of the outsider's historical context and hegemony with those lived and negotiated by the people. The anthropologist needs free passage from one theme to another. Key individuals cannot be easily identified in advance. They are often met through free association of another kind. The writing up is a form of dreaming, just as Freud compared free association to that. Notes and evidence, paperwork and high-tech communications are vital resources. But their interpretation and rethinking are assisted by the free-ranging imagination, which allows seemingly extraneous memories through all the senses to surface. To rephrase Schiller: 'Reason must relax its watch upon the gates;' that is, before the final text can emerge.

References

Agar, M. 1980. *The Professional Stranger*. New York: Academic Press.

Bion, W.F. 1977. 'Attention and Interpretation', in W.F. Bion *Seven Servants*. New York: Jason Aronson.

Breton, A. 1937. *L'Amour fou*. Paris: Gallimard.

Bristow, A.R. and J.A. Esper. 1988. 'A Feminist Research Ethos', in Nebraska Sociological Feminist Collective (ed.), *A Feminist Ethic for Social Science Research*. New York: Edwin Mellen, pp. 67–81.

Brody, H. 1973. *Inishkillane: Change and Decline in the West of Ireland*, London: Allen Lane.

de Beauvoir, S. 1949. *Le Deuxième Sexe*. Paris: Gallimard.

Ellis, C., C. Kiesinger and L.M. Tilmann-Healy. 1997. 'Interactive Interviewing: Talking about Emotional Experience', in R. Hertz (ed.), *Reflexivity and Voice*. London: Sage, pp. 119–49.

Fish, S. 1980. *Is There a Text in this Class? The Authority of Interpretive Communities*. Baltimore and London: Johns Hopkins University Press.

Freud, S. 1900/1954. *The Interpretation of Dreams*, trans. J. Strachey. London: George Allen and Unwin.

———. 1914. *The Psychopathology of Everyday Life*, trans. A.A. Brill. London: Ernest Benn.

Herzfeld, M. 1999. Interview with J. Okely, Copenhagen.

Jackson, J. 1990. '"I am a fieldnote" : Fieldnotes as a Symbol of Professional Identity', in R. Sanjek (ed.), *Fieldnotes: the Makings of Anthropology*. Ithaca and London: Cornell University Press, pp. 3–34.

Lindisfarne, N. 1997. Interview with J. Okely, Oxford.

Mcleod, M. 1996. Interview with J. Okely, Glasgow.

Okely, J. 1983. *The Traveller-Gypsies*. Cambridge: Cambridge University Press.

————. 1986. *Simone de Beauvoir – a Re-reading.* London: Virago and Pantheon, USA.

————. 1992. 'Anthropology and Autobiography: Participatory Experience and Embodied Knowledge', in J. Okely and H. Callaway (eds), *Anthropology and Autobiography.* London: Routledge, pp. 1–28.

————. 1994a. 'Thinking Through Fieldwork', in R. Burgess and A. Bryman (eds), *Analysing Qualitative Data.* London: Routledge, pp. 18–34.

————. 1994b. 'Vicarious and Sensory Knowledge of Chronology and Change: Ageing in Rural France', in K. Hastrup and P. Hervik (eds), *Social Experience and Anthropological Knowledge.* London: Routledge, pp. 45–64.

————. 1996. *Own or Other Culture.* London: Routledge.

————.2000. 'Rootlessness Against Spatial Fixing: Gypsies, Border Intellectuals and "Others"', in R. Bendix and H. Roodeburg (eds), *Managing Ethnicity.* Amsterdam: Het SpinHuis, pp. 13–40.

————. 2001. 'Visualism and Landscape: Looking and Seeing in Normandy', *Ethnos* 66 (1): 99–120.

————. 2002. 'Written Out: *Inishkillane* Revisited'. Paper presented at the AAA conference, November 2005, Washington.

————. 2003a. 'Deterriorialised and Spatially Unbounded Cultures within Other Regimes', *Anthropological Quarterly* 76 (1): 151–64.

————. 2003b. 'The Filmed Return of the Natives to a Colonising Territory of Terror', *Journal of Media Practice* 3 (2): 65–74.

————. 2006. 'Ethnographic Knowledge has the Power to Transform: It May Also Be Ignored, Blocked or Misappropriated', Third Eric Wolf Lecture, International Research Centre for Cultural Studies, Commission of Social Anthropology of the Austrian Academy of Sciences, Department of Social and Cultural Anthropology, University of Vienna.

————. 2007. 'Fieldwork Embodied', in C. Shilling (ed.), *Embodying Sociology; Retrospect, Progress and Prospects.* Oxford: Blackwell, pp. 66–79.

————. 2008. 'Knowing without Notes', in N. Halstead, E. Hirsch and J. Okely (eds), *Knowing How to Know.* Oxford: Berghahn, pp. 55–74.

————. 2010. *Anthropological Practice: Fieldwork and the Ethnographic Method.* Oxford: Berg.

Overing, J. 1996. Interview with J. Okely, St. Andrews.

Parry, J. 1997. Interview with J. Okely. London.

Pratt, M.L.1986. 'Fieldwork in Common Places', in J. Clifford and G. Marcus (eds), *Writing Culture.* Berkeley: University of California Press, pp. 27–50.

Rosaldo, R. 1989. *Culture and Truth: The Remaking of Social Analysis.* Boston: Beacon Press.

Williams, P. 2002. *Gypsy World: The Silence of the Living and the Voices of the Dead*, Chicago: Chicago University Press.

3

Bringing Ethnography Home?
Costs and Benefits of Methodological Traffic across Disciplines

Thomas Widlok

Introduction

Anthropology, it has been suggested, has exploded methodologically, influencing many other disciplines but not necessarily to its own advantage (Mars 2004: 1). Ethnography in particular has been appropriated by neighbouring disciplines; its exploding popularity is a cross-disciplinary success story. However, an explosion, after all, leaves little or nothing intact and useful behind. What are the costs of success for anthropology in terms of its distinctive fields, concepts and methods? Going out to encounter 'other cultures' has gained currency and is now a general possibility undermining the near monopoly that anthropologists had held for much of the twentieth century in terms of 'having been there' to tell their authoritative story. Moreover, key terms such as 'culture' are now being used extremely widely, by biologists dealing with non-humans, by economists dealing with 'corporate cultures' and by many others seeking for a shorthand that invokes difference. The political (ab)uses of the 'culture' discourse have led many anthropologists to give up the concept altogether, if not as a technical term then at least as an explanatory concept. 'Ethnography', finally, is now so widely used that it covers a wide spectrum of qualitative research methods employed by social scientists of a variety of backgrounds. Is the combined effect of losing exclusive claims to fields, concepts and methods necessarily one of a precarious disciplinary identity and of a protectionist closure of the discipline? In this contribution I shall argue that this need not be the case. There are net benefits of having ethnography venture outside its native discipline as long as it can be successfully and productively reincorporated in new ways. Not every borrowing of ethnography by neighbouring disciplines means that it will be 'watered down'. It may in fact be 'enriched' (and enriching). Other disciplines, for instance archaeology, have successfully borrowed from adjacent disciplines, absorbing borrowed techniques. This 'implosion' seems to have been leading to promising developments (Mars 2004: 1; see also Widlok 2004a, 2005a). The costs and benefits need to be assessed in detail for each particular case of the cross-disciplinary traffic of methods. The cross-disciplinary move of ethnographic methods may help to refine these methods by putting them into wider perspectives, which, somewhat paradoxically, may also include the (re)discovery that anthropology is more than ethnography (see Jarvie 1967; Ingold 2007). The case investigated here is that of linguistics, or, more precisely, the implications of integrating ethnography into current language documentation and archiving for anthropological ethnography. The question is whether and how it enhances our understanding of what constitutes good ethnography and good anthropology.

Ethnography in Unlikely Places

The relationship between anthropology and linguistics has a long and multifaceted history which has been summarised and discussed elsewhere (Duranti 1997; Foley 1997). Suffice it to say that it is with considerable enthusiasm that anthropological linguists have embraced ethnography. Current language documentation aims to include ethnography by reinstalling language as a cultural communicative practice and by focusing on this practice as the declared object of documentation. Anthropologists may simply shrug their shoulders, suggesting that 'the linguists have finally learned their lesson', and they may bemoan the fact that the ethnography of anthropological linguists still does not fully reach the high levels of reflexivity, of openness and of serendipity that are being attributed to anthropological ethnography. Linguists may point to their successful strategies of analysing language in its embeddedness in a society's culture and social organisation, strategies that have evolved out of the growing interest in actual events and in naturally occurring talk (see Goodwin and Duranti 1992: 1). But, as Holy has pointed out, to anthropologists this 'does not sound particularly novel' (Holy 1999: 47). What is overlooked, however, is that integrating ethnography into linguist practices also has the potential of changing ethnography as an anthropological practice. In post-postmodernist anthropology the rather technical procedures of linguistics may seem to be a particularly unlikely place to look for methodological inspiration. However, what exactly are the implications of the routines of linguistic work, especially in the field of multi-media documentation, and what would a successful reimport into anthropology look like? In this contribution I want to outline these implications with regard to a number of key features of present-day language documentation, namely the notions of 'corpus', 'session' and 'context'.

The linguistic practices under consideration here are those of current 'field linguists', inspired by anthropological linguistics in particular, but also fuelled by a general paradigm shift away from Chomsky's linguistics of generative-transformational grammar (Tabakowska 1999). The latter type of linguistics, still dominant in some parts, puts an emphasis on the autonomy of language and therefore thinks it can do without ethnographic work. The revolt against this type of linguistics resulted from the inability of the old paradigm to cope well with natural languages and with growing evidence from many 'exotic' languages, documented by anthropologically minded linguists (see Himmelmann 1998; Austin 2003). More recently, this shift in theoretical thinking has been accelerated by funding initiatives of research programmes in field linguistics, in particular with regard to 'endangered' languages (above all the Dokumentation Bedrohter Sprachen – Documentation of Endangered Languages – programme of the Volkswagen Foundation and ELDP, the Endangered Languages Documentation Programme, of the Rausing Foundation). This, in turn, has gone hand in hand with momentous technical developments of language documentation devices through the use of multimedia tools (especially video recording) and of archiving these records in digital archives of hitherto uncharted dimensions. It is the expressed hope of these research initiatives that the documentation will be long-term (beyond individual research projects), of wide reach (using Internet access) and two-way (serving also as a resource base for the community of speakers). In order to achieve these ambitious aims, specific practices and research routines have to be in place, involving the convertibility of recording formats, the standardisation of metadata descriptions and the regulation of data access, amongst other things. Ethnography is considered to be an integral part of the documentation effort, but, as I shall show in more detail below, ethnography is also changed as the new routines are put into place. These changes involve both meanings of ethnography, the product resulting from the work of ethnographers, namely a holistic description, and the process of field research that leads to this product. If ethnography is, in its concise and literary meaning, 'writing about peoples' (Barnard 2000: 141), the changed routines alter the meaning of every aspect contained in this definition:

- 'Writing' is no longer limited to words and to a linear form of presentation since multimedia documentation allows the integration of other media. Hypertext features allow a break with a purely linear form of data presentation.
- 'Peoples' is no longer necessarily understood in terms of ethnic or any other bounded groups being the units of analysis since speech events frequently involve members of different groups and do not presuppose the existence of groups at all even though they may lead to the emergence of such groups in the first place.
- 'About' continues to be a valid preposition only in so far as the editors of the ethnographic corpus need not be members of the speech community, and therefore may come from a distance. However, 'about' now merges into 'with' and 'of' or 'by' to the extent that the there are no reasons why the management and editorship of corpora should not consist of members of the speech community in question.

To be sure, these changes have already gradually made their way into anthropology. Still, it would be deceptive to present them as if they were already firmly established in anthropological ethnography. It is true that there has always been the use of other media than writing in ethnography, such as images, maps, films, charts and 'ethnographica', i.e. materialised culture. However, even the extensive critique of 'ethnographic writing' in postmodern anthropology had the tendency to look at all these forms of representations as 'text' and not as alternative forms of representation with specific entailments. Similarly, there has been a sub-current in anthropological research that has always considered 'folk description' or 'going out and describing the culture ... [and language] ... of a particular group' (Agar 2002: 54) not to be limited to an ethnic group. The notions of 'ethno' and 'folk' do not necessarily denote 'non-Western' but rather the language and culture of ordinary folk i.e. 'just plain folk', not the language and culture of regulators, standardisers and other supervisory bodies whose aim it is to formulate an orthodoxy of how to speak and to write a language. The alternative term 'sociography' has been around for about seven decades (usually attributed to the work of S. Steinmetz in the 1930s). It is used primarily in historical anthropology and social history, while Bourdieu's concept of 'social field' (1979) is widely used but is still considered to be exactly this, 'Bourdieu's term'. Again, it would be misleading to suggest that this recovering of the 'non-non-Western' has been fully accomplished in anthropology. The same applies to the often raised demand for 'dialogical' ethnography in which 'informants' become 'consultants' or 'partners'.

In other words, the innovative input that multimedia language documentation can provide for ethnography is not disconnected from aspirations for improvement within anthropology. As we leave the lofty heights of programmatic reflections and look more concretely, ethnographic practices and routines are altered in the research process itself. I shall look in particular at a changing notion of 'corpus', at changing ways of dealing with 'sessions' and at new approaches to 'context'.

Compiling a Corpus

The importance that linguists attach to 'the corpus' has to do with their conception of 'context' (see below), which in many ways may appear to be rather peculiar from an anthropological point of view. In mainstream transformational linguistics, mentioned above, the linguistic units (words, sentences, etc.) that form part of language as an autonomous domain are defined by their distribution across the environments (or 'contexts') in which they occur (see Hervey 1999: 62). Here, the environment is rather narrowly considered, namely as the context of the surrounding linguistic units of the same type, e.g. what is the phonemic environment in which a phoneme can occur, and what is the grammatical environment in which a certain word can occur, and so forth. In English the phoneme /o/ needs a certain environment to make a word (usually at least a preceding consonant such as /t/), the word 'student' needs a certain environment of other words (usually an article like 'the' and a verb like 'sleeps') to make an utterance. In other words, the aim of this distributionism is to document the utterances in which certain sounds or words can occur and to thereby define the formal identity of these sounds as meaningful sounds and these words as meaningful utterances. The trouble is that in principle the array of utterances in which they can occur is infinite, as is now being realised (Hanks 1996: 141; Hervey 1999: 62). The initial common response to this problem was to replace the open-endedness of real events with the limits of an artificially closed corpus (collected by the researcher in question). There are parallels between this notion of a 'corpus' and that of the traditional ethnographic monograph. Both are considered to be the common product that results from documentation work. Traditional ethnography has for a long time been seen as defining the holistic inventory of cultural materials in a variety of environments. In both cases there is currently a process of redefinition taking place, and the conference sessions from which this collection of texts has resulted is part of that process in anthropology. My argument is that for anthropology some inspiration can come from the ways in which present-day language documentation redefines 'the corpus'.

The notion of a corpus as a domain in fieldwork-oriented language documentation introduces several new aspects. A corpus can be as big and comprehensive as any previous collection of utterances, or as any ethnographic monograph for that matter, but no pretension is made that it covers all parts equally. Rather, the default assumption is that there can be a number of complementary corpora. With traditional ethnographic monographs, the attempt has been made, in the well-known Human Relations Area Files, to standardise monographs so that one could slice them up into traits that could then be compared. This attempt is greatly hampered by the fact that monographs written at different times about different groups by ethnographers with very different backgrounds do not lend themselves to be partitioned into pieces that would easily and productively allow comparisons. Even if the same index words have been used, it is a matter of considerable debate to reconstruct the possibly divergent theoretical underpinnings. With a corpus, in contrast, we now readily assume that the limits of what went into the corpus are indeed set by the researcher and that they are not 'given'. It is also readily accepted that a corpus can and will include some parts that are better and more thoroughly analysed than other parts. This is especially relevant for data collections based on audio and video recordings. As is widely known, the transcription of these records is extremely laborious and time-consuming. There is a growing sophistication in transcriptions that are multilayered, with distinct layers for phonemic transcription, orthographic transcription, various ways of parsing into grammatical units, glossing in another language and free translation, to name but the most common layers. At the same time, it has become much easier to record large amounts of data at little cost and with relatively little effort. The combined result of these two trends is that within a corpus only a fraction of all recordings is being transcribed, the tip of the iceberg. This is especially true in the common situation of an 'endangered' language where priority is usually given to recording, to collect as much as possible, with transcription to follow at some – unspecified – time in the future. In other words, no pretence is being made that all these recordings will receive the same attention and the same degree of analysis. Some sessions contain more 'rich points' (see below) than others, but the sessions that are not used as intensively as others by the researchers who have compiled the record are not edited out of the corpus. This is a major difference from most anthropological ethnography, which cuts out the data that remain 'unanalysed'. A good linguistic corpus should feed more than one researcher, and increasingly it will feed back into the group concerned as well. This is in the interest of long-term critical research, in which new questions are raised by other researchers using the same corpus. A traditional ethnographic monograph is – unfortunately – still very much considered a conclusion, a closed body, while the linguistic corpus in multimedia documentation is a body that is still alive, a resource, not a conclusion.

However, it would be a fallacy to consider that part of the corpus that remains unanalysed to be 'raw data'. It is not in the naive sense that there could be no data without theoretical presuppositions. As Jarvie argued almost half a century ago: 'For the notion of "ethnographic fact" conceals the evident theory-impregnation of ethnography … We should not allow ourselves to be blinded to the theoretical content of ethnographic statements by the low level of the theories' (1967: 26). Low-level theories are included in single-term descriptors, classifiers and glosses, no matter whether they are put on paper or into a file. In both cases, we may have heaps of notes or tapes that remain unanalysed. Moreover, in an electronic corpus, these data are in several ways different from a collection of field notes. While notes, or any other 'analogue' documents for that matter, can be put into an archive and then retrieved unchanged, if slightly yellowed, after a certain period, the multimedia language documentation corpus is different. Archivists like to characterise such a corpus as a 'migrating archive'. This is not only because data are no longer stored in one place – in fact, copies should be regularly transferred between mainframe computers to reduce the risk of data loss – but because they are subject to a routine of reformatting in order to enable access and readability across decades of technological change. Without constantly reformatting the metadata the links between the parts of the archive, the archive's structure, will be lost and the retrievability of data will be greatly impaired or outright impossible. Data links and structure now have to be externalised and to be made explicit in a meta-commentary, the metadata, that explains the ordering of entries and the relationships between them. This will also allow the merging of hitherto separate corpora and a continual restructuring of the overall corpus layout. One could go as far as to say that the notion of a corpus allows the data collection to be varied in size, as heterogeneous as one may imagine, to be cumulative and therefore to be truly open because it is defined solely with reference to an accompanying set of metadata. It is the explicit metadata that ensure that openness and heterogeneity continue to exist. This flatly contradicts the postmodernist claim that the abolition of any meta-narrative would be the prerequisite for an ethnography that is dialogically constructed and dynamically improved in the course of time.

In practice, metadata in this context mean that the corpus has to be divided into sessions and that for each session a metadata file has to be compiled that contains key information about the contents of the session and its place in the corpus at large so that it can be successfully retrieved in the future. Data that are inserted into the corpus are not simply added on top, like new notes put on top of a heap of existing notes. Newly inserted sessions can alter the corpus as a whole, for example, when the transcriptions of a text automatically update the lexical database: The software tools (such as Shoebox and Toolbox) that are now widely used will check the existing database as the researcher interlinearises a new session. Whenever a new entry (word) is found, the researcher will be prompted either to match it to an existing record or to create a new record in the database. Take the corpus under consideration here, that of ≠Akhoe Hai//om, a central Khoisan language spoken by a group of so-called 'Bushmen' or 'San' hunter-gatherers in northern Namibia (Widlok 1999). It originally consisted only of a word list (of about 1800 words) that a Finnish teacher had collected in the 1970s and which had been rescued from a dilapidated shed near the Namibian/Angolan border, where it had become food for the termites. Then it grew by a number of tapes of different types (audio cassettes, Hi8 video, VHS video, DV video) stored in numerous boxes of an anthropological fieldworker (in this case myself) in an orderly, if idiosyncratic, fashion but with increasing difficulties of finding machines that could read and play the tapes. Eventually, the single-handed maintenance of such an archive becomes impossible unless a growing proportion of research time is devoted to maintaining 'old data'. At that point in time, the growing corpus was integrated into the large electronic archive installed by DOBES at the Max Planck Institute for Psycholinguistics, following the same standards that the ELDP archive at SOAS and other international archives follow. The latest addition to the corpus consists of recordings made by a Hai//om NGO as part of an oral history project, and a merger with other Khoisan electronic archives has become possible. In the past, the corpus originally compiled by the Finnish teacher (a collection of stories, a grammar and a lexicon) would be printed as a book and remain basically unchanged by any future research. Archivists would add bodies of material by juxtaposing them. The electronic archiving system that is now being put in place allows the insertion of new data not by creating a separate, new corpus but by transforming the existing corpus, without, incidentally, erasing the information on authorship. I shall argue in the following section that the definition of sessions and the formulation of metadata entries, which may initially be considered to be a prime exemplar for external interferences into ethnography as anthropologists practise it, may in fact be a blessing in disguise or at least a case of benefits outweighing the costs.

Working with Sessions

The current funding initiatives for language documentation have set aside funds for the upkeep of electronic archives for the decades to come. This involves the repeated reformatting of the data, currently converted from various media into digital MPEG 2 format. The corpora should remain accessible, through the use of metadata, no matter what the original format of the ethnography was (text file, photo, video, audio, kinship database) and no matter what future software and formats will be like. In order to achieve this, the corpus has to have sessions and metadata describing these sessions so that they can be found in the corpus. This key requirement of an electronic archive regularly led to raised eyebrows amongst anthropologists particularly committed to ethnography as it may appear to be yet another 'objectifying' means to compartmentalise fieldwork experience into externally defined slots. However, such a hasty reaction can be unfounded at best and self-deceptive at worst. The demarcation of sessions can be as sensitive (or insensitive) to local or emic conceptualisation as any other aspect of ethnography. It forces ethnographers to lay open what otherwise often remains implicit and it suggests a much more systematic use of 'strips of ethnography' (Agar 1986) than is commonly the case. Administrators of language archives frequently insert 'controlled vocabularies' into the descriptions of corpora and sessions, that is a very limited choice of descriptive terms from which one needs to choose to compile a metadata entry. In principle, however, they do not predetermine how sessions are defined in terms of contents.

Quite to the contrary, in practice, sessions may still be demarcated according to the preferences of the researcher. The anthropological litmus test is therefore the degree to which the definition of sessions takes account of the specific situations, positions and locations of speakers 'on their own turf' (see Widlok 2004b). Instead of generalising the everyday cultural background of the researcher into a conceptual grid of categories, the emic definitions of speech genres, events or situations can either replace or complement the established ways of defining what constitutes a piece of ethnography. Moreover, since the minimal definition of a session simply consists of a name, defining its beginning and end (on a tape or any other media) and its relation to other sessions or resources in the corpus, there is no reason why sessions should not be overlapping. Parts may be taken out of existing sessions to create new sessions and existing sessions may be enlarged after connections to preceding or to subsequent events become clearer. This is not just a matter of pragmatically compartmentalising a corpus to make it more manageable. Rather, the function of defining a session is to use this session in order to create frames for understanding what people do when they talk. A session is therefore very much like what Michael Agar (1986) has called a 'strip' of data that helps to resolve breakdowns or gaps in our understanding. Agar attempted to develop a new language for describing the epistemological process of ethnography, which usually does not comply easily with the dominant hypothesis-testing paradigm. Under that paradigm, a hypothesis is defined and appropriate procedures for data collection are designed to test it. In contrast, ethnography follows not the prior formulation of hypotheses but an initial breakdown of understanding as the researcher's first attempt(s) to make sense fail. These breakdowns of understanding occur all the time, not only when we learn a language but more generally when we continue in our attempts to apply categories and concepts. Correspondingly, one session can be used for resolving very different breakdowns of existing frames of expectations.

To make the point clearer, let me introduce a session that was recorded as part of our language documentation project with speakers of ≠Akhoe Hai//om (for details, see also the ≠Akhoe Hai//om home page at www.mpi.nl/DOBES). This session contains several rich points. To begin with, the session is part of a long storytelling tradition, in this case stories featuring Haiseb, a culture hero in the lore of many Khoisan groups. In a nutshell, the plot is about this trickster who once went walking through the bush, like the ≠Akhoe Hai//om (sometimes) still do today. He managed to scare off the lion from its kill and to have the meat for himself and his family, until his children told the lions' children about it and the trick no longer worked. Narratives with this plot, or similar motives, are found amongst other Khoisan-speaking groups (see Schmidt 1989; Widlok 1999) and possibly elsewhere, but what makes this storytelling session particularly valuable as a part of this corpus is that it documents a particular way of telling the story. Witnessing ≠Akhoe Hai//om storytelling is tantamount to a 'mandated breakdown', as suggested by Agar (1986), that is, it challenges our understanding of how narratives spread (or how individual instances of talk are turned into 'a narrative'), namely by one person telling a story to one (or several) listener(s). Witnessing an ≠Akhoe Hai//om storytelling event immediately leads to a breakdown of that understanding which turns out to rest on rather culturally specific expectations: Here it is not one storyteller facing an audience but several, often all, participants actively engage in the storytelling event so that the roles of 'storyteller' and 'audience' merge into one another. No one is only a listener but everyone present is potentially and actually a narrator. Correspondingly, the maximal corresponding session in this case will be archived in the form of a video clip, comprising several hours of video footage showing several people interactively taking turns telling several Haiseb stories. On the particular occasion in question, a man had hunted an antbear and brought it back to his hearth group. It took several hours for the meat to be divided and cooked over the fire, and this is the period that people filled with storytelling. News about the lucky hunt spread so that a number of people came to visit while others went away briefly to get more firewood or water to keep the cooking going. The maximal session captures all of this, but within this maximal session other sessions may be defined in which a specific story is told with a specific constellation of speakers. In this particular case, the 'Haiseb and the Lion's Meat' story is being told with two primary speakers, a middle-aged woman and her son-in-law. The corresponding clip (of about forty minutes) constitutes an ethnographic strip that helps to resolve yet another breakdown of our understanding. Not only may storytelling involve more than one speaker, but it furthermore matters who the speakers are and what their relationship is. In this case the primary (but not the sole) actors are in an avoidance relation of being in-laws to one another. They do not sit close to one another and avoid addressing one another directly, although they belong to one hearth group, share their resources and are very familiar with one another. In other words, they do not form a 'team of narrators' in the sense of two performers or a dance company, who would rehearse their cooperation before performing to outsiders. Hence a further breakdown of understanding occurs following our expectation that a meta-discourse of rehearsal is necessary to coordinate turn-taking when a narrative is being presented. Further sessions at a more microscopic level of resolution may be defined with the aim of showing how participants deal with overlaps, echoing, repetitions. The metadata files for these sessions are the necessary aides to find a session amongst hours of video recordings. The information included in the metadata also situates the recording historically (the place and the persons involved) to avoid the folklorist illusion of a 'closed corpus', in which one session of storytelling, for instance, becomes the typical and authoritative version of a narrative that is in reality distributed dynamically across events in time and space.

Thus, an explicit session definition facilitates an ethnographic strategy that critically differs from that of the folklorist of the old days, who would go around, collect instances of a story and then compose a master exemplar of that story, which was then printed in a collection of folklore. We did not select 'the best' storyteller. In fact, in that instance, I did not mean to record storytelling at all. I was attracted to the scene because of the killing of the antbear, which I took to be a good opportunity to record how meat was divided among kinsmen. The ≠Akhoe Hai//om participants in a sense then hijacked the DV camera by adding more things that they thought should get recorded, namely the Haiseb trickster stories which involve many references to wild animals and to what happened to Haiseb when he went foraging in the bush. The session description, therefore, includes much of what would ordinarily be labelled 'context information'. This leads us to 'context', the third, and maybe the most critical, aspect of current language documentation efforts, which has considerable potential for also enhancing ethnography within anthropology.

Dealing with Context

From the brief description of the storytelling session given above, it will be clear that there are a number of different ways of 'contextualising' this event. First of all, and this is the most likely contextualisation to be put forward by linguists, ≠Akhoe Hai//om storytelling can be contextualised with reference to other types of speech acts in ≠Akhoe Hai//om, for instance arguments, everyday conversation, ritualised language, demand sharing and so forth. Alternatively, it may be contextualised comparatively with regard to storytelling in other Khoisan groups (see Schmidt 1989) or indeed among other people living in the area (see Widlok 1999) or beyond the region, say among other people classified as hunter-gatherers (see Brody 2001).

Then there is a completely separate set of possible contextualisations, given that the session outlined above also documents avoidance relationships, which emerge not only in storytelling events but also in other contexts, some of them linguistic (such as the use of kin terms) and others not (such as the use of physical space). The two main narrators in the storytelling session are a young man, Nomob, and Mais, his mother-in-law. Nomob and Mais would not sit close to one another, so that without a wide-angle lens it would have been hardly possible to get them into the same frame of video recording. The video session documents both the avoidance expressed through their seating arrangement and at the same time the familiarity they both have with the story and with one another. Nomob is living with his parents-in-law as part of a bride-service arrangement (see Widlok 1999). Their avoidance relationship would not be correctly captured by simply documenting the distance between them and by outlining what they avoid doing together. As this session shows, when it comes to telling a story Nomob and Mais work together very closely, they are on equal terms, they do not compete with one another but they cooperate with one another without forfeiting a relationship of respect. In other words the context of avoidance relationships among ≠Akhoe Hai//om elucidates the way they talk to one another and at the same time the shared storytelling sheds more light on what constitutes an avoidance relationship in the first place, namely not the absence of relations but a particular sociality of familiarity and respect. The metadata description of the session in the language archive allows for both types of context to be specified. The template of the IMDI editor (the software tool for designing the metadata: see Widlok 2004b) has controlled vocabularies for both 'speech genres' and 'actor roles', but in principle there is no limit to the context information that can be included in the metadata description. This mix of controlled comparisons (limited choices), on the one hand,

and the openness and limitlessness, on the other, is a compromise between the attempt to prompt the researchers to give as much contextual information as possible without predetermining what the researchers (or speakers of a particular language) will find to be appropriate to be included as context.

Anthropological ethnographers are often quick to assert that what marks their ethnography off from other forms of qualitative research (or from anything that other disciplines call ethnography) is that 'we know the context and how to contextualise'. As Dilley has already pointed out, the importance that anthropologists give to context is only matched by the paucity of attention given to the theoretical and methodological exploration of it (1999: 1): 'Ever since Malinowski, anthropologists have chanted the mantra of placing "social and cultural phenomena in context" .' The mantra continues, despite the fact that Dilley and others have clearly shown that 'context' is far from unproblematic. It has become clear that propagating the 'context of situation' for linguistic analysis (following Malinowski) misleadingly insinuates a facticity of context, something that is out there and only needs to be uncovered (see Fabian 1999: 101). Context is always preselected by the analyst and follows intiuitions about what is considered to be relevant (Hervey 1999: 68). Moreover, if explanations rest on something being integrated into an external context that context in itself would need contextualising, leading to an infinite regress.

Linguists and anthropologists have encountered considerable problems when trying to 'fix the meaning' of even basic key terms in their descriptions. The Hai//om term '*ises*' (glossed as 'story' above) is a case in point. The root verb from which the term is derived can mean 'to appear', in the sense of 'disguise' and 'pretence', as well as 'to happen', in the sense of 'occurrence' and 'event' (see Rust 1969: 208). The same problem emerges in ≠Akhoe Hai//om with other key terms such as /*huru* ('play' or 'ritual'), as I have pointed out elsewhere (Widlok 2005b). Any disambiguation of these terms proves to be very difficult. If the telling of stories from 'the time of the first humans', such as the Haiseb stories, seamlessly merge with 'factual' stories from the here and now, it is by no means clear that the latter are interpreted by extending them 'backwards' into a 'mythical sphere'. The reverse could also be true. For a linguist, this challenges the traditional, formalist, approach to the problem based on a rather strict separation between lexical form and context. In the established academic division of labour, a (formalist) linguist would collect examples of how the linguistic form is being used in a variety of contexts in order to pin down the 'literal' meaning of a word, while anthropologists were usually left the task of concentrating on metaphors and on lexemes that have no clear literal meaning. Anthropologists tend to leave the terms in italics, shifting the burden of making sense to the readers, who have to keep track of the variety of meanings that get attached to a local term in the course of ethnographic writing. But this is exactly what Hervey has identified as the widespread strategy of 'explaining the unexplained by the inexplicable', ultimately shifting it outside the theoretical scope of investigation (1999: 68–69). The underlying problem with this approach is that it proves to be an impossible task and that it is ultimately self-defeating because context is inexhaustible and there is no way of knowing from the data when enough 'applications' of a term have been collected to fix its 'literal' or its derived meaning.

Multimedia language documentation, which includes ethnography, does not privilege either the 'literal' or the 'metaphorical' end of the spectrum but begins by juxtaposing as many diverse speech events as possible. This can be misunderstood to amount to an unreflective amassing of data, but it can also be turned into a routine of analytical movements, that is, moving laterally rather than moving in linear fashion from 'pure form' to 'application'. The analytical movement proceeds from one situation with a particular positioning of participants to another situation with – in all likelihood – a somewhat different positioning. Using hypertext, it now becomes possible for ethnography producers and users alike to follow this lateral movement across the whole corpus without difficulty. In this process the ethnographic unit of speech production and analysis is shifted from that of individual speakers (or interview partners) to that of the participatory framework in which speakers and listeners engage with one another. It replaces the theoretical notion of the unlimited combinational capacity of language production with that of a limited practical feasibility, since speakers – due to their position in ongoing social interaction and communication settings – do not have indefinite or equal access to speech resources but are restricted by the immediate situation, their social position and the overall conditions for interaction and communication (see Hanks 1996). It is only a small step from this improved dealing with linguistic context to an improved understanding and description of non-linguistic action in general anthropological ethnography.

Moreover, a final twist can be added to the point that is equally fundamental. The lateral way of learning to understand and use a language, or any other cultural practice for that matter, is in principle also followed within a language itself by the already competent speakers of the language. They, too, do not start off with abstract 'pure notions' of events, of 'play' or 'story', but they, too, create framelike bridges of understanding as they move from one situation to the next. They may stretch the words that they have available to cover a new experience, or a new experience may lead them to foster or to refrain from the use of certain language resources in certain situations. They make mistakes, not narrowly defined mistakes such as getting the tenses wrong but frame-based mistakes, that is, the situation may not be working in a way that their frame expectations can handle (see Agar 2002). The same happens to linguists and anthropologists as soon as they go beyond observing and start participating ethnographically in 'a language' or 'a culture'. In other words, the relation that the community of speakers have to their own language and their way of life more generally should no longer be considered to be radically different from that of the outside linguist/anthropologist. The upshot of this is that the ethnography in such electronic documentations are now not only in principle but also in practice a resource for both other researchers and the people with whom they have worked. The two are brought together not simply because it is required by the ethics of one's profession or by the rules of one's funding body but because it is an implication of state-of-the-art documentation methods. Researchers learning and documenting a language ethnographically follow the same route and have the same difficulties as already competent speakers of the language themselves who also deal with a changing world and a changing language.

Conclusion

When we see ethnography leaving the confines of our discipline we may look at it as parents do when they see their grown-up child leaving home, coming under the influence of other people without planning ever to completely return to the native family. Ethnography was in fact initially the child of the mixed marriage, so to speak, between linguistics and anthropology, at least in the work of Boas or Malinowski. However, in this contribution I have not advocated a simple return to the roots or an attempt to restore the original state of affairs when linguistics and anthropology were still united in ethnography. Rather, I have suggested that we may in fact benefit from the experiences that ethnography has gained and continues to gain by venturing outside anthropology. The child has grown up but it has not left the house empty when it moved out. I have made this general point by presenting material from current research in multimedia language documentation research.

Thus, my particular concern has been with field linguistics where the term 'ethnography' was adopted some decades ago but where it has only recently been taken seriously as part of multimedia language documentation efforts. Generalising from this experience, I suggest that bringing the child home after it has ventured outside the confines of the discipline, without stopping it from continuing to leave the house, may indeed be the way forward for anthropology. There are many good reasons for encouraging ethnography in the context of language documentation (see Widlok 2004b). Conversely, tracing the ethnography as it enters other arenas, such as that of language documentation, helps anthropologists to concentrate on what continues to be their most important methodological task, namely to sharpen their problems, to articulate their conjectures (see Jarvie 1967: 27) and to realise that this brings the rich points of ethnography home.

References

Agar, M. 1986. *Speaking of Ethnography.* Qualitative Research Methods Series 2. Beverley Hills: Sage.

———. 2002. *Language Shock. Understanding the Culture of Conversation.* New York: Perennial.

Austin, P. 2003. *Language Documentation and Description.* London: Hans Rausing Endangered Languages Project.

Barnard, A. 2000. *Social Anthropology. A Concise Introduction for Students.* Taunton: Studymates.

Bourdieu, P. 1979. *La Distinction: critique sociale du jugement.* Paris: Éditions de Minuit.

Brody, H. 2001. *The Other Side of Eden. Hunter-gatherers, Farmers and the Shaping of the World.* London: Faber and Faber.

Dilley, R. 1999b. 'Introduction: The Problem of Context', in R. Dilley (ed.), *The Problem of Context.* New York: Berghahn: 1–46.

Duranti, A. 1997. *Linguistic Anthropology.* Cambridge: Cambridge University Press.

Fabian, J. 1999. 'Ethnographic Misunderstanding and the Perils of Context', in R. Dilley (ed.), *The Problem of Context.* New York: Berghahn: 85–104.

Foley, W. 1997. *Anthropological Linguistics*. Malden: Blackwell.

Goodwin, C. and A. Duranti. 1992. 'Rethinking Context: An Introduction', in A. Duranti and C. Goodwin (eds), *Rethinking Context: Language as an Interactive Phenomenon*. Cambridge: Cambridge University Press: 1–42.

Hanks, W. 1996. *Language and Communicative Practices*. Boulder: Westview Press.

Hervey, S. 1999. 'Context, the Ghost in the Machine', in R. Dilley (ed.), *The Problem of Context*. New York: Berghahn: 61–72.

Himmelmann, N. 1998. 'Documentary and Descriptive Linguistics', *Linguistics* 36 (1): 161–95.

Holy, L. 1999. 'Contextualisation and Paradigm Shifts', in R. Dilley (ed.), *The Problem of Context*. New York: Berghahn: 47–60.

Ingold, T. 2007. *Anthropology is NOT Ethnography*. Radcliffe-Brown Lecture in Social Anthropology, 14 March 2007. London: British Academy.

Jarvie, I. 1967. *The Revolution in Anthropology*. London: Routledge.

Mars, G. 2004. 'Refocusing with Applied Anthropology', *Anthropology Today* 20 (1): 1–2.

Rust, F. 1969. *Nama Wörterbuch*. Pietermaritzburg: University of Natal Press.

Schmidt, S. 1989. *Catalogue of the Khoisan Folktales of Southern Africa*, Part 2: *The Tales*. Hamburg: Buske.

Tabakowska, E. 1999. 'New Paradigm Thinking in Linguistics: Meaning is the Context', in R. Dilley (ed.), *The Problem of Context*. New York: Berghahn.

Widlok, T. 1999. *Living on Mangetti. 'Bushman' Autonomy and Namibian Independence*. Oxford: Oxford University Press.

———. 2004a. '(Re-)current Doubts on Hunter-gatherer Studies as Contemporary History', in A. Barnard (ed.), *Hunter-gatherers in History, Archaeology and Anthropology*. Oxford: Berg: 217–26.

———. 2004b. 'Ethnography in Language Documentation', *Language Archive Newsletter* 1: 4–6.

———. 2005a. 'Theoretical Shifts in the Anthropology of Desert Hunter-gatherers', in P. Veth, M. Smith and P. Hiscock (eds), *Desert Peoples. Archaeological Perspectives*. Oxford: Blackwell: 17–33.

———. 2005b. 'The Relational Resourcefulness of the Body', in K. Sugawara (ed.), *Construction and Distribution of Body Resources*. Tokyo: Tokyo University of Foreign Studies: 18–30.

4

Ethnography at the Interface
'Corporate Social Responsibility' as an Anthropological Field of Enquiry

Christina Garsten

Introduction: In the Thick of Corporations

In exploring globalisation processes, one can hardly escape the role of corporations and of the market. With recent social change, such as the remodelling of welfare states and intensified globalisation of trade, the spirit of Western market capitalism colours our ways of thinking about the dynamics of societies as well as the make-up of social relations. We learn to gear our minds to market reasoning and to corporate interests, all the way from day care through the school system, into professional life – and sometimes even sociability is modelled with market thinking lurking behind. We spend of lot of time and energy within and in the vicinities of corporations, through work, through the experience of being a customer or otherwise being affected by their operations. Whether we like it or not, much of our lives are lived in the thick of corporations, as it were, locally as well as translocally.

Corporate structures and ways of thinking reach far beyond our local communities and are tangled into everyday lives at translocal levels. Their impact is often wide-ranging, affecting not just the economy, but also the environment and social and cultural structures. With the gradual dismantling of national regulations and trade barriers and the establishment of flexible and entrepreneurial corporations as the template for organisational design, disorganised capitalism has taken a strong grip on the world. Contemporary large-scale global economies leave us with a fragmented political authority with limited power to oversee and regulate the workings of markets (Palan 2000). In some senses, the state has left open an area for corporations to enter and in which to establish new markets for regulation as well as new arenas for diffusion of normative ideas.

This new situation also challenges established ways of thinking about states, markets and corporations. We have been taught to think in terms of a split between the benevolent state on the one hand, and the profit-oriented market populated by greedy corporations, on the other. A commonly held view among corporate leaders, at least in Western capitalism, is that getting involved in wider societal issues risks taking a corporation's eye 'off the ball' as well as intruding on the arena of the nation state. The economist Milton Friedman's view (1970) that 'the business of business is business' and the sole social responsibility of a corporation is to maximise profits for its shareholders is indicative of this view. More recently, however, we have seen the development of a slightly different set of ideas positioning a new role for corporations in the global economy. Corporate leaders have had to respond to concerns about the potential negative effects of their activities, to growing grass-roots critique and political action and to tougher and closer media coverage. A growing number of corporations are engaging in what may be seen as a normative add-on to capitalism, attempting to make sure that they do not contribute to human rights violations or violations of workers' rights. The idea that business has a broader social responsibility or citizenship role has, in some ways, strengthened with the globalisation of markets (see, for example, Compa and Diamond 1996; Addo 1999; Andriof and McIntosh 2001; Sullivan 2003). 'Corporate social responsibility', commonly referred to as CSR, has since the 1990s emerged as one of the priorities in the policy documents and yearly reports of corporations. Corporate actors are seeking to develop or adopt codes of conduct and ethical guidelines into their corporate cultures and management systems (see, for example, Leipziger 2003). In this way, they wish not only to respond to stakeholder pressure but also to project an image of business as not just profit-seeking, but also socially responsible and ethically minded.

An important milestone for CSR was the launch of the UN Global Compact in 1999. Since the United Nations Secretary General Kofi Annan challenged world business leaders to 'embrace and enact' the Global Compact initiative, a large number of corporations have joined. Non-governmental organisations (NGOs) work to support the UN in their efforts to promote the basic principles of a market informed by human rights principles and codes of conduct. Also, consultancies specialise in counselling business leaders in social accountability.

In this gap of global governance, a number of new tools and professional roles have emerged. Social standards, policies, codes of conduct and assessment practices abound (see Brunsson et al. 2000). Corporations undergo ethical certification and enter into partnerships with other organisations to manifest accountability to the state, to the wider public and to potential consumers. There is also a host of new professional positions for the pursuit of corporate social responsibility – 'corporate social responsibility manager', 'manager codes of conduct', 'ethical trading manager', and the like. The field of corporate social responsibility has also become a favourite concern of the media, with a number of magazines targeting CSR issues all round the world.

What we see is the development and growth of a new policy area, with an intricate network of organisations, new forms of partnerships and its own particular language to support it. In this policy web, relations and interconnections between the social, on the one hand, and the economic, on the other, between moralities and markets, are increasingly complex and constantly negotiated. In discussions of corporate social responsibility, managers try out partly new ways of combining profit with social accountability and what it means to be a 'global player'. In the process, they negotiate bottom-line reasoning with sustainable futures, markets and moralities, and they interact with the interests of state agencies and non-governmental organisations (see Garsten 2004b). We are seeing the development of an organisational landscape that is made up not so much of clearly identifiable entities with completely differing interests, but of organisations that cross-cut and intermesh. The field of CSR is, in other words, made up of an assemblage of corporate capital, human rights advocacy and regulatory interests.

The ethnographic approach may reveal specific alignments of corporate interests and rationalities with other collective concerns and interest. But doing fieldwork in and among translocal organisations invites a number of methodological challenges. This chapter discusses the challenges of studying the 'corporate social responsibility' movement by doing ethnography in and among translocal organisations, with a particular focus on the problems associated with fields that are discontinuous in both time and space. For a start, it is not easy to determine what makes up 'the field' as such. The organisations involved are often dispersed across national boundaries, and the actors tend to be highly mobile. The central ideas manifest themselves in a number of different localities and appear difficult to pin down. The field of corporate social responsibility, it seems, is 'here, there and everywhere' (see Hannerz 2003).

The field of 'corporate social responsibility', I suggest, may be studied by the anthropologist positing herself at the crossroads, or interface, of such linkages and connections. It is at the very interfaces of organisations that one may come to understand what 'corporate social responsibility' is all about, where one can get a sense of the different versions that are played out and the temporary consensus that may emerge, following negotiations.[1] We are dealing here with interactions of people representing different organisations, different interests and with their own individual preferences, experiences and perspectives. At the interface, we may find that interactions and relations in the field may be quite dense around the topics at heart, that differing interests are twinned together in quite complex ways, and that ethnography in translocal fields may very well be 'grounded' in its own particular way, in reference to the character of the field. While this methodological stance enables us to track processes of meaning-making that may be translocal, it also invites some serious questions regarding the 'thickness' and density of ethnography in practice.

CSR Conferences as Anthropological Fields: Contingencies, Continuities

Doing fieldwork in the area of corporate social responsibility leaves the door open for some tricky methodological challenges. Given that '[a]n extended spell of "participant observation" is still the irreducible minimum of professional credentials required in the discipline', as Sherry Ortner (1997: 61) notes (citation from Comaroff and

Comaroff 2003: 153), studying the CSR movement entails having to scrutinise and reflect on methodological approaches. To begin with, it is not easy to determine where the field starts and where it ends. The field seems to appear in a number of different localities, only to evaporate or diffuse again as easily at it emerged. It may appear in a countryside village outside Stockholm, on the premises of the Swedish Ministry of Foreign Affairs, at the European Commission in Brussels or in luxury hotels in Brussels or Miami, to mention only a few of the places I have visited in the field. The field of corporate social responsibility, it seems, is all over the place and nowhere at the same time. Caring little for national or other boundaries, the CSR movement exists on a scale that does not yield itself easily to classic fieldwork.[2]

For me as an anthropologist, this proved as frustrating as it was positively challenging: not least since the 'subjects' of study hardly inhabit stable social contexts for which we possess conceptual tools. The people in the field, i.e. the corporate leaders, the consultants, the representatives of NGOs, states or international organisations, have travel across the world built into their calendars and do much of their work 'on the move', as it were. Moreover, they seem, at first, to be continuously new ones, giving the impression of a field that continuously renews itself or keeps on adding new members and associates. For the initial period of research, I was truly troubled by the degree of apparent discontinuity of the field.

Conferences are temporarily localised, temporally organised sites where the content of corporate social responsibility and its boundaries are tried out and manifested. And it is exactly at the interfaces of different organisations – state agencies, corporations, non-governmental organisations – that these conferences are situated. To a large extent, corporate social responsibility is about conferencing. This does not mean to say that they may not have important consequences: sometimes they do. The impact is judged at local level, down the supply chain, in factories, sweatshops, domestic units and elsewhere. My point is rather to emphasise the importance of conference participation as a way of 'doing' corporate social responsibility. Much of the field of corporate social responsibility is about corporate leaders presenting their cases and their experiences, discussing among each other, debating with NGO and union representatives and setting up new meetings. Conferences are arenas for the performance of corporate social responsibility talk, arenas where the discourse of CSR is created, negotiated and elaborated upon. They are sites for drawing lines of inclusion and exclusion; for the marking of identity between those who believe in CSR and others; and, not least, for the creation of visions and action plans and for making a difference. Conferences are thus also part of what makes up 'the local' in this widely dispersed and globalising field. They are 'where the action is' (see Strathern 1995). Hence, I set my mind on attempting to attend a number of conferences, workshops and meetings that appeared to be of some weight for the people involved. These were people I had previously interviewed and established a certain rapport with. Following them along to conferences thus seemed to be a promising way forward.

As elsewhere in the world of conferencing, the official agendas are often complemented by less official but equally important ones, organised on the spot. The very possibility of meeting informally with representatives of different kinds of organisations is a main attraction of conferences. Informants have told me that they often go to conferences in order to meet with other professionals engaged in the same business sector – outside the conference programme. Another reason often stated for conferencing is that it offers valuable opportunities to socialise with other CSR professionals of the same nationality, who may want to discuss a proposal for new legislation or a political move. Among the CSR 'insiders', some conferences are also better known than others for facilitating such extra-programme meetings. And they are not necessarily those that take place in the more attractive big cities. Doing conference fieldwork thus also seemed reasonable from the aspect of providing another, less formal, arena for engagement.

After having attended a few conferences and meetings, I began to realise that some people tended to appear now and again, that the issues discussed were quite similar across contexts and that there were, after all, some patterns in the field. As I tried to let go of the idea of locating the field in space, as it were, and instead set out to 'follow the metaphor', the 'plot' or the 'story'(Marcus 1995), a degree of continuity began to appear.

Much of the relative continuity was to be found in the vocabulary of the conference delegates, which also set a distinctive mark on the field at large. The field of corporate social responsibility is to a great extent a discursive arena, replete with keywords, metaphors and plots, such as 'accountability', 'transparency', 'corporate citizenship' and 'partnership'. These keywords are used in a great number of organisational settings and types of activities, in policy documents, in yearly reports, in internal discussions and, not least, at conferences. They have a mobilising function, with the capacity to energise and give direction to thoughts and actions, and they function in this sense as 'attention direction devices' that facilitate coordination across time and space (see Power 2003: 14). The conference delegates at the Ethical Corporation's conference in Brussels, one of the many conferences I attended, were well aware that they were part of a discursive coalition or community, where the members spoke the same lingua franca, and where they used the same words as signifiers.[3] There were several mentions of the particular language of CSR during the conference. Moreover, there was a sense of awareness of the fact that skilful use of this language determines who is 'in' and who is 'out'. By way of short comments or joking remarks, delegates would let the other participants understand that they were aware of their 'proper' usage and meaning and when boundaries were stepped over.

As a particular type of language, the CSR lingua franca also serves an exclusionary function. This is why even people who tend to be sceptical about the inherent meanings of a concept or phrasing might choose to engage in the lingua franca in order to communicate with the other actors in the field. Although they may not agree with the business version of CSR, union and NGO activists often choose to employ the same terminology as the corporate people, and vice versa.

The different categories of actors in the field of CSR may from this perspective be looked upon as part of a 'discourse coalition', in Hajer's terminology (Hajer 1995: 65). In this discourse coalition, actors might perceive their interests and positions as being widely different, but are attracted to a specific and common set of storylines, that is, the discursive elements that keep the coalition together. At CSR conferences, the members of this discourse coalition get together, try out their positions, negotiate the meanings of concepts and tools and visualise ways ahead. Conferences are thus venues for people with different interests to mobilise other stakeholders to be positively tuned to their ideas, to evangelise and spread the word, so to speak.

From the perspective of doing an ethnography of globalisation processes, the people who are engaged in the corporate responsibility area may be said to constitute a particular 'tribe' of transnationalism (see Field 1971; Hannerz 1990: 243). As mentioned above, the upsurge in the demand for corporate social responsibility has meant the creation of new professional positions and roles in corporations, NGOs and state agencies. Their particular role in the organisations they represent, their knowledge and expertise in the area, their experiences and perspectives, and their capacity to mediate between the global and the local make this 'tribe' an important collectivity in the globalising of markets.

It is among this 'tribe', and in this field of production and use of motivational language, 'doing-good' aspirations, bottom-line calculations and contingent social landscapes that I have engaged with the methodological challenges of ethnographic work at the interfaces of organisations. It is to these challenges that we now direct our attention.

Single-purpose Communities and Transient Fields

The way in which we 'do ethnography' is to a great extent related to how we perceive the problem we wish to study and how we perceive the field. In the above, I have suggested that the field of CSR may be understood as a policy area that spans several organisations and that is essentially constituted in the interface between them. The actors share a common vocabulary, they have similar interests – or negotiate around them. The people involved represent different types of organisations – corporations, NGOs and state agencies – and they rarely meet outside professional engagements. But, when they do meet, they come together to discuss and present their views and cases, to negotiate and to share a sense of 'doing good'. The 'local', where the action is, is not to be found in any particular place, at least not continuously. It appears in different places and goes latent as soon as the conference or meeting is over, only to reappear again in a place agreed upon by the central actors in the field.

CSR may thus be understood to constitute an ethnographic problem, where the area of problematisation is constituted through economic relations, professional knowledge and organisational actors. The interactions between corporate interests and profit, on the one hand, and social responsibility, labour rights and human rights, on the other, crystallise ethical problems of contemporary society. The proponents of corporate social responsibility propose normative guidelines and ethical claims for a more humane capitalism. The way in which CSR is understood and put into practice eventually has implications for how corporate activities impinge on individual and collective life and for relations between state and market. The site, or the location, of these problematisations is organisational, but subject to shifts and irregularities.

At a more general level, we may note that this regular shifting of locations is quite common in the corporate world. Generally, it is used as a way to introduce a sense of dynamism and change in organisational routines. Whilst the popping up of organisational events here and there, as it were, may give the impression that things are constantly 'on the move' and ever-changing, we should not be too quick to assume that a degree of organisational stability is not there. Although continuity may not be found in the regularity of spatial organisation of CSR conferences and meetings, it should be looked for in the articulation of interests, in the maintenance of relational links and in the constellations of ideas and systems of knowledge that tie the actors together. In other words, continuity is relational, rather than spatial.

A number of researchers have brought to the fore the fact that globalisation and the increasing complexity of cultural distribution question central concepts such as 'community' (see, for example Hannerz 1996; Albrow et al. 1997; Bauman 2000; to mention only a few). In his writings on 'liquid modernity', Zygmunt Bauman suggests that communities now tend to be volatile, transient and 'single-aspect' or 'single-purpose'. Their lifespans tend to be short but intense and 'full of sound and fury' (Bauman 2000: chapter 5). The communities of liquid modernity centre round common interests that are dormant and then awakened in otherwise disparate individuals, thus bringing them together for a stretch of time when other interests – those that divide instead of uniting them – are temporarily laid aside. Such 'carnival communities' offer a temporary respite from daily solitary struggles; they break the monotony of everyday solitude and let off pent-up steam, he suggests. The types of field I have been engaged in when studying the CSR movement in many ways resemble the single-purpose communities described by Bauman – carefully staged, with intense discussions and a strong sense of 'doing good'. They materialise for limited stretches of time, in changing places and with people moving in and out of the field. But they are stabilised by the relational links among and between organisations and in the assemblage of ideas and interests that cut across them.

Hence, fieldwork in such a 'single-purpose community' tends to be of a different character than 'classic' anthropological fieldwork. Since the field is made up of several fields, rather than one, fieldwork tends to and often has to be multi-sited. Doing fieldwork in the CSR area has meant following the connections and threads among sites that together constitute the field (see Marcus 1995, 1998). Once 'the logic of association' (Marcus 1995) between different sites, which may have little in common except for the fact that they are sites where the CSR people meet, had been figured out, the multi-sited character of the field appeared as evident. In the case of CSR, the logic of association was made up of a shared interest in corporate social responsibility and some kind of involvement and stake in the voluntary regulation of transnational trade.

There is also a sense in which the field of CSR goes beyond the notion of the multi-sited field. To the extent that my material has been collected in a variety of different sites, my fieldwork is distinctly multi-sited in character. But, considering the extent to which CSR is made up not so much by the collection of sites as by the relations between these sites, the sites may fruitfully be seen as part of one and the same network of sites (Hannerz 2001). The emphasis on the forms of association between sites, the connections, takes precedence over the sites as such. Having done fieldwork for a number of months, it became clear to me that I was tracking a field less made up of the geographical sites to which I went to meet my informants, but by the imbrications or intersecting of ideas, knowledge, interests and visions and of the tools envisaged to put these to work. For instance, the ways in which the normative ideas and knowledge fields of corporate CSR managers intersected with those of activists in non-governmental organisations or with those of servants in the EU agencies was one of my focal concerns. That they would share a vocabulary of accountability did not mean that their interests were in any way entirely overlapping. On the contrary, beneath the surface consensus, there were long negotiations over central priorities. And these were poised in relation to those of other organisations.

Moreover, fieldwork in the CSR area has for me involved what Wulff (2002) refers to as 'yo-yo fieldwork', a continuous movement back and forth between home and the multi-sited field. Rather than following the CSR people along in their everyday lives, I have chosen to maintain relations with my informants over time by going back and forth. This has meant that I have had to decide when and where to engage with my field again, which has not always been an easy decision to make. Again, I have tried to choose the meetings, conferences and other occasions that have addressed the topic of my research in a broad sense. While such a choice may involve a loss of context in some sense, in that I did not really get to see much of their whereabouts in the respective organisations, it may also open up for the construction of another, and perhaps more relevant, kind of context. It has allowed for a degree of temporal continuity and for sticking with 'the logic of association' as a way of defining the field. Context, in this case, is more a matter of mapping the topography of ideas, interests, relations and resources at play than a matter of situating the people involved in a territorially based field. By carefully following the field from my own home base and entering it as conferences and meetings were announced, I was able to problematise and define the larger context of CSR and to enter it at moments of peak engagement by its actors.

Single-stranded Relations and the Issue of Depth

The type of fieldwork I am sketching here brings to the fore questions regarding the character of relations between the researcher and the informants and the density of participant observation. In general, a great deal of emphasis has been put on high levels of participation, tight social interaction and multiplex relations as indications of the quality of research. A high degree of participation and dense and multiplex relations have been taken to suggest that the anthropologist has been fully accepted and 'found her feet' and hence that the material gathered may be reliable and not influenced too much by the researcher's presence as an outsider.

In my research in the CSR area, relations to informants have varied greatly, some being short-term and defined by topicality only, some stretching over time and across places, with discussions ranging from the mundane and everyday to the core topic. My informants were always busy and often travelling. Since I did not spend time with them in their respective organisation, time with them was always scarce and never enough. Much as Rabinow has described his engagement with the 'entrepreneurial managers' of biotechnology (2003: 86), time with my informants in the CSR field was also 'precious and given to active questioning, listening, and observing'. To begin with, time spent on CSR may, for each corporate manager, not be full-time. More often, the person responsible for CSR in any corporation has other responsibilities alongside those of manager of CSR. CSR may be coupled with managerial responsibilities for public relations, marketing or human resources. And, even when CSR does make up the full position, the person in question is not always conferencing, but is performing other administrative, operative and social duties. In essence, then, time spent with corporate managers was valuable. Likewise, the time I had with representatives of non-governmental organisations and of state agencies was also precious. These two categories would also often have CSR as one of several areas to cover. The different categories of informants gave varying accounts of their work, interests and ways of engaging in CSR. These accounts were poised at these conferences, at the intersection of their organisations. The conferences were, in this sense, 'experiential and experimental sites', to borrow Rabinow's expression (2003: 87), where different versions of CSR were aired and tried out.

My 'participation' has, from one angle, been limited to being one of the conferences or meeting delegates. On the other hand, my presence as a researcher in large, semi-public events represents the same level of participation as experienced by most of the audience. Based on my experiences, I would thus agree with Charlotte Aull Davies, when she states that:

> the more important indication of good research is the nature, circumstances and quality of the observation. Such observation must also include reflexive observation – that is, the ethnographer needs to be sensitive to the nature of, and conditions governing their own participation as part of their developing understanding of the people they study ... This tendency of both ethnographers and readers of ethnography to evaluate the quality, and validity, of ethnographic findings on the degree of participation which an ethnographer is able to achieve is unfortunate. A more useful guide is the way in which ethnographers ground their observations in critical reflection on the nature of their participation and suitability to the particular research circumstances, and the relationship between researcher and subjects. (Aull Davies 1999: 73–4)

In much the same vein, and in response to the anxieties related to a perceived loss of depth in ethnographic research, Marcus argues that 'the standard of depth in ethnography must be understood with reference to a differently identified community of scholars in relation to subjects ... The old question of *depth* in the creation of functionalist ethnographies is now mediated by questions of *identity* – the anthropologist's preexisting extent of relationship and connection – to the object of study' (Marcus 1998: 246). Along these lines of thinking, I believe my earlier experiences from doing fieldwork in the corporate world and in labour markets (see for example, Garsten 1994, 1999, 2004a, 2008) have equipped me with some knowledge as to the context of corporate activity, of ways of thinking, tropes and metaphors in use, and the like. There is a familiarity with language and an experience that have proved to be great assets for me in achieving some sort of depth in my fieldwork, despite the discontinuity of the field. Equally important is the fact that the corporate world was never a natural habitat of mine, but one I have come to know through years of ethnographic experience, trial and error and a critical gaze.

Doing fieldwork in this way may involve the experience of a particular kind of 'inverted temporality' (Hannerz 2001), in which the anthropologist finds herself being more of an 'old-timer' than her informants. While the reverse has tended to be the case, I believe we shall increasingly be experiencing this inverted temporality in researching complex cultural groupings and organisations, in which our informants move in and out of fields, change positions and roles, and then move on to other interests, assignments and preoccupations. Whilst it may mean that relations with informants tend to be shorter in time, it may not necessarily mean that they are more superficial and thinner in character. Short-term relations and encounters may be just as emotionally and ideationally significant. Often I was given the role of the responsive interlocutor, and sometimes even the informed interlocutor. By conversing with me, members of the field could also receive news from 'the other side', test out their own tentative viewpoints and talk more freely about the huge challenges ahead in working towards corporate social responsibility. I gladly accepted these roles as best I could, wary of the preciousness of each engagement as I was. For my informants, these encounters may well have meant stepping out of the role of 'organisation man' (or woman) for a moment.

In studying a fluid and discontinuous field like CSR, I believe we also need to turn our attention to the structures that constitute and sustain the field – organisational, social and ideational structures. In studying policy-related questions, it may well be that the trajectory of an idea, such as CSR, provides the logic of association and the continuity to a greater extent than the people working on these issues in different organisations. It is these structures, often stretching across and paying little attention to national boundaries, that infuse the gatherings, events and meetings with relevance, meaning and power, even though they may appear to be hidden from view, simply because they appear as 'extraterritorial', temporary and contingent.

Concluding Notes: Stitching it Together at the Interface

Since my interest in the field of CSR is centred on the dynamisms of a policy field that spans multiple countries and localities, it may not provide the reader with as much of a flavour of the different sites and a sense of 'being there' as one would wish for. Whilst there are good reasons for doing multi-sited, translocal or otherwise unorthodox types of fieldwork, there are certainly challenges. With reflections on the nature of anthropological fields, concerns have been raised that anthropology may be turning away from the study of locality to reflections on 'epistemological and political issues of *location*' (Burawoy 2000: 340–41; see also Gupta and Ferguson 1997). Is ethnography turning towards an interpretive exercise, justifying the thinnest of accounts, the most fleeting engagements and the most unsystematic of observations? I believe worries of this kind, however legitimate, to be reflective of the changing nature of our empirical fields and the kinds of engagements we are able to establish with them. 'Grounded ethnography' in complex and transient fields may ask more of us as ethnographers in terms of defining what actually makes up the field, what is really at stake in the field, where boundaries are being drawn and what the connections are between its sites. It may involve meeting the informants where they are, going 'where the action is' – whether in Brussels, Stockholm or some other locality. It means understanding the perspectives and problematising the accounts of organisational actors, spatial and temporal, and exploring their local and translocal contexts. Mapping out the distinctive cultural and political terrain of CSR people and understanding their role in the fashioning of global markets are truly multi-site and yo-yo-like endeavours.

An alternative route was also possible. I might well have chosen to do fieldwork in a single organisation, much as I have done before, thus creating less of a methodological challenge for myself. So why complicate things? I chose to do it this way because the field of CSR is neither constituted nor realised or otherwise worked out in one single organisation. It is rather constituted at the interface of a number of different types of organisations – state agencies, NGOs and corporations. In fact, it emerges from the differing interests and perspectives on these different organisations as stakeholders confronting each other and having to negotiate. It is at the very interface of these different types of organisations that we may understand what 'corporate social responsibility' is really about. The problem area and the policy field span across organisations and involve interactions of people representing different interests and with their own individual preferences, experiences and perspectives on top of it all. At the interface, we may find that interactions and relations in the field may be quite dense around the topics at heart, that differing interests are twinned together in quite complex ways and that ethnography in translocal fields may very well be 'grounded' in its own particular way, in reference to the character of the field.

And so I have been involved in tracing the relationship of capitalism and social responsibility across cultural, national and geographical boundaries. The story that emerges is one of complex and contradictory discourses and practices, of benevolent capitalism and exploitation, trust and betrayal, vulnerability and power, of negotiated and contested ideas and values. It is also a story of the creative agency of men and women who are trying to carve out their own niches or to push their own interests alongside those of their organisations.

Notes

1. In an article on contemporary forms of civil administration and labour market policy in the US, Emily Martin (1997) draws on Donzelot (1991) and his notion of an 'interface zone' between individual and environment to explain the nature of the cultural moulding and the power of individuals today. In this view, change and movement are constitutive of contemporary social conditions. Not only do individuals circulate among the points on a grid of positions, but the parameters defining the axes change over time. And no grid or sets of grids can completely describe any individual, since the categories in terms of which each individual faces the world will be the result of processes the individual has manifested from within his own course of development. As a result, '(t)he individual comes to consist of potentials to be realised and capabilities to be fulfilled' (Martin 1997: 247). In the interface between subject and environment, a world of possibilities for the production of knowledge, for the operations of power, for exploration and development opens up. The interface zone is also a

field of constant response, endlessly varied and in constant change and transformation. Although one must be careful not to move from the individual to the organisational level without critically reflecting on the use of terms and methodological approaches across levels, I find the idea of an interface zone as a site of study to be a promising one. In my own research, I have often found the more intriguing events to take place in the interface between organisations.

2. The chapter builds on multi-sited, mobile fieldwork in a number of different arenas, such as conference venues, meetings, seminars and the like, where the fashioning of socially responsible markets is discussed. As part of the research process, interviews with corporate leaders in different positions in large companies in Sweden and with representatives of non-governmental organisations and consultancies were also conducted, and documents were analysed. The research project started in 1998 and is still ongoing. I am grateful to Raoul Galli, Mita Bhattacharyya and Annika Malmsten for their assistance in the project, not least by conducting interviews and gathering background data. I wish to thank the Bank of Sweden Tercentenary Foundation and the Swedish Research Council for funding this project.

3. Ethical Corporation is a magazine that also organises conferences and workshops in its areas of coverage.

References

Addo, M.K. (ed.). 1999. *Human Rights Standards and the Responsibility of Transnational Corporations*. The Hague: Kluwer Law International.

Albrow, M., J. Eade, J. Durrschmidt and N. Washbourne. 1997. 'The Impact of Globalisation on Sociological Concepts. Community, Culture and Milieu', in J. Eade (ed.), *Living the Global City*. London: Routledge, pp. 19–34.

Andriof, J. and M. McIntosh (eds). 2001. *Perspectives on Corporate Citizenship*. Sheffield: Greenleaf Publishing.

Aull Davies, C. 1999. *Reflexive Ethnography*. London: Routledge.

Bauman, Z. 2000. *Liquid Modernity*. Cambridge: Polity.

Brunsson, N., B. Jacobsson and associates. 2000. *A World of Standards*. Oxford: Oxford University Press.

Burawoy, M. 2000. 'Grounding Globalization', in M. Burawoy, Joseph A. Blum, Sheba George, Zsuzsa Gille, Teresa Gowan, Lynne Haney, Maren Klawiter, Steve H. Lopez, Seán Ó Riain, and Millie Thayer (eds), *Global Ethnography*. Berkeley: University of California Press, pp. 337–50.

Comaroff, J. and J. Comaroff. 2003. 'Ethnography on an Awkward Scale: Postcolonial Anthropology and the Violence of Abstraction', *Ethnography* 4 (2): 147–79.

Compa, L.A. and S.F. Diamond (eds). 1996. *Human Rights, Labour Rights, and International Trade*. Philadelphia: University of Pennsylvania Press.

Donzelot, J. 1991. 'Pleasure in work', in G. Burchell, C. Gordon and P. Miller (eds), *The Foucault Effect*. Hemel Hempstead: Harvester Wheatsheaf, pp. 251–80.

Field, J.A. Jr. 1971. 'Transnationalism and the New Tribe', *International Organization* 25: 353–62.

Friedman, M. 1970. 'The Social Responsibility of Business is to Increase its Profits', *New York Times Magazine*, 13 September: 32–33.

Garsten, C. 1994. *Apple World: Core and Periphery in a Transnational Organisational Culture*. Stockholm: Almqvist and Wiksell International.

———. 1999. 'Betwixt and Between: Temporary Employees as Liminal Subjects in Flexible Organisations', *Organisation Studies* 20 (4): 601–17.

————. 2004a. '"Be a Gumby": the Political Technologies of Employability in the Temporary Staffing Business', in C. Garsten and K. Jacobsson (eds), *Learning to Be Employable: New Agendas on Work, Employability and Learning in a Globalizing World*. Basingstoke: Palgrave Macmillan, pp. 152–71.

————. 2004b. 'Market Missions: Negotiating Bottom Line and Social Responsibility', in C. Garsten and M. Lindh de Montoya (eds), *Market Matters: Exploring Cultural Processes in the Global Marketplace*. Basingstoke: Palgrave Macmillan, pp. 69–90.

————. 2008. *Workplace Vagabonds: Career and Community in Changing Worlds of Work*. Basingstoke: Palgrave Macmillan.

Gupta, A. and J. Ferguson. 1997. 'Discipline and Practice: "The Field" as Site, Method, and Location in Anthropology', in A. Gupta and J. Ferguson (eds), *Anthropological Locations*. Berkeley: University of California Press, pp. 1–46.

Hajer, M.A. 1995. *The Politics of Environmental Discourse. Ecological Modernisation and the Policy Process*. Oxford: Oxford University Press.

Hannerz, U. 1990. 'Cosmopolitans and Locals in World Culture', in M. Featherstone (ed.), *Global Culture: Nationalism, Globalisation and Modernity*. London: Sage, pp. 237–52.

————. 1996. *Transnational Connections*. London: Routledge.

————. 2001. 'Introduktion: När fältet blir translokalt', in U. Hannerz (ed.), *Flera fält i ett*. Stockholm: Carlssons, pp. 86–107.

————. 2003. 'Being There … and There … and There! Reflections on Multi-site Ethnography', *Ethnography* 4: 229–44.

Leipziger, D. 2003. *The Corporate Responsibility Code Book*. Sheffield: Greenleaf Publishing.

Marcus, G.E. 1995. 'Ethnography in/of the World System: the Emergence of Multi-sited Ethnography', *Annual Review of Anthropology* 24: 95–117.

————. 1998. *Ethnography through Thick and Thin*. Princeton, NJ: Princeton University Press.

Martin, E. 1997. 'Managing Americans: Policy and Changes in the Meanings of Work and Self', in C. Shore and S. Wright (eds), *Anthropology of Policy*. London: Routledge, pp. 239–60.

Ortner, S.B. 1997. 'Fieldwork in the Postcommunity', in S. Bamford and J. Robbins (eds), *Fieldwork in the Era of Globalisation* (special issue of *Anthropology and Humanism*), 22 (1): 61–80.

Palan, R. 2000. 'New Trends in Global Political Economy', in R. Palan (ed.), *Global Political Economy: Contemporary Theories*. London: Routledge, pp. 1–18.

Power, Michael. 2003. *The Invention of Operational Risk*. Discussion Paper No: 16. London: ESRC Centre for Analysis of Risk and Regulation.

Rabinow, P. 2003. *Anthropos Today: Reflections on Modern Equipment*. Princeton: Princeton University Press.

Strathern, M. 1995. 'The Nice Thing about Culture is that Everyone Has It', in M. Strathern (ed.), *Shifting Contexts*. London: Routledge, pp. 153–76.

Sullivan, R. (ed.). 2003. *Business and Human Rights: Dilemmas and Solutions*. Sheffield: Greenleaf Publishing.

Wulff, H. 2002. 'Yo-yo Fieldwork: Mobility and Time in a Multi-local Study of Dance in Ireland', *Anthropological Journal on European Cultures* (issue on 'Shifting Grounds: Experiments in Doing Ethnography') 11: 117–36.

5

Notes from Within a Laboratory for the Reinvention of Anthropological Method

George E. Marcus

This chapter provides me with the opportunity to articulate some basic orientations that inform a memoir I am beginning to write on supervising doctoral dissertation research projects over the past two decades. This work has occurred in a department that renewed itself on the back of the 1980s Writing Culture critiques (Clifford and Marcus 1986) of mainstream ethnographic writing and method at the core of anthropology's disciplinary identity, and then, in the spirit of this critique, moved from the 1990s into the present period of developing research on topics and under circumstances that have come to challenge the basic assumptions and vision on which the Malinowskian design of fieldwork was inculcated for several generations of professional culture. Both the objects of the 1980s critiques and their purview were well within this Malinowskian design, and it still dominates ideologically, at least in the classroom model for training graduate students in research, as well as in the rhetoric and form of most ethnographies produced from it. But, indeed, as anyone mentoring and supervising research at present might agree, this traditional design does not capture what fieldwork is in fact like for many career-making dissertation projects these days (Marcus 1999), nor does it give much guidance about how to assimilate and analyse much of the material that such fieldwork accumulates as data.

Some articulation of this subtextual or subterranean process by which the Malinowskian design is in fact being transformed today in the work that professional apprentices do as ethnographers in the making is badly needed, I would argue, if only because the standing, status and viability of ethnography, especially as practised by anthropologists, are at stake among its broader academic constituencies.[1] Now it is true that the research and writing of senior anthropologists have diversified greatly. For many of them, there is nothing strictly ethnographic about what they do, certainly nothing that would conform rigorously to the Malinowskian fieldworker (in part, my evocation of the trope of multi-sitedness [Marcus 1998]) was meant to reflect upon the rise of this diversity of projects). Senior research in anthropology has been profoundly influenced by the eclectic styles of the past two decades of interdisciplinary modes of cultural analysis under a number of different guises (e.g. cultural studies, feminist scholarship, postcolonial scholarship, media studies, the study of emergent literatures). A commitment to a distinctive anthropological ethos that ties the analyst empathetically (though not necessarily methodologically) to certain historically situated and generally disadvantaged human groups still characterises senior work, but often it ranges far more widely in perspective than this. It is clearly not a model for what those who enter the discipline to be trained in anthropology can or, some would say, should do. And, indeed, many of the students entering graduate study, certainly our own, are those whose conception of and desire for anthropology have been shaped by the influence of this interdisciplinary arena, in which anthropology has prominently circulated and to a certain extent towards which it now orients itself, with certain traditional inflections and sentiments.

In this sense, then, the challenge of supervising graduate dissertation research in topical domains (e.g. media studies, the study of the changing forms of capitalism, topics in science and technology studies, the study of professional middle classes and intellectuals, the study of new social movements) for which anthropology has not defined clear collective projects of research for itself remains a major challenge for its disciplinary future (in the past such topical domains defined the outer perimeter of anthropological research, to which it had contributed usefully as a result of its core culture area specialisations; now this outer perimeter is where research at the heart of the discipline has moved, but without a disciplinary sense of purpose yet in these terrains of the modern, the postmodern, and the contemporary). And in my view the challenge at this juncture is one neither of alternative theory nor of grand vision or purpose, but of method, and of method as it is taught to apprentice scholars. The problem of method now in anthropology, consistently with how method has always been constructed in anthropology, is not about the inculcation of disciplined practices through formal rules or protocols for research, but a rethinking of what anthropologists do and come to believe that they do in the activity of fieldwork. I think of this as a matter of design in undertaking fieldwork at a level that is actually more meta-methodological than methodological in the traditional framework of social science. Issues of design engage more with the 'soft' literature on the experience of fieldwork than they do with those who even now would seek to create formal models of fieldwork method. I do not believe devising a new handbook of methods would be useful here, nor are exemplars of senior work useful either, since they to a considerable degree have broken free of training models and care little for issues of method. What remains is a systematic, ethnographic-like consideration of the predicament of graduate dissertation research for gaining some grasp of the changes in the basic paradigm of fieldwork, on which the future of many of the most ambitious of current anthropological research initiatives depends, as well as of the possibility that a collective sense of these initiatives and their reception might arise within the community of anthropologists themselves, who at the present time are probably the least able to assess the value of what their most ambitious and innovative practitioners are doing. These changes are occurring de facto, but an articulation of what they might be could be useful at this point for generating discussion of practices that remain largely invisible because they are located in the intimate relations between teachers and students in the production of dissertations. These relations are still dominated by storytelling in the Malinowskian mode. What is needed is a modified or alternative narrative frame for fieldwork in the context of pedagogy – one that reflects on the current imaginaries in which projects are conceived by teachers and students and on the pragmatic designs for what a student is able to do within constraints.

It is in this pedagogical context that I want to make an intervention, not only because the changes I have personally seen as a supervisor – the successes and failures of particular projects, what resources and strategies are available to give order to such work and lend it disciplinary legitimacy – have been fascinating to me because of my participation in them, but because this is also the context where the crucial structural changes in the discipline are actually occurring, and where altered norms and forms of practice will eventually need to be ratified by discussion, debate and new expectations in the training of students. If there is ever to be an anthropological community of discussion about its own new work, then it must evolve from where what is understood as 'standard' work or 'normal' science is forged. At present, I argue, this is in graduate training, a domain of great unarticulated innovation. To my knowledge, this view of the state of anthropological research from the perspective of graduate student teaching, emphasising its changing, experimental nature, has not been a subject of much open discussion in contemporary anthropology. It is crucial to develop such a discussion now, since graduate programmes are the veritable laboratories for the reinvention of method. Behind the strongly valued preservation of the research ethos, in which there is a commitment to the study of marginalised, everyday lives, there has been a displacement of the conditions, means and modalities of traditional fieldwork, which requires a systematic expression of its own.

Of course, present involvement in these laboratories will not lead to the production of a single alternative design derived from the Malinowskian one. Indeed, what is being evolved now as method will be quite a bit more diverse than the traditional frames in terms of which anthropologists considered themselves to be doing fieldwork and ethnography in the past. Still, it is important to understand the various alterations that derive from classic conceptions and aims of fieldwork, as well as what the limits of ethnography are in its alternative modalities and what concomitant changes might be necessary in the training protocols for the career-making first projects of apprentice anthropologists. I believe all of this is occurring willy-nilly; encouraging discussion and debate about the changing nature of fieldwork as a problem of design constitutes an act of critical reflexivity at a time when a large and prominent sector of social/cultural anthropology is changing profoundly in its sense of purpose and in its desired objects of study.

In my own work and teaching, I have been contemplating one major stream of conditions of research through which the classic design of fieldwork has been modified. This is fieldwork that emerges in conception through crucially orienting ethnography in the first instance within domains of reason, power and knowledge, which exhibit some kinship to the institution of academic anthropology itself that sends the anthropologist into the field. Annelise Riles (2000), following Marilyn Strathern (1991, 1992), has written of this as the problem of working anthropologically within the domains of modern knowledge, of the already known. Here, for such a circumstance of research, I want to outline three orientations that inform my own alteration of the classic conditions of fieldwork.

I am fascinated by the ethnography of contemporary forms of knowledge or knowledges, and it is the politics or ecology of such knowledge forms with which every project of ethnography of the contemporary (the recent past moving into the near future) begins. This is both the context and the scaffolding of fieldwork projects. This hypersensitivity to the ethnography of zones of discourses as an integral part of every ethnographic project comes, I suppose, from the emphases of the 1980s critiques on reflexivity, representation, rhetoric and especially their politics. But, rather than locating these within the traditional boundaries of the Malinowskian project, I see them as shaping a different and methodologically more challenging sense of the field. The practice of reflexivity that is most valuable is one that positions anthropology within a field of already existing discourses and debates to which it is sensitive and of which it makes an ethnographic object itself. If there is one enduring success of the 1980s critiques, it was to turn ethnography upon representations and discourses as socially produced. The study of the fast-moving contemporary builds on this strength. Ethnography moves from orienting understandings of expert points of view to contexts of everyday life that are found within the ethnography of distributed knowledge systems.

For better or worse, I have become associated from the mid-1990s with discussing this development as the emergence of multi-sited research (Marcus 1998). This could mean a mobile traditional ethnography that pursues novelties of social process through connected sites of intensive fieldwork enquiry. Anthropology cannot remain local but must follow, so to speak, its objects and subjects as they move and circulate. Well, yes, this is true, and there are special problems with this, practical and theoretical. But, alternatively, multi-sited research arises more specifically from this noted hypersensitivity of anthropology to the ecologies and politics of knowledge in which it operates to pursue any subject today. It cannot bracket these in the name of disciplinary authority, as in the past, but must incorporate them within the frame of fieldwork itself. This in itself leads to multi-sitedness, since there is no doubt that anthropological analyses take the form of examining the relation of institutions to subjects, of systems to everyday life, of forms of domination to resistance embedded in cultural practices. It is just that these relations must be encompassed by designs for how they emerge in fieldwork. These are new challenges to method that threaten to stretch fieldwork thin across disparate sites until anthropologists articulate norms and forms of alternative practices stimulated by the need to constitute fieldwork from within initial sites of ethnography which take expert perspectives as 'native points of view'. Multi-sitedness comes into being from this need to move out from, but within, the purview of counterpart or even collegial perspectives 'made strange' as orienting ethnographic objects.

From this comes a whole set of issues on fieldwork to rethink – complicity instead of rapport, the explicit necessity of collaborations, the uneven distribution of depth of knowing in ethnography, the changing nature of the object of study. In earlier writing I alluded to the problem of passing through zones of representation that require incorporation into fieldwork. This immediately generates a multi-sited field and the confronting of doing ethnography among elites. Most of my early career was devoted to the study of elites of various sorts and how ethnography might be applied to them – a real outlier of research whose only space was the anthropology of elites always deferred, still to be developed in the future. I strongly resisted this way of constructing a research interest as just another inventory, archive or topical arena for mere coverage. In terms of my current concern to understand ethnographic research as an interest in distributed, multi-sited objects of study, the study of elites most significantly turns out to be a key phase in the reflexive politics of positioning and orienting collaboration with expertise for any project on contemporary relations of change and emergence. The zones of representation to which I referred on the periphery of the focal sites of ethnography turn out to be themselves integral sites of the ethnography of elites within a broader concept of the multi-sited design of fieldwork.

And, finally, in an almost fundamentalist sense, I am interested in asking what is distinctive about ethnography in these projects on the contemporary, different from other influential eclectic styles of cultural research, not so much ideologically (the space that ethnography symbolically defines and legitimates in this regard I consider to be extraordinarily valuable and precious), but what sorts of unique materials does it present and work through? And what does it present as material in the 'results' it reports – cases, stories, anecdotes, illustrations, quoted remarks of subjects? Yes, but what is the body of material, data in the traditional sense, on which the claims of ethnography depends in depth and in reserve? I think ethnography from anthropology has been less accountable in this regard (epitomised in the sentiment I have heard more than once nowadays from older anthropologists that there is very little ethnography in current ethnographies) for complex reasons. In new settings, it is hard to know what Malinowskian materials are. Ethnographic data tend to get evacuated from ethnography in favour of some mix of theoretical reflection, moral purpose and advocacy and merely felicitous citations/exposures of cases. Ethnography, once conceived as a straightforward, limited purpose genre in anthropology (although the Writing Culture critiques helped to belie this conception), has now taken on multiple discursive purposes, which it can hardly bear. In any case, some reinstantiation of the norms and practices of evidence – the exposed working through of material, a literal sense of the weightiness of ethnography, rather than its mere presentation – is necessary at this point.

How to accomplish this with grace while sustaining interest is a considerable challenge, requiring innovation in forms. This will undoubtedly involve viewing ethnography as a more complex process of textual production and attention given to field materials in different forms (e.g. the forms of data, how they are displayed and shared, how to handle interview materials, the inadequacy of anecdotes, etc.). For example, does the material of a situated native point of view offer anything distinctive? Is the grasp of such a perspective still a main object of ethnographic analysis now under the presumptions of 'reflexive modernisation'? Reflexivity is a primary characteristic of all contemporary subjects, and that within such a situated reflexivity is the equivalent of a de facto para-ethnography that anthropological ethnography as a second-order exercise could probe, interpret, translate/describe and appropriate for its own goals of enquiry. Is the distinctive material of ethnography, then, not so much explicit doctrines or premises that are already articulated and staged by contemporary subjects, but potentials, possibilities, imaginaries that haunt accessible and known discourses and lie in the domain of reflexive judgement and perception and to which ethnography might be distinctively committed and suited to accessing? What materials does fieldwork oriented in this way generate? And, to materialise the reflexive, the possible, and the imagined, what analytic operations on evidence must such ethnography perform to be convincing and accountable to professional and other constituencies? So it is not simply the presentation of more interview material and anecdotes that is called for in putting a sense of ethnography back into ethnography, but a working through of material that defines a distinctively anthropological interest in certain dimensions of how the human subjects in fieldwork (once informants) are differently conceived these days. Especially in the orienting ethnography of expertise or overlapping counterpart systems of knowledge with which many fieldwork projects begin (e.g. several such projects with which I am engaged in supervising dissertation research), this task of finding the boundaries of fieldwork within embedded perspectives of knowledge systems on the ground, so to speak, is most acute. The movement and purview of a project of anthropological ethnography of this sort are very much staged and proceed within the realm of an imaginary of possibility and reflexive thought that must be appropriated from a domain of the already articulated, expressed and known, which as such needs no further anthropological articulation. So, in the very constitution of fieldwork, the orienting act of ethnographic enquiry bears the heaviest burden of evidence and the appropriate exposure of the thickness of ethnography in the most fundamental and traditional senses. All of these issues are intimate matters of contemporary laboratories of anthropological method, to which I now turn.

Exhibits from Pedagogy

As I indicated, what I know of ethnography and its challenges today I know less from my own work or that of my contemporaries than from the problems and ambitions of the students I supervise. Students whom we train have a very different situation of graduate study from that of my own generation or even succeeding ones. Because of our association with 1980s critiques and the particular interdisciplinary ferment of which that was part, we cater to certain kinds of students, but by now the latter are not very different from those who define the applicant pools for many programmes. These are students whose idea of anthropology has been shaped by its role and reputation within these interdisciplinary spaces. They are defining the present legacies of that period of interdisciplinary ferment and present a challenge to the settled training cultures of the disciplines that they enter. In anthropology what they seem to want is a certain orientation to social and cultural difference as it plays out in the contemporary world and, more fundamentally participation in a distinctive research experience – the fieldwork/ethnography tradition in the spirit of Malinowski, but adapted to very different conditions. It is in working with students on their dissertation projects that the norms and forms of a distinctive anthropology of the contemporary are being devised – e.g. what can be experimented with, what it is wise to leave alone, how far such a research idea goes in implementation towards a larger but practically unmanageable imaginary for it – these are all vital questions on which the kind of reinventions to which I have alluded depends. Common elements of this alternative model of method in development are the idea that fieldwork, no matter where it ends up, locally begins at home; that the pre-design of projects is much more important than it had been previously in anthropological pedagogy; that projects are always multi-sited in that they move through and within pre-existing zones of expertise, which must themselves be taken as objects of ethnographic curiosity. One moves into the field – indeed, one constitutes it – by moving through local professional and intellectual routes that must form part of the explicit mosaic of any fieldwork project. Technologies of communication have reshaped the ability to stay in touch from the field – to develop parallel perspectives while being immersed elsewhere. In our department, for example, blogs have become a major vehicle of such staying in touch. In sum, the pedagogy of dissertation projects is where the future of the remaking of this established technology of ethnographic enquiry is being remade in complex ways.

In conclusion, I present two sample exhibits from our particular laboratory: one that briefly characterises the successes and failures of particular dissertation research that immerses itself in cultures of expertise; the other that describes a modality of research – that of nested dialogues – which we are evolving from the expected practices of traditional fieldwork but in contexts where the literal site-rootedness that gives classic ethnography its sense of location is not possible or practical (i.e. where there is no ethnographic there there!).

1. We have dissertation projects that begin in conventional locations and progressively move towards contacts, interviews and observations within systemic hierarchies and institutional networks, like government bureaucracies, schools and centres of media (e.g. a recently completed project on national cultural heritage in Mexico based on initial close observations of the administration of archaeological sites, and a project in progress on the politics of remembrance in former Khmer Rouge strongholds in Cambodia, which also moves from a conventional locale to connections and ties to diverse persons and sites elsewhere in the country), and we have other projects that from the start get caught up in circles and communities of interest around a particular issue or policy with questions of debate, expertise and a politics of knowledge at stake. Two recent projects for which the fieldwork became contained, and organised within these webs concern: (1, completed) perspectives on risk and local capitalism among financiers in Seoul, South Korea; and (2, in progress) debates, scandals and opinion around the initiation of freedom of information legislation in post-socialist Warsaw, Poland. These were projects squarely embedded in zones of expertise and representation and methodologically intended to move beyond them,

but they remained the focus of fieldwork in each case. Here, I am more interested in these kinds of cases than the former ones since they pose issues of the nature of fieldwork that begins (and circumstantially ends) in such webs and circles, which challenge aspects of the Malinowskian ideology of fieldwork. In neither of these cases did the students set out to do ethnographies of the cultures of finance or of law, as such. Each was after more abstract objects (What does the move to democracy mean with particularity within the local forces producing globalisation in very different settings?). If they had more time they could have fulfilled a design that moved from such circles that produce discourse to sites of everyday life. Each did to some degree, but each produced materials most intensively in certain milieux defined by self-conscious problematisation around current events, reflecting local expressions of a global process, in which styles of producing knowledge itself were at stake.

The fieldworkers in each case were trying to gain leverage and collaborations within diffuse circles. They were largely successful, but it was also clear that anthropology provided little guide for how to proceed in these settings where the interview, the formal contact or work as an apprentice of sorts was the main mode of access to subjects. What these projects lacked most of all was a comprehensive design based on norms or expectations of what is to be accomplished in ethnography of this sort, especially at the dissertation level. What was needed was an explicit model of ethnography as bounded partial knowledge within a conceptual universe that maps or defines a terrain for fieldwork yet to be done. Also needed was some design of fieldwork that would not have the researcher relying on one or two key informants or on some general cultural model of Koreanness or Polishness to rescue these projects from their lack of conventional contextualising devices. Finding an orientation relevant to anthropology and also embedded in the reflexive understandings of subjects is indeed the challenge of ethnography in such settings. After all, anthropologists, and others, are not very likely to be interested in a restatement simply of what the 'native' knows or does as professional practice in these settings (journalists are better trained to provide this sort of account, or experts and consultants are also sometimes better able to do this themselves). What might be of interest is the way in which the social impinges on and is increasingly imagined within these sites of the remaking of local orders. The wager is that in the reflexive capacities of key institutional operators are para-ethnographic perspectives, unspoken possibilities that are worth grasping and appropriating by anthropologists who then plan to move within them or out from them into other sites of juxtaposed and related enquiry. The problem is that realistically fieldwork projects, especially at the dissertation level, are indeed fortunate if they are successful only in grasping the so-called reflexive modernisation that is going on in the expert and intellectual circles in which they move.

Yet this is quite enough if only the trajectories, horizons, incompleteness and typical course of development of this sort of fieldwork project were understood and explicitly normalised in the training model of graduate research. Actually, de facto, this is how career research is developing in anthropology today, out of dissertation research. Simply, students are taking on projects of a scope that cannot be fulfilled by a project of ethnography in terms of which dissertations are defined. To recognise this incompleteness is a virtue; it allows for the ethnography that is accomplished in the dissertation to be thorough, while partial. For example, the Korean dissertation fieldwork sent the researcher on a postdoctoral fellowship back to the academic and professional culture foundations in finance on matters of risk. This was not seeking an alternative academic reception for her work but a move to another related domain or site of fieldwork itself. What was closely observed and understood in Korea is actually part of a network (rhizome? assemblage?) of distributed knowledge and practice regarding risk in financial markets that is being developed from an ethnographically appropriated Korean orientation. While a project of this scope – an appropriate scope for the phenomenon in which the researcher was interested – could have been designed in outline as a dissertation project, realistically only a strategic, orienting part of the fieldwork could be done. And retrospectively this is what the student accomplished. But as a training project, defining the scope of this research in relation to expectations about anthropological method was much more like 'feeling her way'. My sense is that much fieldwork like this has this experimental quality these days. The student produces a dissertation in the guise of an ethnography of a local culture of some sort (in this case, of the Korean culture of finance), but as evidenced by later work, this dissertation project is actually part of something with a broader empirical and theoretical horizon, which demands ethnographic coverage as well. This was obvious in preparing for the initial fieldwork, but it also became obvious in working locally within the culture of Korean finance. All that is missing here – crucially missing – is a revised model of ethnographic method for training anthropologists that allows for the research process that is de facto being pursued beyond the confines of the professional culture of graduate training in the Malinowskian ethos. The Polish project, now in progress, seems to be developing in the same open-ended, experimental way, but also under the regulative norms of the reigning fieldwork model about how to produce research, what it should be about and what form it should take from the experience of fieldwork.

In both cases, what these studies are in fact doing in extended multi-sited and transnational enquiries is much better than answering questions posed by Western academic discourse through experience in local settings elsewhere. In retrospect, the point of the dissertations is to evolve the terms of discussion themselves from local cultures of considerable cosmopolitan knowledge about the social systems in which they are operating. The trajectory of these works is quite different from those that begin as rooted in a people or a place and move into global issues of change from there. I am most interested in the fieldwork/ethnographic models that become embedded in the ecologies of knowledge, and their local forms, in the first instance – a situation that absorbs the time available to produce a dissertation and thus forces a reconsideration of the boundaries and limits expected of ethnographic research itself.

2. In projects that I have described, there is rarely a vantage point from which to do traditional fieldwork – living in a community among subjects, opportunities for sustained interactions and observations, etc. More usually, fieldwork consists of organising and waiting for interviews and attending events, where access is limited. Fieldwork of the density that the Malinowskian ethos evokes is virtually impossible. How is the researcher to accumulate materials that generate the texture of ethnography

– of 'thick description' – without the classic conditions for doing ethnography. In thinking about the challenges that fieldwork of this sort poses, it is also important to understand that working within circles of expertise does not have the same aims of classic ethnography either. This is working within the already known, for which description is not the goal, and the interpretations developed by the anthropologist are more obviously dependent on and derivative from the collaborative contexts of such fieldwork. Rather, in such projects, the anthropologist is after the reflexive dimensions of cognition and discourse in these circles, which are developed among subjects themselves in local idioms or can be elicited by techniques imposed by the fieldworker in partnership with subjects.

One such technique is what I call nested dialogues, with which I have experimented in work that I did with Portuguese aristocrats to whom I had both remarkable and uneven access, and which has also been the subject of training projects conducted by Chris Kelty in our department. Over the course of a semester, Kelty and a group of graduate students organised sustained and related series of occasions with computer scientists at Rice. They conducted in-depth interviews with three computer scientists, probing how in their work their awareness of the importance of the social has emerged – through ethical reflection (and requirement these days), through consulting (e.g. on the emergence of digital voting machines in national elections) and through autobiographical recounting. There were individual and collective interviews, seminars and group meetings in different venues, which generated reflexively discussed bodies of field material, which in turn served as commentaries on preceding sets of material. This is something akin to focus groups, but in contexts of depth and use in which, to my knowledge, focus groups have never been developed. What motivates this technique is the need for ethnography or the characteristics of ethnography by other means.

At the end of the semester two days of seminars were held in which researchers and subjects discussed transcripts of earlier meetings. In sum, there was no natural or obvious setting in which to collect such eminently ethnographic material. It required the design and creation of occasions that were nested, in which relations changed among fieldworkers and subjects as the reflexive stakes in the material increased. The most interesting discussions following the climactic seminar were about what analytic protocols were most cogent to apply to the materials; how to use Internet resources to make them available and dynamic; and what further uses in enquiry they might have.

Work in contemporary arenas common to ethnographic research will require more such improvisations and designs inspired by the processes of enquiry within the Malinowskian paradigm but without its governing conditions. Whether this is classic ethnography or not, it is what fieldwork is becoming in important domains of research, requiring reinventions of the established senses and ideologies of method in the veritable laboratory of graduate training.

Notes

1. The various receptions and constituencies for ethnography and the implications of these for redesigning the forms of ethnographic research are worth an essay and more. Ethnography remains popular, but primarily in terms of its known, established and frankly well-worn functions, and not in terms of the more challenging norms and forms to which it aspires. Ethnography is an intellectually subordinate form in all of the senses that make it popular; there is very little context in the disciplinary community of anthropology itself for appreciating or evaluating ethnography's more ambitious trajectories which are virtually invisible to its external constituencies. Conventional ethnography has much to say to others and this is a real contribution, but there is very little room for intellectual growth in the discipline itself in repetitively fulfilling this worthy function in different domains. In its mature form, as an instrument of critique, ethnography articulates the conditions and interests of the disadvantaged; it makes clear and questions the assumptions and premises of the informal cultures that animate structures of power and domination, and, yes, it still provides the raw material for those, mainly in the West, who want to contemplate the primitive and the primordial. The kinds of research that transform ethnographic design have, with few exceptions, no dense reception in anthropology itself, but depend more on other constituencies for recognition and approval. And these constituencies tend to see not what is new in such ethnography but how well it functions in terms of its traditional capacities. This creates difficult problems for addressing how anthropologists themselves are to set standards for their own products of research, which represent the most ambitious and innovative efforts to modify the well-worn ethnographic research instrument. So one turns, I would argue, to the context of teachers and students developing dissertation research, a veritable laboratory for examining the limits and possibilities of the fieldwork/ethnographic mode of research, in a controlled, intensive way available nowhere else.

References

Clifford, J. and G.E. Marcus (eds). 1986. *Writing Culture: the Poetics and Politics of Ethnography*. Chicago: University of Chicago Press.

Marcus, G.E. 1998. *Ethnography Through Thick and Thin*. Princeton: Princeton University Press.

——— (ed.). 1999. *Critical Anthropology Now: Unexpected Contexts, Shifting Constituencies, Changing Agendas*. Santa Fe: School of American Research Press.

Riles, A. 2000. *The Network Inside Out*. Ann Arbor: University of Michigan Press.

Strathern, M. 1991. *Partial Connections*. ASAO Special Publications No. 3. Savage, MD: Rowman and Littlefield.

———. 1992. *Reproducing the Future: Essays on Anthropology, Kinship and the New Reproductive Technologies*. New York: Routledge.

6

Making Ethics

Sharon Macdonald

The Association of Social Anthropologists of the UK and Commonwealth and the American Anthropological Association have had codes of ethics for some decades now; and debate about ethics and ethnographic research is likewise long-standing and ongoing.[1] In recent years, however, there has been a proliferation of additional ethics codification, emanating from a wide array of organisations, including research councils and governments. A key difference from the codes of professional organisations is that these are generally to be implemented at institutional (i.e. university) level, which has led many universities to draw up their own codes of ethics and procedures for the review and management of research undertaken by their staff. Unlike the codes of ethics of professional organisations, those of institutions generally need to cover all disciplines and their multiple types of, and approaches to, research; and, accordingly, they also need to take into account the regulations, codes and guidelines of numerous organisations. In addition, as part of a public performance of being ethical that is generally required by research sponsors, institutions are required to put auditable procedures in place for scrutinising research undertaken by their staff. This includes prospective research, the plans for which must be approved by ethics review boards before it is permitted to go ahead, as well as, in many cases, mechanisms for monitoring ongoing and sometimes completed research.

This move towards increasing codification and bureaucratisation of ethics, especially by universities, has been the subject of much discussion and two major areas of concern in anthropology. One of these is over the processes of codification and bureaucratisation themselves, which some see as part of a culture of audit in which these act as a publicly performed 'proxy of moral judgement', which, according to Lynn Meskell and Peter Pels, can entail 'a distanciation from the ethical practice that practitioners should aim at' (2005b: 21; see also Brenneis 2005). Ian Harper and Alberto Corsín Jiménez similarly argue that codification involves a 'process of exteriorizing ethics, such that they become something external to the discipline' and 'less a quality of relationships than an aspect of managerial processes and cultures' in which 'professional judgment is displaced in favour of defendable process' (2005: 10; see also Corsín Jiménez 2005a). What these commentators call for instead is an ethics that is 'embed[ded] in scholarly practice' (Meskell and Pels 2005b: 3) and, as such, located 'at the *core of* rather than exterior to research' (ibid.: 10). On the basis of this principle, the European Association of Social Anthropologists (EASA) has decided against producing a code of conduct but has instead established an ethics network to allow for 'the constant renegotiation and re-contextualization of ethical thinking and standards' and to act 'as a think-tank to advance ethics debates and as an advisory body' (http://www.easaonline.org/networkspage.htm, accessed July 2007).

The other, related, area of concern has been over whether ethnographic research can be accommodated within pan-disciplinary ethics regulations that seek to demonstrate high levels of research governance. Particular difficulties are seen to lie in the fact that, as Rena Lederman puts it, '"doing fieldwork" is all about embedding oneself in social situations not designed by the investigator' (2006a: 477). This is typically over long periods of time, during which one may come to be related to less often only as a researcher. This means that ethnography is inherently responsive, indeterminate – we do not always know in advance what the focus will end up being – and difficult to codify, and that the boundaries between 'research' and 'not research' are often unclear and fluid. Ethics codification, in contrast, presumes 'clearly bracketed research' (Lederman 2006a: 477) rather than such 'informality' (ibid.). Some of the specific requirements of ethics codification may, for these reasons, be inappropriate and even misleading to those among whom we conduct our research. Signed informed consent forms, for example, may run counter to the aim to provide information by implying a more tightly specified and narrow research approach than is usual in ethnography; or they may be deemed insulting by research participants, who see themselves as 'experts' rather than research 'subjects'. Likewise, anonymisation – another technique of assumed 'good practice' in many institutional and other disciplinary ethics codes – may in some cases be judged an affront to intellectual property or denial of recognition. But we may only learn the local ideas and expectations after having been immersed in them (see, for example, Silverman 2003 for a sensitive discussion).

Whatever concerns anthropologists may have, institutional ethics review and research governance are not likely to go away and, indeed, look set to spread,[2] though it is worth noting that in the United States, in what have been dubbed the 'institutional review board wars', legal scholars in particular have argued that aspects of review procedures violate the US First Amendment, that is, they infringe upon the freedom of speech (Hamburger 2005; Lederman 2006a). Given that ethics review of prospective research is almost certainly a requirement (if not now, then in the near future), what can we do? One option is for ethnographers to pretend compliance, 'going through the motions' of institutional review but undertaking research in the manner they think most appropriate (and ethical) (see, for example, Katz 2006). This clearly puts the researcher in an invidious position. Another option is to participate in ethics review procedures in order to try to ensure that the specificities of ethnographic research are recognised and accommodated and that at least some of the dangers of codification and its implementation are averted.

This chapter gives an account of my own participation in the drawing up of a university ethics policy and procedures. Like a number of other scholars, including Vered Amit (2000), Don Brenneis (2005, 2006) and Rena Lederman (2006a, b), who have participated in institutional research governance procedures, I became involved in my university's ethics developments largely because of concerns about ethnographic research of the kind noted above. During the years in which I participated, although there were times of frustration, I was fairly optimistic – as I reported at the 2004 EASA meeting, at which the workshop on which this volume is based – that we would be able to produce a policy with sufficient subclauses, exceptions and procedural flexibility to make ethnographic research possible and to allow for some embedding within disciplinary specialism. I noted in that account, however, that I was aware that:

> my confidence partly rests on the rather flimsy basis of words such as 'normally' and the fact that most of those who have chosen to become involved in matters of ethics at present are open, reflective people who do not see their task as one of laying down absolute laws and insisting that they are followed to the letter, caveats notwithstanding.

As the policies were put into practice in my own department, I was also relieved to see this being done with sensitivity towards and understanding of the nature of qualitative work, including ethnographic;[3] and throughout I remained impressed by the thoughtfulness, sagacity and commitment of most of those involved.

Nevertheless, when, for the purpose of revising my original paper for this volume, I came to look back at the ethics policy that was finally produced in 2005, I was struck by how much less the policy seemed to concede to ethnographic research than I had imagined at the time. The wording was such that it seemed to me now that were an ethics reviewer to follow the policy to the letter, rather than generously interpreting its nuances, they would probably not give approval to most ethnographic research. In part, my more pessimistic reading was shaped by awareness of a turn towards 'regulatory hypervigilance' (Lederman 2006b: 489) in US universities, where, especially following changes in federal legislation in 1991 and some prominent cases of medical research malpractice, institutional ethics review boards have been reported as often being more conservative in their assessments, rejecting or requiring amendment of more proposals and extending their remit to disciplines (e.g. literature) that were formerly off the review radar (see Lederman 2006a; Shweder 2006). Another reason for my more pessimistic interpretation, I think, was that I was reading the policy 'cold' and disconnected from the social relationships of its production, and so without my earlier sense of either it necessarily being operated by known reasonable people or my heightened attention to the hard-won 'get-out clauses'. But, even beyond these different interpretive moments, there was a question to be addressed of how, even in a context where there was an express intention to make sure that there was understanding of the nature of ethnographic research and provision for it within the policies, this did not end up in the final policy in a more substantial way, as well as why I had not seen this more clearly at the time. This chapter is an attempt to reflect back on the ethics making in which I was involved to try to unravel how this had happened.

Examining this question is not intended just as a personal working through of individual disquiet. Rather, by reflecting back and trying to understand how this came about, my aim is to explore what are likely to be wider processes at work. As is a common endeavour in anthropology, I investigate how particular ways of going about things, of framing debates, of shared assumptions and so forth can shape an outcome – sometimes in ways that are unanticipated and perhaps not fully realised by participants at the time. Doing so can also, I hope, be useful to others engaged in drawing up similar policies and procedures, amending or challenging them, for, as Vered Amit says (2000: 232), 'knowing and understanding these structures and practices are crucial for framing any kind of informed stance' – even though her own experience of trying to participate in her university's ethics committees left her disillusioned about the possibility for intervention. So, although my account to some extent corroborates Amit's conclusion that it is harder to make a difference than we might have hoped, I want also to investigate further how this happens, as well as to recognise the value of what might seem fairly small achievements and possibilities for the future.

Reflecting on Ethics in the Making

Below, then, I take an anthropological look at some of the aspects of the making of a university ethics review policy that led to ethnographic research being less well accommodated than I had originally hoped. This means reflecting back on the work of the committees of which I was part over a number of years. The ethical status of such reflection itself deserves comment – and to some extent illustrates some of the wider dilemmas of ethnographic research, including the retrospective revisiting of 'the field' to think about it in light of new themes, which is fairly commonplace in anthropology. When I participated in committee work, I did so as a colleague concerned to ensure that ethnographic and related approaches would be accommodated within the ethics policy and, officially, as a representative of social science research interests more generally. Although one committee member once joked that I might make an interesting study of 'this bear pit', I was not there to conduct research and did not anticipate writing about the committee work (though I did write about ethics regulations more generally in relation to my own fieldwork, as for the original conference presentation). I decided to do so initially, however, in order to work out for myself what had happened; and then, after fairly extensive discussion with some of those involved directly in the committee work as well as others elsewhere, to share this and open it up to wider collegial debate through publication.[4]

In doing so, I have been careful to avoid as far as possible identifying particular individuals with specific positions or breaking any confidences. For this reason, and as this is 'unintentional ethnography' that seeks to present general reflections, I include less concretising detail (e.g. participant portraits, dates, numbers of meetings, direct examples of dialogue) than an ethnographic account would more usually contain; and I seek to draw out more general matters rather than dwelling too much on the specifics, though the latter are not irrelevant and some need to be outlined. Luckily, perhaps, the story that I have to tell is not itself about any kind of malpractice or incompetence (except occasionally my own). It is instead about relatively routine procedures and ways of framing debates that are likely to have wider currency.

Between 2003 and 2006, I participated in several committees involved in initiating, drawing up and putting into practice the University of Sheffield's ethics policy. These included university meetings at which I was present as a research director of my department, during which I voiced concern about possible risks to other forms of research if a general ethics review policy was devised only with consideration to biomedicine; this led to my being drafted on to an ad hoc committee, consisting primarily of biomedical and health-related researchers, whose task was to map out the university ethics policy, which was then presented to the university senate for approval. A more wide-ranging group, drawn partly from the ad hoc committee, then drew up the terms of reference for establishing a university research ethics committee (UREC). This, on which I served as representative for social sciences, was concerned with identifying governing principles and operating procedures, as well as some reviewing of research proposals.

The immediate prompt for the University of Sheffield to create an ethics policy and set of procedures for reviewing research proposals was a decision by the Wellcome Trust, which funds mainly biomedical, though also some social science and other, research, that it would only fund research undertaken in universities that had such codes and procedures.[5] It was widely anticipated that other research councils would follow suit, as some have since done (e.g. the Economic and Social Research Council). The ethics policy produced (University of Sheffield 2005) acknowledges this 'continuing trend towards ensuring that, where applicable, sponsored research is prior to ethics approval' in a list of 'several, significant developments over recent years [that have] strengthened the case to develop an Ethics Policy' (ibid.: 3). Four other developments are also identified: '(ii) A continuing trend towards collaborative interdisciplinary and international research'; '(iii) Developments in UK and EU legislation and policy concerning research ethics';[6] '(iv) A series of well-publicised scandals that adversely affected public confidence in health and social care research (e.g. the Royal Liverpool Children's Hospital Alder Hey Inquiry)'; and '(v) The development of research ethics policies by other Russell Group Universities' (ibid.).[7] These 'trends' neatly sum up some important features of the context in which the ethics policy was produced and which helped shape it: in particular, the sense that doing so was inevitable and, moreover, the policy must be put in place rapidly if university research was to be funded at all; awareness of a plethora of national and international developments under way; and the understanding that this was as much about public performance as about the 'real ethics' of research.

Medicine Matters

Also evident to some extent in the list and elsewhere in the policy document, as in the initial prompt to create the policy and the predominance of medical and health researchers and representatives involved, especially in the early stages, was the predominance of biomedicine in developing the ethics policy. This was not unusual: institutional ethics policies elsewhere, including institutional review in the US, have also generally been devised primarily to address the ethics of biomedical practice. As others have noted (e.g. Hamburger 2005; Lederman 2006a), such policies typically employ a model of relations between researchers and researched in which the latter are conceived as 'patients' or 'human subjects' in need of protection from possible medical research malpractice – a model that does not necessarily readily encompass other ways of construing the research relationship. At Sheffield, we avoided the language of 'subjects' and instead used 'participants', a change of terminology that at the time I thought important in that it might better cover the more participative relationships of some kinds of social science research as well as the active acquiescence that the medics also wanted to procure through the ethics procedures. In itself, however, it did not necessarily leave space for participation (of the kind discussed earlier in this chapter as well as in other chapters in this volume) beyond that defined by the ethics procedures.

Medicine does, of course, matter. Few other disciplines face the regular risk of causing their research participants physical injury or even killing them. As such, biomedicine had 'risk-clout' – its greater potential for serious harm was one important and justifiable reason why it tended to dominate discussions. In an ethnography of the Science Museum that I carried out in London, where I charted a process that did not turn out quite as its participants had anticipated, I coined the term 'institutional regression' to describe how, when decisions became hard to make and time pressure was on, there was a tendency to revert to more conservative approaches and to legitimise these through phrases such as 'we're the Science Museum after all' (Macdonald 2002). In the Sheffield ethics discussions, despite attempts to consider a wide range of disciplines, there was a similar process of what might be called disciplinary regression, a return to the biomedical case and accepting the need for this to be central (by me included), especially when the pressure was on.

In addition, as noted above, in what might be called prior framing, so many existing debates and broader networks of ethics procedures and policies were already centred upon biomedicine. Ethics policies from elsewhere, including other universities, which were consulted as part of drawing up the Sheffield code, were predominantly framed in terms of biomedicine. In addition, National Health Service (NHS) ethics policies and procedures[8] – which any research involving National Health Service patients, staff or premises had to comply with – were familiar to many on the Sheffield committees and so tended to act as something of a model, albeit partly as one to avoid replicating, NHS ethics review being legendary for its slowness, and its bureaucratic and restrictive nature. Although the Sheffield committee made a decision that any research to be submitted to NHS committees would not also need to go through the university procedures, it nevertheless felt it important to create something that was no less ethically robust, even if it was more straightforward and less gruelling. Here was another more general phenomenon that also came into play in various different contexts during discussions – an avoidance of seeming less ethical than others, an 'as-ethical-as-thou-ism', which sometimes affected me too.

Nevertheless, there were important divergences from the NHS regulations. One interesting area concerned the boundaries between scrutiny for 'ethics' and for 'scientific quality' – two matters taken as discrete by most committee members while being recognised as related. NHS ethics committees often rejected research on 'scientific grounds' (e.g. ethnographer colleagues have reported to me that they had their research proposals rejected for having 'sample sizes' that were 'too small to be statistically significant'). Although in other contexts I would have wanted to argue for an 'embedded' approach which would surely reject a separation of 'ethics' from 'science', here – in a pragmatic shifting for more immediate ends – I was relieved that we collectively concluded that the ethics committee should not see its remit as also judging the scientific merit of research.

There were also numerous discussions on the committees about the boundaries between the NHS and the university procedures, partly because emerging government policy on this was changing as we tried to create our own, and partly because there were areas of research for which the policies and procedures would need to coordinate.[9] Indeed, the ad hoc ethics committee, although charged with drawing up guidelines for all university research, had initially been constituted to address certain developments in Department of Health procedures, and, as such, its initial and core members were from medical fields; and the chairs of both the ad hoc committee and the UREC worked in health research. Other people, including myself, later came to be added in. But the initial constitution and the fact that discussions were already under way meant that intervention was always into an existing debate in which the terms had already been established. The difficulty of entering these debates was exacerbated by the complexities of the existing and changing networks of biomedical research regulation and the numerous acronyms involved. This had a feedback effect of making those who could join these debates seem more knowledgeable and competent to deal with the matters in hand. Although the chairs and some other committee members tried to make an effort to consider other disciplines, they were most likely to do so as part of a well-meant logic of encompassment – an 'of course this will affect you too' – rather than opening up gaps for difference. They also, on good grounds, tended to take it for granted that these kinds of discussions were both more advanced and more pressing in relation to their own field.

In addition, as others have outlined (e.g. Mills 2003), ethics codes are often produced in response to key cases of malpractice. As noted above, the university's ethics policy itself mentions that certain cases of malpractice, such as Alder Hey, were part of the motivation for producing the policy. Alder Hey was shorthand for a series of scandals erupting in 1999 concerning UK hospitals, in which dead bodies (including those of children) had been stripped of various organs without informing relatives. Although a main perpetrator was prosecuted under regular criminal law and expelled by the General Medical Council for malpractice that was contrary to the existing code, the scandal generated wider concern over staff supervision and the way in which the hospitals had handled the allegations. A public inquiry into the scandal in 2001 recommended tighter institutional scrutiny and legislation making informed consent mandatory – though some scholars criticised the report for its inconsistencies and 'inappropriate conflation between seeking redress for past wrongs and shaping future policy' (Dewar and Boddington 2004: 463). Nevertheless, it acted as a key or motivating case in various discussions during the making of Sheffield's ethics policy and was one reason for the wider 'fetishization' of informed consent (as Harper and Corsín-Jiménez 2005 put it). What happened, then, was that debates easily became framed in terms of making sure that such a *worst case scenario* could not occur again.

'No Philosophers Please'

On the committees it was generally taken for granted that medical and health researchers held relevant ethics expertise. The ad hoc committees also intermittently included lawyers. These too, however, had biomedical expertise and were there to contribute their knowledge about existing and sometimes speculated future legal frameworks affecting 'research' (almost always used as a general term, even where it might refer only to medical research – though this was often hard to ascertain). If biomedicine had risk-clout, law had a technical-clout – it seemed to present fixed parameters. Nevertheless, there were often arguments about interpretation, with some of the medical and health researchers feeling that some of the lawyers' interpretations or speculations about the future were too restrictive and pessimistic. Where this was the case, there was a tendency to switch the focus, to look at other regulations on which the medics had greater expertise and that were already having more immediate effect. As one medic said to me, the problem with at least some lawyers was that they tended to work too much in the abstract and, unlike medics, were not engaged in the daily task of trying to do research in the face of the regulations.

The UREC, however, did not include any lawyers in its constitution. When at one point I suggested that it might do so, in order to provide specialised expertise that others did not possess, I was overruled by the argument that such expertise could be drawn on when it was needed. Moreover, few individual lawyers would cover all possible areas, so it would be better to call up specialists in times of need than to have a single 'resident' lawyer. I also ventured early on that the constitution might include a philosopher, for a contribution from the discipline with most obvious professional expertise in ethics debates. This produced a hush and, once I had spent more time in the committees, I understood that it had been foolish to have suggested adding a contribution that might quibble with the existing definitions and basic premises that had already taken so long to hammer out.[10] While it was a good point, I was told (probably indicating to the contrary), what really mattered was having people involved who, because of the nature of their research, would be subject to the regulations. That, indeed, was a main reason why I was there – because social sciences research would be affected. At work here too was a bounding process, through which what was seen as extraneous to the key task in hand was defined as irrelevant or unnecessary.[11] The distinctive constitution of relevant expertise in terms of being subject to the effects of the regulations could also be seen in the emphasis on including 'lay members' ('ordinary people' who are not connected with the university) in the committees. Such 'lay members' represent the potential subjects of the potentially risky university research. Their presence is also part of a performed transparency that, as others have observed, is also a feature of such systems and of audit more generally (Strathern 2000). I argued during the early phases that such a framework denigrated university expertise and was based on an unjustified premise of researchers as lacking in integrity (see Corsín-Jiménez 2005b), but this was also effectively irrelevant as some funding bodies required them. The terms had already been set.[12]

Spaces for Difference

The discussion above provides a partial account of why it was hard to find space for the kinds of concerns about ethnography that I had wanted to interject into the process. It was partly squeezed out by what needed to be in and by the sheer scale and complexity of the task. Along the way, we looked at numerous different ethics guidelines, including those from professional organisations, conventions and reports, and heard from various experts on matters such as university insurance and indemnity and the Data Protection Act. Just getting something produced that would meet all of the different demands without being hopelessly complex became the overriding task in itself.

Most of those who participated were keen to minimise complexity and bureaucracy – the chairman of the UREC, who did a particularly excellent job of steering the process, often emphasised this at the beginning of meetings. Many committee members grumbled about the overall rise of bureaucracy and 'form-filling' in university life. My more specific concerns about ethnographic research were, I think, sometimes understood within this framework – as part of a general weariness with bureaucratic overload rather than as a case for why some aspects of the policy should not apply to all research. As such, there might be nodding of heads – but then moving on. Involved here too was the fact that matters such as 'informed consent' were seen as so fundamental – and so much part of the rights of the 'research participant' – in biomedicine that it was hard to convey why they might be problematic elsewhere. Here, the fact that some colleagues from some non-medical disciplines – such as Politics and English – who attended information meetings were very vocally in favour of increased 'ethical rigour' in their fields made my own position even more at odds with the general consensus. They surely had good reason for their positions, especially as they did not much use discipline-specific ethics codes, their concerns being variously with misleading interviewing tactics and lack of care over anonymity or acknowledgement. For my part, however, it added to the difficulty of also needing to act as a representative of social science in general, which included disciplines such as Politics and a broad spectrum of research techniques. Indeed, I sometimes worried that perhaps I was trying only to protect my own research approach and began to wonder whether I should have used signed informed consent forms in earlier projects. These moments of self-doubt, which grew in the face of widespread acceptance of the policies among many colleagues, also damped my initial zeal to intervene as I had imagined initially.

Ethnographic research was not, however, the only approach that sought exception from aspects of the policy. Psychology, while in favour of signed forms for agreeing to participation, argued for a concession to permit 'deception' in 'exceptional' circumstances in order, say, to investigate racist views. At the time, I saw that as a useful concession that might be used by social researchers too, reasoning with myself that we were rarely talking about 'deception' but just a surely more acceptable inability to be fully informative about things that were outside our control. This was part of a more general tendency on my part to seize upon spaces within the policy that I thought might be conducive to ethnographic research and to overplay their significance in my own mind – a process of over-optimistic interpretation. In the face of a specific concession that formal consent might not always be fully informed, however, the argument that it might not be acquired at all became in some ways even harder to justify. Probably more useful was the concession that I managed to get inserted into the policy that 'research in public contexts and with groups' might not necessarily always obtain informed consent from all participants. This was framed in terms of feasibility, which was only one strand of my original set of arguments. But partly because the policy was evaluated in terms of its robustness in the face of providing possible escape routes for malpractice, the feasibility argument was all that remained. As such, it could only open up a bit more space in which, with optimistic interpretation, such a case might be made.

Here, I should also briefly note the processes by which drafting the actual policy took place. This was not done by all sitting down and jointly writing out each sentence – a procedure that would have been extraordinarily difficult with such a large group. Indeed, as discussions were often lengthy and engaged it was hard enough for the secretary of the committee to keep track of which points had been agreed. Rather, as is probably usual in these circumstances, drafts were produced by the chair and the secretary, and these were commented on and debated by the rest of us during meetings, and then the versions were redrafted and re-presented to the committee. Although the version of the ethics policy currently available on the Web says 'version 3', there were also numerous pre-versions and versions of specific sections that were reworked over the months. I have no doubt that those directly engaged in the difficult task of drafting and redrafting attempted to take into account all of the points that were raised; but they also did so within an overall framework in which the avoidance of harm and preventing unethical research not unreasonably (as was part of the dilemma) took precedence over enabling 'minority' forms of research.

As with many other knowledge systems about which anthropologists have written, arguments that questioned the overall framework or its premises tended to be defined as irrelevant or impossible to address. I tried, for example, to argue that we might not always want to make the prevention of harm or discomfort to research participants our overriding consideration – if, for example, an organisation was engaged in pernicious or corrupt practices. Indeed, the word 'truth' also increasingly entered my own private and uttered vocabulary. After initial puzzlement about the point I was trying to make, another committee member helpfully translated it into exposing the corrupt behaviour of estate agents,[13] which received lots of laughter and enthusiastic agreement. (As Don Brenneis observes of the research panel discussions of which he was part, 'The more extreme opinions expressed were almost always made relatively safe through the use of humour or indirection' (2005: 245).) But it did not find its way into the final wording.

This did not mean that the points were totally ignored, however. Instead, the attempt was to leave space for the differential implementation at departmental/disciplinary level. This was recognised in statements early on in the documents about the diversity of research:

> The Ethics Policy ... has been designed to allow a certain degree of flexibility at the individual Department level in recognition of the diverse and dynamic nature of the University's research base. The decision regarding whether or not an individual research proposal ... raises ethical concerns ... is made on a case by a case basis within the parameters of the University's Ethics Review System. (University of Sheffield 2005: 2)

These were important statements in which I, and other committee members, put much hope that future committee members would act flexibly and deal thoughtfully with some of the troublesome cases that were not easily contained in the more specific details of the code. I was also told that some of the kinds of points that I was making were already covered elsewhere, in commitments to academic freedom in university statutes.[14] What the university ethics policy needed to do was to demonstrate to funding bodies and others that the University of Sheffield had as rigorous a policy and procedure in place as any other similar institution.

I also put faith in the procedures that we devised. These involved devolving ethics scrutiny as far as possible to departments – to those who held subject expertise – with the UREC acting as a body for adjudicating disputes and monitoring practice. This, I thought, ensured that the potential for overly restrictive interpretations of policy would be limited. My initial observations in my own department seemed to confirm this. However, shortly after this was all agreed, new regulations from the Economic and Social Research Council seemed to imply that research that they funded and identified as requiring ethics scrutiny would have to be reviewed for ethics by the UREC (or another extra-departmental ethics review board) and not by subject specialists. Since then, and indicative of the slipperiness of this area, this seems to have been amended to allow for subject-specialist review procedures as long as some non-specialists are also involved.

Conclusion

This chapter has outlined some of the conceptual frameworks and discursive practices – including my own – that contributed to the university ethics policy that was produced at the University of Sheffield. It is a policy that manages to be robust while also relatively open, leaving room for negotiation in its use of phrases such as 'wherever possible' and 'proportionate to the nature of the research activity'. How this will be interpreted by future committee members or other university staff as they prepare their research proposals, however, is less clear. Vered Amit tells of how what began as a set of 'guidelines' in Canada rapidly transformed into 'a priori prescriptions' (2000: 224–25); and Richard Shweder, among others, has documented 'mission creep' – the extension of application of narrower interpretations of federal rules at local level – in US universities (2006). More generally, as Don Brenneis observes, 'institutional review boards constitute a critical nexus in the shaping of research ethics across many disciplines … The anticipation of review may shape the design of research and, indeed, the range of topics considered feasible' (2005: 240). How far such self-limiting occurs is difficult to assess. In the Department of Sociological Studies at Sheffield University, where there were lively forums for debating methodology and ethics, the local implementation of the policy suggested that this could be avoided. At the same time, however, several colleagues around the university expressed concern to me (which I tried to alleviate) that the new ethics regulations would prevent them from conducting research in the more open-ended way that they would do otherwise, one wearily remarking that they would switch to more formal interviewing, which was 'in any case … easier to do than ethnography'. Confronted with multiple demands and time pressures, taking on what was envisaged as a 'fight' with an ethics committee was not something that this colleague could face. Understandable risk aversion operates at personal as well as institutional levels.

By highlighting the negotiated process of the making of an ethics policy, I hope to emphasise that, rather than being the product of a single-minded application of a set of thoroughly agreed principles, it is a more tentative and only partially settled achievement. As such, it should be understood as open for further and ongoing negotiation – something recognised in the policy's proposed annual self-review. In addition, identifying some of the particular discursive processes involved in the making of an ethics policy may help others involved in such processes to recognise these earlier and address them more directly than I did. Some of these, such as the tendency to use worst-case scenarios as motivating cases, however, are easier to address than others. The fact that such codes or policies attempt to encompass all disciplines sets up particular difficulties; and in retrospect I think that institutional ethics policies should attempt to include more and stronger statements about specific disciplinary methods and their underlying philosophies, and the kinds of risks commonly faced in different types of research. This might also contribute to a task that Rena Lederman has recently argued for – that of 'educating' ethics review boards (2007b). To help do so she has proposed a 'boilerplate' – a statement about the nature of ethnographic research, its underlying ideas and why it needs to tackle ethics in particular ways – for anthropologists to use when they face institutional review.[15] Her argument is not only that such a boilerplate provides each of us with a useful template for our own arguments but that if review boards become used to seeing these arguments repeatedly, in the same or similar words, these are more likely to become more common currency and better understood and transmitted between committee members. Her initial experience of this at her own university has been encouragingly positive.

Education is, as Lederman emphasises, necessarily an ongoing rather than a one-off process. It is also multi-directional – a process in which anthropologists (and others) need to learn about review boards, partly in order to both face and educate them. It is towards such an ongoing task that this chapter is intended as a contribution.

Acknowledgements

While taking full responsibility for this chapter, which is based on recollections and interpretations that may not be shared by others involved, I would like to thank colleagues at the University of Sheffield with whom I have discussed ethics over the years, including those who worked on the various ethics committees and in the Department of Sociological Studies. I especially acknowledge helpful comments on versions of this chapter from Darren Shickle, Richard Hudson, Tim Birkhead and Nicky Gregson, and, beyond Sheffield, Mike Beaney. I also thank Rena Lederman, Alberto Corsín Jiménez and Don Brenneis for invaluable wise words and insightful (including unpublished) articles on the subject; and the original workshop organisers and participants, and volume editors, for providing the impetus for thinking about these matters.

Notes

1. For details of these respective guidelines and accompanying information see the Associations' websites: http://www.aaanet.org/committees/ethics/ethics.htm and http://www.theasa.org/ethics.htm (accessed July 2007). For histories of the development of ethics codes in anthropology see Caplan (2003b) and (Mills 2003); and for further discussion see Caplan (2003a), Fluehr-Loban (2004), Meskell and Pels (2005a, b) and the recent special issue of *American Ethnologist* (2006 vol. 33, no. 4) edited by Rena Lederman.

2. There are already some journals in the medical field that will only publish research for which evidence of having passed ethical review is provided (Hamburger 2005).

3. This may have been partly due to the fact that the Department already had a culture of discussing and teaching ethics, and, for example, already expected postgraduate students to write about ethics in their research plans and for these to be approved before beginning fieldwork. The Department had also long formally stated that it followed the British Sociological Association code of ethics in its staff and student research.

4. Similar ethical questions have been faced by others (see especially Lederman 2006b). This also raises the related interesting question of what counts as 'research' (see also Lederman 2007a), reflective commentary not counting as such according to some ethics regulations (including, tightly interpreted, those of Sheffield University). As I learnt during my ethics-making participation, various disciplines bypass ethics review by employing narrow definitions of what constitutes research. In medicine, for example, 'routine testing' is often excluded in this way.

5. See http://www.wellcome.ac.uk/doc_WTD002757.html (accessed July 2007). The history of the concern over funding is also indicated by the fact that Sheffield University's website at which these policies are to be found is under a link on 'winning grants' (http://www.shef.ac.uk/researchoffice/support/winning/governance-ethics-grp.html, accessed July 2007).

6. These included, in particular and as mentioned elsewhere in the document, the Council of Europe's *Convention for the Protection of Human Rights and Dignity of the Human Being with Regard to the Application of Biology and Medicine: Convention on Human Rights and Biomedicine* (www.conventions.coe.int/Treaty/en/Treaties/html/164.htm, accessed July 2007) (1997); the World Medical Association Declaration of Helsinki (http://www.wma.net/e/ethicsunit/helsinki.htm, accessed July 2007) (original 1964, amended 2004); the UK Council for Science and Technology's *Rigour, respect and responsibility: a Universal Code for Scientists* (www.cst.gov.uk/cst/business/files/ethical-code.pdf) (2005); the UK Data Protection Act (1988) and the Human Rights Act (1998).

7. The Russell Group is, in its own self-description, 'an association of 20 research-intensive universities in the UK' (http://www.russellgroup.ac.uk/, accessed July 2007).

8. See the National Research Ethics website http://www.nres.npsa.nhs.uk/ (though this is the 2007 version, accessed July 2007).
9. For example, there were some suggestions that, in future, universities might have their own NHS-approved ethics committees. See also the website in the previous footnote.
10. I also learned later that there had been one meeting at which basic philosophies had been discussed (though with no professional philosophers present) but that this had produced such disagreement that it was not pursued and explicit reference to philosophical positions was not included in the policy documentation. Some members of the committee also had some philosophical training.
11. There were many other disciplines that would potentially be affected – such as history, archaeology and music – that were not included until after the policy itself had been drawn up, at which stage all heads of department were contacted to ask whether there was research in their departments that fell under the definitions that had been devised. Many that surely do such work seemed to believe that they did not (perhaps because the language of 'human subjects' and 'data and tissue' meant that they perceived it as medically oriented) or else they ignored the request for information. The UREC, however, was constituted to include representatives from all faculties, including arts and humanities.
12. I should also emphasise that those lay members who participated in this case were extremely clear-sighted and helpful.
13. Estate agents are the mediators involved in buying and selling property in the UK.
14. The first of the university's statutes concerning academic staff is 'to ensure that academic staff have freedom within the law to question and test received wisdom, and to put forward new ideas and controversial or unpopular opinions, without placing themselves in jeopardy of losing their jobs or privileges' (http://www.shef.ac.uk/calendar/statute31.html#part1, accessed July 2007).
15. A first version of this boilerplate and Lederman's excellent discussion is available at http://savageminds.org/author/rena-lederman/ (accessed July 2007); and a further developed one, with further excellent discussion, in *AAA/Anthropology News* (Lederman 2007b).

References

Amit, V. 2000. 'The University as Panopticon. Moral Claims and Attacks on Academic Freedom', in M. Strathern (ed.), *Audit Cultures*. London: Routledge, pp. 215–35.
Brenneis, D. 2005. 'Documenting Ethics', in L. Meskell and P. Pels (eds), *Embedding Ethics*. Oxford: Berg, pp. 239–52.
———. 2006. 'Partial Measures', *American Ethnologist* 33 (4): 238–40.
Caplan, P. (ed.). 2003a. *The Ethics of Anthropology: Debates and Dilemmas*. London: Routledge.
———. 2003b. 'Introduction: Anthropology and Ethics', in P. Caplan (ed.), *The Ethics of Anthropology: Debates and Dilemma*. London: Routledge, pp. 1–33.
Corsín Jiménez, A. 2005a 'Failing to Re-describe: Universities as Public Knowledge', *Description and Creativity Conference*. Cambridge.
———. 2005b. 'After Trust', *Cambridge Anthropology* (special issue, *Creativity or Temporality?*, edited by E. Hirsch and S. Macdonald) 25 (2): 64–78.
Dewar, S. and P. Boddington. 2004. 'Returning to the Alder Hey Report and Its Reporting: Addressing Confusions and Improving Inquiries', *Journal of Medical Ethics* 30: 463–69.
Fluehr-Loban, C. (ed.). 2004 (2nd ed.). *Ethics and the Profession of Anthropology: Dialogue for an Ethically Conscious Practice*. Walnut Creek: Altamira.
Hamburger, P. 2005. 'The New Censorship: Institutional Review Boards', *Supreme Court Review*, October 2004 Term: 271–354.
Harper, I. and A. Corsín Jiménez. 2005. 'Towards an Interactive Professional Ethics', *Anthropology Today* 21 (6): 10–12.

Katz, J. 2006. 'Ethical Escape Routes for Underground Ethnographers', *American Ethnologist* 33 (4): 499–506.

Lederman, R. 2006a. 'Introduction: Anxious Borders between Work and Life in a Time of Bureaucratic Ethics Regulation', *American Ethnologist* 33 (4): 477–81.

———. 2006b. 'The Perils of Working at Home: IRB "mission creep" as Context and Content for an Ethnography of Disciplinary Knowledges', *American Ethnologist* 33 (4): 482–91.

———. 2007a. 'Comparative "research": a Modest Proposal Concerning the Object of Ethics Regulation', unpublished paper forthcoming in *PoLAR.*

———. 2007b. 'Educate your IRB: Fieldwork Boilerplate (or, an experiment in cross-disciplinary communication)', *AAA/Anthropology News*, 48 (6): 33–34.

Macdonald, S. 2002. *Behind the Scenes at the Science Museum.* Oxford: Berg.

Meskell, L. and P. Pels (eds). 2005a. *Embedding Ethics.* Oxford: Berg.

——— 2005b 'Introduction: Embedding Ethics', in L. Meskell and P. Pels (eds), *Embedding Ethics.* Oxford: Berg, pp. 1–26.

Mills, D. 2003. '"Like a horse in blinkers"?: a Political History of Anthropology's Research Ethics', in P. Caplan (ed.), *The Ethics of Anthropology: Debates and Dilemmas.* London: Routledge, pp. 37–54.

Shweder, R. 2006. 'Protecting Human Subjects and Preserving Academic Freedom', *American Ethnologist* 33 (4): 507–18.

Silverman, M. 2003. 'Everyday Ethics. A Personal Journey in Rural Ireland, 1980–2001', in P. Caplan (ed.) *The Ethics of Anthropology: Debates and Dilemmas.* London: Routledge, pp. 115–32.

Strathern, M. 2000. 'New Accountabilities: Anthropological Studies in Audit, Ethics and the Academy', in M. Strathern (ed.), *Audit Cultures.* London: Routledge, pp. 1–18.

University of Sheffield. 2005. *University of Sheffield Ethics Policy for Research Involving Human Participants, Data and Tissue.* Retrieved July 2007 from http://www.shef.ac.uk/content/1/c6/03/25/85/ethics_policyvs3.pdf

7

Ethnographic Practices and Methods
Some Predicaments of Russian Anthropology

Alexei Elfimov

My aim in this chapter is to reflect on ethnographic field practices as they have developed or remained underdeveloped in the Russian tradition of anthropological research. As in many other anthropological traditions, the past decade in the Russian tradition was a period that highlighted the uncertainties in regard to the field – that is, in regard to its location, its status, its accessibility, the methods of studying it and other aspects. Most of these uncertainties, indeed, seemed, or seem now, rather global; but their actual apprehension was locally coloured and in many ways was a product of the local academic tradition and local social anxieties. The realisation that Russian anthropologists increasingly came to face in the past decade was that the 'field' became closer than before but at the same time less accessible than before; it suddenly became more important but at the same time it became less clear how that very importance was to be grasped or even approached. This realisation, however, in the Russian case was embedded in a set of rather particular dilemmas, which I would like to discuss here in more detail.

One observation that you can draw from a comparative look at different disciplinary traditions in the last quarter of a century is that each anthropology, while willing to tackle similar issues, has to struggle with its own past. At any rate, this observation is applicable to the Russian case. In fact, I would go so far as to stress that, for anthropology, as for other humanities disciplines in Russia (and anthropology is a humanities, rather than social science, discipline in Russia), the struggle with the past has traditionally been a more defining factor than concern with the present. This is a complex issue that extends beyond the scope of this chapter and which I attempted to analyse in a more focused manner in another account (Elfimov 2003), but I shall have to touch on some of its principal manifestations. The manifestations, actually, are multiple. One of the less important ones, for instance, is a rather peculiar backward attitude ('That's not the way we used to do it') with which Russian ethnographers, save for the youngest generation, often like to meet new realities and new research challenges. This attitude is not so much a matter of sticking to the old canons of work; for in fact few ethnographers today want or are able to keep doing things the way they used to do them. It is a kind of belief that all meaningful reference points remain in the past and the present cannot supply anything that would efficiently organise the disciplinary order or serve as coherent points of departure in research. What is much more important, however, is that 'the way we used to do it' is, in reality, very often not remembered as such. While this rhetorical formula has been gaining currency, many of the actually useful ways of conducting research have been abandoned. On the positive side, a welcome outcome of this attitude has been an awakened interest in the discipline's past. The number of publications dealing with the history of Russian/Soviet anthropology has grown steadily over the course of the last decade, but one cannot help seeing that that interest has been pursued to a certain detriment of the interest in the actualities of research.

Yet another manifestation of the same issue has been the proliferation of what some Russian anthropologists call the 'revivalist mood' in ethnographic practices. This is basically the idea, not altogether novel, that ethnographers' practices should be aimed at uncovering the dormant past and bringing it back to life. By the end of the last century, the idea became so popular that even the executive director of the Russian Academy of Sciences' Ethnology and Anthropology Institute had to voice his puzzlement. 'For some reason', he commented, 'this mythic idea of a rebirth as a return to the old is appealing to anthropologists ... I was always curious about what it was they wanted to revive. Bast shoes? Samovars? Wagons on the roads?' (Elfimov 1997: 784). Indeed, one aspect – an applied aspect – of the problem is that ethnographers today very often want to revive what people they study want to abandon. But the problem has a reverse – methodological – aspect as well. It consists in a very peculiar pattern of mapping the field by ethnographers. Ethnographers tend to designate field sites as relevant when the latter display the presence of vestiges of the past. One telling episode comes to my mind in this connection – an episode that has recently been commented upon by a number of senior anthropologists in Russia (Tishkov 2003a). A group of ethnographers who made a preliminary exploration of field sites in a Russian region marked by ethnic tensions and other social problems returned to their institution and reported to the project director that they decided they were going to look for other villages that would be more interesting for field research. To the director's question 'Why so?', they replied, 'There were few elders in these villages, and we could not find anything old at all that would be of value.' This episode is probably not unusual in the history of anthropology, but it has caught the attention of Russian scholars today precisely because it is no longer an anecdote but a case that tells much about the wider conceptual framework that ascribes relevance to field research.

What is important, however, is that the roots of these problems in Russia are not just 'cultural' but have a rather firm institutional basis. Ethnography, as I have mentioned, is a humanities discipline in Russia. Not only is it a humanities discipline, but in essence it is also a subdivision of history. Administratively, it belongs in schools and faculties of history, and many of its practitioners take it for granted that what they practice is in fact a historical discipline. This model of institutionalisation goes back to the late 1920s and early 1930s when all academic disciplines in the Soviet Union went through the infamous ideological cleansing. Before that, two notions of the discipline coexisted: there was 'ethnography', understood as a kind of descriptive discipline; and there was 'ethnology', understood as a social science with more conceptual and theoretical ambitions. The general bias among leading scholars seemed to be in favour of institutionalising ethnology as the principal discipline and granting ethnography some sort of dependent status. In the course of the ideological cleansing, however, ethnology was officially banned as a 'bourgeois social science' on the grounds that there could be no alternative to the Marxist social science, which was declared to be the only valid social science. Ethnography, nevertheless, was allowed to exist and charged with the task of illustrating the Marxist scheme of social development with appropriate examples. Essentially, what was required of ethnography was to explain why in the modern Soviet state there still remained some 'backward' peoples. All instances of 'backwardness', obviously, were to be explained as survivals or vestiges of the past. In the modern present, there could be nothing ethnographic. Ethnography, as a discipline called on to account for the presence of 'social awkwardness', was thus in the strict sense turned into what Johannes Fabian (1991: 193) once called a 'discipline with a negative object'. Therefore, the logic demanded that ethnography be equated with historical research, and so it was placed in history divisions.

More than half a century of training within such a system has been, of course, instrumental in producing a rather distinctive type of ethnographer with rather distinctive views of what ethnographic practice is or should be like. In this light, it is perhaps not surprising that, in the period of general social revitalisation of the 1980s, a reaction toward this state of affairs in the discipline began to emerge. The last decade, indeed, was marked by an increasing interest in overcoming this specific understanding of ethnography. But it is important to note that this interest also set the development of Russian anthropology on the way that in some sense ran counter to the ways along which anthropology moved at the time in some Western traditions. While those traditions, over the course of the last century, displayed a fairly distinctive trajectory from the understanding of anthropology as a natural science through the understanding of it as a social or behavioural science to the understanding of it as one of the humanities, the Russian academic tradition of the last quarter of the century witnessed a contrary urge to free anthropology from the humanities and move it closer to the social sciences. In short, the desire to practice ethnography as a kind of social science while it remains institutionalised as one of the humanities is a very tangible predicament of contemporary Russian anthropology.

I began by pointing out this predicament not only because it highlights some of the differences between Russian anthropology and anthropology in other national traditions, but also because it is essential for understanding a number of other issues related to ethnographic practices. One such issue is that of method. It constitutes a predicament of a separate kind, and, interestingly, seems to be inscribed in a local trend that also diverges from the trends that have been becoming pronounced elsewhere. To put it briefly, while in other anthropological traditions participant observation as a classic method of research has been seriously questioned lately and there could be observed a distinct interest in embracing an array of techniques that would suit research needs in the face of the globalisation era, in Russia there can be observed a tendency towards abandoning the array of techniques that Russian/ Soviet anthropology had experimented with and an interest in embracing participant observation in its classic form as a method supposedly constituting a more efficient type of field practice.

The relationship that Russian and Soviet anthropology had with the participant observation method may be characterised at least as uneasy and unresolved. On the one hand, Soviet textbooks customarily made a mention that ethnographers employed the participant observation method; on the other hand, they customarily avoided elaborating on what employing that method actually meant. On the one hand, it was informally understood that the enigmatic method was actually a borrowing from the West (an 'alien academic tradition'); on the other hand, there could be observed a clear desire to internalise it, make it one's own.

The method, however, was never made one's own. Or, to be precise, it was appropriated but never domesticated. Again, much of the difficulty with making it comfortable and dutiful had to do with the discipline's development in the past. The kind of activity that participant observation prescribed had rather uncomfortable historical connotations and something of a political hue. In the Russian tradition going back to the tsarist time, those who lived for long among the remote peoples usually did so for political reasons. That is to say, reasons could be various (ranging from geopolitical exploration missions to exiles); but, one way or another, they were politically sponsored and invariably situated within larger imperial concerns. It was not academic reasons that made most Russian and Soviet ethnographers go to the field for prolonged periods of time. And, indeed, it was not the Stalinist regime that set this unfortunate trend. Vladimir Dahl, one of the outstanding early Russian ethnographers and folklorists, conducted his remarkable research in the Orenburg steppes, being a member of the imperial mission to the Central Asian borderlands. The brilliant research of the later Russian ethnographers Vladimir Bogoraz and Waldemar Jochelson in north-eastern Siberia were made possible by their political exile. In Soviet academia, the trend continued, although the line between being on a mission and being in exile certainly became much more thin and shaky. Boris Dolgikh, for instance, carried out his early research on the circumpolar peoples as a state census registrar, his later research as an exile. Examples actually abound. Quite recently, a thick two-volume collection, 'Repressed Ethnographers', has been produced by Russian scholars, and the third volume is already said to be planned because the first two have failed to mention all the personalities that fall into this category (Tumarkin 2002–3). But, whether it is possible or not to reconstruct the vicissitudes of all the ethnographers in Russian history, one of the results of this particular trend of development of Russian anthropology in the last two centuries is that the type of field practice that came to be labelled as 'participant observation' gradually became associated with social outcasts in the Soviet academic imagination.

It must be added that another level of reality that underlay this picture and was not in the least conducive to the promotion of research based on participant observation was the rigid social structure of the Imperial Russian and Soviet states, enforced with very precise – indeed quite ethnographic – mechanisms of police surveillance and informing. In Imperial Russia, local police officers and informers employed techniques that much more closely resembled participant observation routines than methods used by ethnographers did. Such police officers and informers, who could be local administrators, schoolteachers, doctors and often priests, ordinarily kept notebooks in which for years they painstakingly recorded various aspects of everyday life of communities, part of which they were. Ethnic details, among others, were always in the focus of their attention. For example, one of the police officers in a town of the Udmurt region wrote, 'The Votiak people, when not drunk, are quiet, shy, secretive, do not socialise with foreigners, live in large families and are quite friendly. The Votiak distrust Russians but are open towards the Tatar, with whom they quickly and willingly make friends, although the latter tend to abuse that friendship' (Berdinskikh 2003: 175). Individual movement in Russia and the Soviet Union was always difficult. Going to unclear places for unclear purposes was not a welcome endeavour in any sense. The romance of the lone scientist in the field was flawed in the Russian case in a number of serious ways.

Still, these were not the only reasons why Russian anthropology went in the direction of looking for other kinds of field practices. Another impediment to the institutionalisation of participant observation as a reliable method of anthropological research was the character of the cultural – or intercultural – setting in which Russia and Russian ethnographers had been situated since the very beginning of anthropology as a meaningful project in the country. The neighbour cultures and lands that traditionally attracted the attention of the Russian state and, consequently, Russian ethnographers (the Caucasus, Central Asia or even endless expanses of Siberia, which could be administratively within the empire, but culturally were entities that did not recognise the empire and lived as though it did not exist) were the territories in which the infiltration of an ethnographer as a kind of participant observer was usually a bleak prospect. For instance, Central Asian states, such as the Bukhara emirate or the Khiva khanate, remained extremely difficult to penetrate for foreigners throughout what is considered the classic period of anthropology's development. The same Vladimir Dahl conducted his research on the area mostly by gathering information from merchants and locals coming to the Russian–Central Asian borderlands, and never ventured into the 'heart of darkness' himself, for stories of those who had were known to be instructive. British missionaries Charles Stoddard and Arthur Connolly were killed in Bukhara, in what was a widely publicised case. The isolated attempts at settling in the region by Russians were not very encouraging either. A few endeavours, such as I.V. Vitkevich's one-and-a-half month trip to Bukhara, were actually successful. But the resulting accounts were not usually publicised. Thus, Vitkevich's account of his travels, which was mentioned in memoirs of his close friends as extremely interesting, was promptly classified by the government as apparently containing rare information that was of strategic interest, and it was published for the first time more than a century later, in the 1980s (Khalfin 1983).

In the phase of Russian anthropology's development as a professional discipline, therefore, the main objects of that anthropology were, so to speak, hostile borderlands of the empire. The figure of the lone anthropologist was not a viable one in the setting that produced in the imagination of the Russians, as tellingly reflected in literature, so many stories of captives turned into slaves, 'prisoners of the Caucasus' and explorers that vanished in the unreachable lands of the north.

And yet another observation may be made to help explain why the Malinowskian type of field venture did not move Russian/Soviet anthropology even when it was at its height in Great Britain and began to spread over to the United States. In the 1920s, when participant observation began to capture professional imagination in the West, Russia witnessed an eclectic period of social constructivism, marked by the carnival of socialist utopias and the heteroglossia of mass culture. In other words, while Western anthropology started to display a tendency towards analytical individualism, Russian/Soviet anthropology found itself immersed in what was a tendency toward polyphonic collectivism – although it would be fair to note that both were equally romantic. The kinds of projects, for instance, that the Academy of Sciences' ethnological branch favoured at the time were complex collective projects involving ethnography, physical anthropology, linguistics and psychology. Alexander Luria's experiments in measuring social modernisation, which in some ways anticipated the social change studies that would attract American social science by the mid-century, were a remarkable example of that trend. The individual fieldworker, just as in the earlier Imperial Russia, was not a favoured character; and, on top of that, the romance of the primitive – or, rather, of *Volksgeist* – was rapidly being overpowered by the utopias of social modernisation.

Thus, participant observation – due to specificities of the understanding of ethnographic research as a kind of historical enquiry, due to difficulties with accessing important 'field sites' by individual researchers, due to uncomfortable connotations that prolonged stays in remote places carried with them – never materialised in Russia as a fully legitimate method of ethnographic involvement.

This does not mean, however, that Russian anthropology was left to make use of historical and quasi-anthropological methods only. Indeed, from the very beginning, it seemed to place emphasis on other kinds of field practices, which supplied it rather well with an appropriate body of knowledge. In particular, the two practices that assumed importance in the social context of Russia were the practice of large-scale statistical and qualitative surveys and the practice of what one might call multiple case studies.

The practice of large-scale surveys, which was indeed made possible by the highly centralised and hierarchised nature of the Russian state, was a rather interesting case. It was constituted, if one wished to draw a graphical representation of it, as a kind of evolutionary tree turned bottom-up, at the top of which there was a group of professional anthropologists, at the mid-levels of which there were semi-professional or amateur anthropologists and regional administrators and at the bottom of which (which implied actual 'fieldwork') there worked ordinary people, particularly those whose occupations made the process of observation and interviewing less complicated and less demanding. These were typically, as mentioned earlier, police officers, local administrators, schoolteachers, doctors and priests. The data that were gathered by such fieldworkers were processed and sorted out by the mid-level scholars and then forwarded to professional anthropologists at the top, who used them according to their research design and purposes.

One of the better-known examples of the official institutionalisation of such a practice was the Tenishev Ethnographic Bureau, which has been at times considered by some Soviet/Russian scholars as the centre of early Russian anthropological functionalism; but in fact the practice was employed rather widely and the activities of the Russian Geographical Society constantly promoted it. Needless to say, the data obtained from such surveys were always of great use to the state authorities and were regularly inspected by various administrative committees. But, leaving the beyond-dispute question of the institutionalisation of anthropology as an imperial discipline aside, it is worth stressing the relative efficiency with which this type of research practice was implemented in Russia. What made this practice work was, indeed, not only the political coercion – which, of course, made it difficult for ordinary people at the bottom of the hierarchy to refuse to comply with directives coming down from the top – but also the energy which metropolitan and regional scholars invested in the dissemination of anthropological knowledge among these groups of people. The motives of such scholars were often romantic and deeply permeated with the philosophy of *Volksgeist*, which was in turn intertwined with the specific ideological notion of 'duty to the people', which gained wide currency among the gentrified strata of Russian intellectuals by the end of the nineteenth century. The combination of the V*olksgeist* philosophy with that particular notion was still prominent among the intellectuals in the Soviet time, being certainly popular among anthropologists, and in some important ways it accounted for the conservationist attitude that manifestly spread through the humanities in the last quarter of the twentieth century (see Elfimov 2003: 114–18). Thus, it was typical of scholars to elevate the task of studying anything related to peasant culture to the status of moral obligation. For example, Professor I.N. Smirnov of Kazan University, one of the many defenders of the idea of promoting ethnographic education in small towns of the regions, declared, 'Those who live amongst such surroundings [i.e. rich in ethnographic detail] have no right not to pay attention to them – they have a moral duty towards science and mankind' (Smirnov 1891).

This practice, which bore fruit in the context of Imperial Russia, continued to be important in the context of the Soviet state. However, in the latter context its application began to change. It was now decreasingly applied to surveys of traditional culture and increasingly applied to the notorious 'national question', the state-building process, which, as Francine Hirsch put it, 'involved "re-imagining" the former Russian empire as a socialist federation of nationalities' and required that 'ethnographers, statisticians, and linguists from Minsk to Vladivostok … have to decide which tribes, clans, and peoples belonged to which nationality' (Hirsch 1997: 251). In a word, the statistical aspect of this type of research was advanced to the foreground, whereas its qualitative aspect became much less prominent, as *Volk* culture now began to be ideologically positioned as somewhat of a rudiment in the modernising society. In the last decades of the Soviet era, this type of research was still important in national census campaigns; but, as some recent analyses demonstrate, at that time it was already removed from ethnographic research as such and became essentially the prerogative of the state administration (Sokolovski 2001: 163).

The type of qualitative ethnographic research that Soviet anthropologists learned to pursue most successfully was based on the second practice developed within the Russian anthropological tradition – that of multiple case studies. It essentially consisted in recurrent short-term field expeditions to a number of chosen localities, which in some cases might either be initially planned within a framework of a long-term large-scale investigation project, or, as was more often the case, spontaneously assume the shape of such a project. Not infrequently, these expeditions were undertaken for so many years in a row and with such regularity that the studied people got to know anthropologists very well and came to expect their arrival at this or that time of the year as a taken-for-granted event. Since this was the dominant type of field practice that mediated the encounter between anthropologists and their studied 'others' for over half a century, it could not but result in the shaping of a specific kind of relationship between the two parties. On the one hand, this type of encounter was short enough not to allow for any contact that would be too close, as well as short enough not to involve the discomfort of a prolonged stay (on the part of either the anthropologists or the locals); on the other hand, it was frequent enough to allow for the establishment of a more or less trustworthy and lasting relationship. On the one hand, it seemed shorter than needed for producing reliable or desired knowledge; on the other hand, being repeated, it gave anthropologists a sense that their research findings were verifiable and that they had a continuous opportunity to double-check their facts and conclusions.

In sum, this type of relationship was marked by advantages and disadvantages. To begin with, anthropologists seemed to be practising a rather cautious approach – the 'other' seemed to be kept at bay, never too close; but at the same time the relationship was continuous – it was marked by perennial mutual reacquaintance, which kept the two parties together. On the one hand, anthropologists seemed to be enjoying a position that was much less vulnerable (than that, say, of a participant observer) and therefore implied that they could feel relieved of certain constraints; on the other hand, the prospect of having to come back placed a heightened sense of responsibility on them. In fact, this relationship eventually began growing into one that allowed for a fairly open system of feedback, as the studied people at some point began showing an increasing interest in learning how to reach anthropologists outside the field situation. This, undoubtedly, added a positive dimension to the anthropological understanding of field practices and their broader implications. However, it must be mentioned that the very same feeling of rapprochement had something of a sedating effect on anthropologists' conceptual vision of the field. The illusion of 'verifiability' – that is, of a supposedly always present secure opportunity of 'dropping by' and double-checking the field facts – perhaps the Russian variant of what Alcida Ramos (1990: 458) has aptly called 'the field-in-our-backyard syndrome' – produced a strangely static view of the field as something lying halfway between a historical manuscript, in which one could always – today, tomorrow, in a year – look at the previous page and find what one had forgotten, and a provincial scientific lab in which the same experiments were carried on and on from year to year, always with the same results.

But, whatever advantages and drawbacks this practice of field research might have, in the Soviet tradition it was developed better than the classic participant observation method. What was occasionally practised in the guise of participant observation, in reality was hardly ever participant observation. There was a pretence that it was, but, as Moscow University anthropologist Alexei Nikishenkov once noted, it rarely amounted to anything more than 'the ritual duties of questioning the village elders' (Elfimov 1997: 780). In fact, those who wanted to question its validity could do so, and indeed sometimes did, by questioning the very term as it was used in Russian. The Russian translation of 'participant observation' (*vkliuchennoe nabliudenie*) is inexact and means literally 'plugged-in observation': that is, the reference to 'participation' is absent as such. At best, the phrase implies that one observes from within the community, but it does not mean that one must 'participate'. In accordance with this usage, getting within the community was usually seen as a rather straightforward process too. Not burdened by challenges of becoming a participant, it was generally understood simply as being physically located at a field site. Whether the community accepts you as a member, or even as a trustworthy outsider, was not an issue. Much as in Marvin Harris's reductionist notion of 'etic' field practices (1979), it was presumed that, once you are physically at a site, you can make objective observations that are valid regardless of what natives think and what natives do.

In the 1980s, the last decade of Soviet ethnography, long-term participant observation was actually discouraged in anthropological training and students were initiated solely into the method of short-term case studies. Indeed, the disciplinary inertia was so strong that even in the 1990s, which witnessed rapid changes in attitudes of all sorts, many practitioners kept resisting participant observation as a dubious idea that carried with it various century-long anxieties and connotations. Thus, reacting to the emerging interest in rediscovering the value of the classic participant observation practice for ethnographic research, senior Soviet anthropologist Viktor Kozlov wrote:

> Fieldwork implying one or another level of immersion in the studied ethnic group, especially if the group has a semi-nomadic way of life in taiga or tundra, is hard and rather dangerous. It is worth recalling a tragic case of the early 1950s, when one of the younger fellows of Institute of Ethnography's Leningrad branch went out to wander with the Chukchee nomads and was turned into a concubine who was passed from one clan to another. Many dangers await men as well. (Kozlov 1992: 6)

Yet the 1990s, the period when the structure of Soviet academia began to crumble, reopened not only the interest in classic long-term ethnographic studies but also structural holes through which engaging in such studies became in fact occasionally possible. The disarray in employment regulations and unbearably low academic wages under Yeltsin produced in both students and professors a sense of striking indifference towards the official rules of the academic process and made many feel that they were morally free to do things the way they pleased. The situation not only made unplanned leaves of absence possible, but also seemed pregnant with opportunities in general (although the sense of open opportunities began to rapidly diminish in the second half of the 1990s). This is not to say that all ethnographers rushed into the field, but some indeed started to probe the reality of the classic participant observation practice in an unsanctioned way.

Even though the results of that probing were mixed, the course of the decade continued to witness the decreasing interest in ethnographic methods that had been practised in the Soviet time. In a certain sense, the trend might be seen as part of a more general tendency – quite distinct in the Yeltsin era – towards repudiating anything Soviet and regaining things associated with the pre-Soviet past. I discussed the profound effect this tendency has had on the Russian humanities in another account and in more detail (Elfimov 2003); but it would be worth mentioning that one of its odd consequences was a rather uncritical acceptance of the idea that things dwarfed by the Soviet regime had been inherently progressive and that the best way of proceeding into the future was, thus, through the things forgotten. This mood has been recently recaptured, for example, in the address to the Russian anthropological community by one of its leading institutional figures, Valery Tishkov, who has stated, 'The future belongs, as the past does, to the fieldwork conducted in small groups by the participant observation method. It is time to supplement the graduate student training with a ten-to-twelve-month season in the field' (Tishkov 2003b: 18). Although Tishkov's own vision of why participant observation is important is by no means simplistic (as he indeed makes a reservation that both the method and the 'field' itself have to be rethought), the general understanding of the issue still more or less comes down to the notion that the method is very important simply because it has been neglected for so long.

But there is also a different sense in which the old method seems to have assumed importance lately. From the practitioners' point of view, the potential value of participant observation is sometimes seen not so much in what it vaguely promises to provide for ethnographers, as in what it much more distinctly promises ethnographers to overcome. What it promises them to overcome is, of course, some of the flaws associated with the established field practices. For the younger generation of anthropologists in particular, the most obvious flaw is the very design of fieldwork as a type of formalised practice devoid of close contact, of meaningful immersion in the actual life of the studied culture, of opportunities for getting to know the culture more intimately and, of course, of romance. For others, the problem is in what is sensed to be deeper structural deficiencies of the implementation of field research procedures in the Russian/Soviet tradition. For instance, one of the remnants of the way the old large-scale survey system, and in some sense the short-term case-studies system, had been implemented in Russia and the Soviet Union is the wide gap between the mastermind anthropologist-theoretician at the top and fieldwork functionaries at the bottom. This gap remains quite pronounced up to the present day and has been variously commented upon. Moscow anthropologist Sergei Sokolovski observes that 'there has not been any substantial flow of theoretical knowledge from the theoreticians to the fieldworkers and vice versa. They have been two separate castes' (Elfimov 1997: 779). Siberian anthropologist Andrei Golovnev concurs, 'In Russia, the holistic study of cultures (or peoples) is held to be a privilege of a small cohort of eminent anthropologists-theoreticians ... but not ethnographers' (Golovnev 1995: 14).

The reverse aspect of the very same type of implementation of field procedures has been a certain lack of concern for fieldworkers' training. As it was routinely assumed that, on their way from the bottom to the top, fieldwork notes would be sorted out by 'professionals' anyway, the issue of fieldwork skills became not so consequential.

Minister Nikolai Blinov, who had conducted field research for one of the large-scale ethnographic surveys in nineteenth-century Russia, wrote in his memoirs:

> I had to get familiar with statistics techniques by looking into randomly available writings of researchers who published in the *Proceedings of the Geographical Society* ... As for the method of obtaining data and information from the peasants, I had to make up one of my own. I made a notebook, in which I listed all [people to be interviewed] and charted lines at the margin for marking such things as family status, cattle owned, crops, and so on. During a trip to a village you have plenty of time to talk with a peasant and ask him all about his life. Once you are back, you promptly fill the figures in the notebook – the memory holds for an hour. (Blinov 1981: 179)

This passage is strikingly reminiscent of how Soviet students learned, and Russian students nowadays more often than not still continue to learn, fieldwork methods. The amateurishness of this procedure, in the imagination of many students (and professors), is often counterposed to the supposedly higher standards of participant-observation-based fieldwork that is thought to require much more substantial preparation, for the ethnographer embarking on that type of research cannot hope that his or her notes would be sorted out by some professional intermediary before they are put to use by some theoreticians at the top.

To sum up, the methodological predicament of contemporary Russian anthropology is that the classic participant observation method is beginning to be seen as a way out of the crisis, which itself is understood as an effect of holding on to the old field practices, while the conditions in the field are actually becoming increasingly complex and unaccommodating for relying on the classic participant observation method, and while the method itself is increasingly subjected to rethinking by anthropologists elsewhere as inadequate in the face of globalisation processes. Reflecting on this situation, I would like, however, to conclude with a number of observations and questions.

First of all, recognising the predicament of Russian anthropology as a humanities discipline that is struggling to become a social science as a particularly problematic one, I cannot but think of the methodological predicament of the discipline as a tangle of opportunities, rather than a deadlock. It seems to me that the disappointment and discontent with the local field practices should have become grounds for their reassessment, rather than their abandonment or replacement. Indeed, it is not that the method of multiple case studies, for example, was deficient in itself; it is rather that what were thought to be its deficiencies were actually consequences of its misuse. It does seem to me that its potential was not developed, just as the potential of early Soviet approaches to research inspired by the constructivist mentality was never explored in full measure. My first question, then, is whether, in the era of cultural globalisation, it would not be worth making an effort to adapt the practice of multiple case studies to the new conditions (and possibly recalling the abandoned projects of the constructivist period), rather than trying to replace it with the classic Western model of participant observation. In fact, it appears that the technique of multiple case studies could, indeed, be adapted in some interesting ways to the fragmentary nature of contemporary cultural worlds.

Secondly, I wonder whether the pattern of the relationship between the ethnographer and the studied other, which has crystallised over the course of the last century as a result of particular field practices, is not worth developing further. Considering the positive facets of this relationship, such as the anthropologists' accountability and the openness to feedback, it may be premature to discount its usefulness.

Thirdly, it seems to me that the predicaments of ethnographic practice in the Russian case are still entangled with the dilemma of having to choose between catching up with the West and exploring the ways that seem meaningful within the context of one's own society. Due to particularities of historical development, Russian anthropology traditionally focused attention on the other within, like, for instance, early American anthropology. But, if American anthropology eventually discovered the other without and to an extent transferred its internal anxieties on to it, nothing like that happened in Russia. Russian anthropology never found the other without and remained absorbed by the other within. This is to say, much in the desire to reappropriate the classic participant observation method is to make the other within seem like the other without – that is, to romanticise the practice, which has come to be seen as too familiar and perhaps in a way uninspiring. But the question whether anthropology can or cannot do without romantic motives is, of course, a theme for another debate.

References

Berdinskikh, V. 2003. *Uezdnye istoriki*. Moscow: Novoe Literaturnoe Obozrenie.
Blinov, N.N. 1981. 'Dan svoemu vremeni', *Ural* 2: 178–82.
Elfimov, A. 1997. 'The State of the Discipline in Russia: Interviews with Russian Anthropologists', *American Anthropologist* 99 (4): 775–85.
———. 2003. *Russian Intellectual Culture in Transition: The Future in the Past*. Münster: Lit Verlag.
Fabian, J. 1991. *Time and the Work of Anthropology*. Chur: Routledge.
Golovnev, A.V. 1995. *Govoriashchie kul'tury*. Ekaterinburg: Russian Academy of Sciences.
Harris, M. 1979. *Cultural Materialism: the Struggle for a Science of Culture*. New York: Random House.
Hirsch, F. 1997. 'The Soviet Union as a Work-in-Progress: Ethnographers and the Category Nationality in the 1926, 1937, and 1939 Censuses', *Slavic Review* 56 (2): 251–78.
Khalfin, N.A. (ed.). 1983. *Zapiski o Bukharskom khanstve*. Moscow: Vostochnaia Literatura.
Kozlov, V.I. 1992. 'Mezhdu etnografiei, etnologiei i zhizniu', *Etnograficheskoe obozrenie* 3: 3–14.
Ramos, A.R. 1990. 'Ethnology Brazilian Style', *Cultural Anthropology* 5 (4): 452–72.
Smirnov, I.N. 1891. *Zadachi i znachenie mestnoi etnografii*. Kazan.
Sokolovski, S.V. 2001. 'Klassifikatsia i perepis', in *Obrazy drugikh*. Moscow: Put', 157–205.
Tishkov, V.A. 2003a. *Rekviem po etnosu*. Moscow: Nauka.
———. 2003b. 'Rossiiskaia etnologia', *Etnograficheskoe obozrenie* 5: 3–23.
Tumarkin, D.D. (ed.). 2002–3. *Repressirovannye etnografy* vols. 1 and 2.

8

Getting the Ethnography 'Right'
On Female Circumcision in Exile

Aud Talle

For the last few years I have been trying to write an ethnography of 'female circumcision in exile'.[1] Basically, my aim has been to describe and analyse a social practice that within a brief period of time has moved from its 'place of origin', where it is deeply encoded in cultural forms and ways of living, to unfamiliar and hostile surroundings far away. This ethnography is in other words about a social and cultural practice that has 'travelled', and actually still travels (see, for example, Clifford 1997; Gupta and Ferguson 1997; Marcus 1998). The spatial fluidity of the subject matter, its dramatic and violent character, inflicting severe pain on young girls, and its bodily nature, carving human flesh, do not lend themselves easily to straightforward ethnographic fieldwork and writing. My objective in this chapter is to try to construct an ethnography of people's lives that stretches out both in space and time and of which memory is an integral part.

The excision of vital genital organs of the female body in order to create a 'complete' and beautiful woman is a social practice historically localised in north-eastern Africa. Recent mass emigration from this part of the world to Europe, North America, Australia and elsewhere has brought the practice into new cultural and political contexts. For the last decade or so the world has seen a flow of circumcised female bodies across the globe, to the extent that the practice, in fact, has never had a wider geographical distribution than it has today. This current dispersion, however, has not meant a proliferation of diverse circumcision practices, entrenched in cultural valuations and symbolic representations, such as was the case when the practice spread over the centuries on the African continent (Murray 1974; Mackie 1996; Shell-Duncan and Hernlund 2000). Rather, in exile the opposite is the case: the further the practice of female circumcision travels out of Africa – in that process becoming circumscribed by a global discourse – the more it seems to lose in cultural elaboration and complexity.

My account deals with Somali refugee women in London, their situated lives in a world city and how in that context they live and experience being genitally cut. The Somali women have experienced the most radical form of circumcision, called infibulation (from Latin *fibula*, 'clip') or pharaonic circumcision (*guudninka pharonika*, the term referring to a practice of great antiquity). At about the age of six to ten years, the outer genitals of the girl are pared away and the vulva stitched together leaving only a tiny opening for urine, and later menstruation, to pass. In London, as in an increasing number of places all over the world (also gradually in Africa), the hegemonic discourse defines female circumcision as a mutilation practice and a serious human (and women's) rights issue (Nussbaum 1999). In order to draw attention to the medical severity of the intervention on the bodies of girls and women as compared with the less harmful circumcision of men, female circumcision as a term has been replaced by 'female genital mutilation' (its abbreviation FGM is more commonly heard; see, for example, Toubia 1995; IAC 2007).[2] The reterritorialisation of a local practice such as female circumcision in the contemporary European context powerfully demonstrates the point that the 'primitive' has 'come home' to us (Moore 1999).

Fieldwork and Context

This ethnographic material derives chiefly from shorter sojourns of fieldwork (between two and four weeks at a time) in an immigrant-dense suburb of the British capital.[3] My engagement with Somali women in London has not been classical anthropological fieldwork in terms of 'intensive dwelling' in one locality (Clifford 1997: 190). Quite the contrary; I have moved in and out of the 'field' in a rather unsystematic manner; whenever time has permitted, I have either travelled to London from Oslo or made a stopover in London on my way to and from other places. The depth of my fieldwork exercise can certainly be questioned in this regard; extended fieldwork is undoubtedly a 'mark of disciplinary distinction' (Clifford 1997: 216) and continues to be the foundation of thick ethnographic analysis (Geertz 1975; Marcus 1998). The longer, the better has often been a sort of commonplace truism in anthropological discourse. I am not questioning the merit of long visits in the field, far from it. My message here is solely to give the notion of fieldwork (and ethnography) a widened consideration by specifically seeing my engagement with Somalis in London in conjunction with my field experiences among women in Somalia some years ago. My knowledge and experience of Somali communities at a previous time, however, is more than background material – something formally defined and 'outside' the actual scene; rather, it is indeed part of the 'context' that will be evoked in my analysis of female circumcision in exile (Hastrup 1995; Dilley 1999).

In the title of the chapter I have used the phrase 'right' ethnography; right is, of course, put in quotation marks. Being fully aware of the invalidity of such a phrasing, particularly if it is meant to be normative, I nonetheless found it worthwhile to use for my purpose here. 'Right' ethnography may look like an oxymoron, a contradiction in terms, because the production of ethnography, unless we think of it as only getting the details right, is never pure descriptions devoid of interpretations and theory

(Sanjek 1990; Carrithers 1992). Seeing social and cultural phenomena in their cultural context has always been a guiding principle for anthropological analysis. Context in contemporary anthropology has to do with interpretations and making relevant connections (and disconnections): how do we as anthropologists in our analytical practice on the one hand, and our informants in their beings and doings on the other, make sense of life and make claims to truths? 'Right' ethnography alludes to contextualisation as a deeply meaningful exercise, never neutral, but always emanating from creative intersubjective encounters in a variety of fieldwork settings as well as the researcher's interpretative strategies (Hastrup 1995; Dilley 1999).

The specificity and distinctiveness of this particular ethnography is an interconnection and disjunction of space and time, of intercontinental and historical movements mediated through female bodies. Much like Liisa Malkki's study of uprooted and displaced Burundian refugees in Tanzania, this is also an ethnography of 'processes and interconnections' rather than a comprehensive account of 'a community' or a place, a situation and 'its people' (Malkki 1995a: 1). Malkki's story is about the condition of 'refugeeness' in a neighbouring African country; mine is about the refugee condition in a faraway and distant place. The ethnography of this chapter, however, is not about refugeeness as such; rather it is about an interconnection between a local practice and a global, universal debate – a relationship that in this particular case is at once circumscribed by institutions of hegemonic power and embedded in bodily memory and experiences of pain.

Disrupted Lives

My involvement with female circumcision in exile was to some extent a coincidence. During the 1980s I did fieldwork in Somalia, both among women in the capital of Mogadishu and among camel nomads on the Ethiopian border. Among other things, I studied the practice of female circumcision and how that practice was meaningfully related to the construction of gender and lineage identity (Talle 1993). In the late 1980s, the political situation in the country became increasingly repressive. My last trip to Somalia was in 1989. One year later, a full-blown civil war broke out – and in fact this has still not come to a complete halt all over the country.

For many years it was impossible to return to Somalia. Furthermore, my collaborators had left for different parts of the world. Sadiya, a gynaecologist and close friend, who is at the centre of this tale, was among the last to leave. She and her husband, an employee of the foreign ministry, belonged to the ancient urban community of Mogadishu, *xamar*, a population of mixed Somali and Arabic descent. By being racially diverse, urban and cosmopolitan and pursuing a livelihood based on commerce and the arts, the *xamar* people have through history remained outside the ethnic configuration of mainstream nomadic Somalia (see Casanelli 1982). Due to their unique position in the landscape of clan-based ethnic politics, they saw themselves as marginal (and immune) to the core of the conflict of the civil war. At the height of the political mayhem, however, nobody could avoid being involved. Late one evening a gang of armed men attacked Sadiya's house, and only by crafty negotiations with the attackers and a good portion of luck did she and her family escape catastrophe. The following morning the family fled to another part of the city where they remained for some time in the house of a clan relative of Sadiya's mother. In 1992, one year into the civil war, she and her family embarked on a long journey through Kenya, Zambia and Yemen before they by coincidence landed in London in 1994. 'We could have been anywhere,' she concluded to me when we met for the first time in London, pointing to the chancy character of the refugee mode of existence.

My first meeting with Sadiya in London was in 1999, five years after she had settled in Britain. We met on the premises of the health centre where she worked temporarily as a volunteer. When I arrived, the receptionist asked me to sit down and wait, and within a short moment Sadiya walked across the floor to greet me. I immediately noticed her changed appearance: she was dressed in a floor-length skirt, long-sleeved woollen sweater, thick socks, boots and a scarf folded around her head – all in black and brown colours. The sight took me aback.

Memories flashed back to Mogadishu, where I had often visited Sadiya at the gynaecological and obstetric hospital where she worked, and where so many pregnant women and young girls had arrived in agony as a consequence of a severe circumcision or obstructed labour. There, in the tropical climate of a coastal town, Sadiya always wore the transparent and loose female dress, the *dirie* – hers was often in a blend of grey and white colours – and the one-coloured matching *garba saar* draped lightly over her head and shoulders. The architecture of the hospital was such that it allowed a maximum of breeze to enter the premises (there was no air conditioning in the hospital) giving women an elf-like gait as the gentle wind moved their gauzy clothes.

The figure in front of me was a less sophisticated 'European' and not the attractive Somali woman I used to know. Sadiya had taken on to her body the dreariness of the place she lived in. The cold, misty climate of Britain surely required warm clothes, but the scarf kept tightly around the head carried a meaning to her life that I only learned about later and to which I shall return shortly. As much as it was the beginning of a new story, our first encounter in London was also an extension of an old one. The discontinuity in her life, as I observed it, was nevertheless a continuity of our relationship and indeed a part of this tale.

Sadiya in London was 'different' from Sadiya in Mogadishu not only in terms of clothes. The trauma of her flight – which she told me about in detail – the brutal assassination of a close colleague at Benaadir hospital shortly after she left (along with the murder of many others), the rape of her young cousin (whom she had to examine and stitch afterwards, and who later disappeared for a period in Canada), her status as a refugee in Britain, her unemployed husband and her lack of a licence to practise as a medical doctor were experiences she now embodied and which had become part of her situatedness in London. There appeared to be nothing ordinary or everyday about her life any longer (Malkki 1995b). Even the place where she presently lived was frequented by rapists and drug abusers. 'We are the lower classes now,' she commented to me, both of us terribly mindful of a disrupted life career.

Many other Somali refugee women in London incarnated similar abnormal and extreme life experiences. Khadiya, for instance, in her mid-thirties, had fled with her husband and two children in a car from Mogadishu southwards, towards the Kenyan border. Only about 100 km along the road their car was shot at and her husband and two children were killed. She had to continue the journey towards Kenya on her own and through benevolent assistance in Nairobi she got on a plane to England. She did not know any English nor did she have relatives or friends waiting for her there. Sitting in front of me at a Somali women's support centre shrouded tightly in her clothes – her face barely visible – Khadiya incorporated the burden of an exiled and deprived woman. Her withdrawn bodily appearance, in her clothing as well as her remarkably dispassionate face, bore witness to great distress. 'She is much better now,' said Anab, a lawyer volunteering her services at the centre.

The refugee narratives of Sadiya and Khadiya are just two stories; there are many others to be told. Refugee lives I encountered in London were typical and idiosyncratic at the same time: some were as traumatic as Khadiya's, some less, some worse, while others again told of narrow escapes, sheer luck or extraordinarily fortunate circumstances. All stories, however, carried the drama of sudden losses and abrupt changes in individual lives.

The Emergence of a Field

What kind of 'field' did this material constitute? Disparate Somalis, with considerable internal animosity and divisions (Griffiths 1997), with extreme life experiences, uprooted and dispersed in alien surroundings and subjected to new power structures and institutions of support and surveillance, but nevertheless trying to work out a normal life and reconfigure new ethnic identities, challenge descriptive practices as we know them in anthropology. Confronted with this field situation, surely '*ethno* in ethnography [took] on a slippery, nonlocalized quality' (Appadurai 1991: 191). Although in recent years we have become quite familiar with the deconstruction of conventional concepts and methods within the discipline, the conception of ethnography as a localised coherent totality lingers on in anthropological discourse and practice (Hastrup and Hervik 1994; Gupta and Ferguson 1997).

For reasons noted below, female circumcision is a difficult issue to study in a European, 'out-of-context' situation. Thus the main reason for choosing London among several exile options was the presence of Sadiya. Our earlier collaboration in Mogadishu, her knowledge of and experience with the practice of female circumcision (from hospitals and awareness-raising campaigns) and our long-standing friendship made London an optimal choice as a fieldwork locus for this project. In most countries in Europe (and in North America and Australia), the practice is criminalised, thereby rendering many people mute or secretive about the topic. Furthermore, in their exiled condition, women who have been subjected to the operation are often pitied, scorned or reprimanded by representatives of the mainstream society. Being a criminal act, in some places also researchers and others are legally obligated to report violations against the law, putting the anthropological project under insurmountable ethical dilemmas (Janice Boddy, personal communication). Thus, in order to perform useful research on this issue in exile, close relations with members of the community appear to be essential. Trustful and intimate relations have always been important in anthropological fieldwork; intimate relations represent 'depth', that is, closeness and intensiveness in field relations, which the discipline regards as a prerequisite for ethnographic description of high quality. In London, Sadiya was the 'methodological peg' on which this study hinged. I literally found my way through Somali London following in her footsteps.

I began travelling to her flat, on the thirteenth floor in a delapidated high-rise building in a run-down working-class area in north-east London. The building was to come down shortly. Two similar buildings had already been demolished. Here, Sadiya lived in a four-room flat with her two teenage sons, her unemployed husband and her elderly mother. After a few years, the family moved to a semi-detached house in the same borough. During the day, her sons were at college, while her husband and mother stayed at home.[4] The husband used to watch Arabic and Somali television programmes and the BBC, read the *Guardian* or *The Times*, meet friends and run errands. Sadiya herself travelled between different refugee centres and health clinics, where she offered her interpreting services. After several years of voluntary work, Sadiya was permanently employed as a health assistant adviser by the municipal health authorities. With full-time employment, she was a busy woman, trying to work out a daily schedule of servicing at the clinics, cooking for her diabetic husband, attending to her mother while she was alive and sometimes entertaining relatives visiting from other exile countries outside the UK. In between, she found the time to visit friends, to participate in weddings and to offer her condolences to grief-stricken people. She attended meetings, seminars and conferences in other parts of the city (a few times abroad), but she almost never travelled to the city centre of London for theatre, cinema, restaurants or any other entertainment (except when I took her to such places).

Sadiya's life had many similarities to other refugee women's lives in London (and elsewhere in exile), but their life conditions were not identical, far from it. Her academic education and fluency in English and the fact that she was beyond childbearing age made her free to move around in quite a different way from, for instance, many younger women. Younger women, often married to men living in another exile country or in Somalia/Somaliland, have reported 'crippling' and depressive experiences of isolation in tiny flats (see Tiilikainen 1998). Considering that Sadiya has a job at a health clinic, is trained as a gynaecologist and belongs to an ethnic group outside the major lines of conflicts, she enjoys easy access to Somali women of many different political and ethnic affiliations. Her politically neutral position, coupled with her medical skills and her friendly personality, make her trustworthy in the eyes of many refugee women. They confide in her, particularly in matters related to their reproductive health. Although Sadiya is not permitted to work as a medical doctor, of which people are aware, Somali women nevertheless approach her for a second opinion on the doctor's diagnosis.

An important aspect of Somali women's lives wherever they live is their preoccupation with childbearing. They experience frequent gynaecological and abdominal problems and their relationship with health authorities in Britain, as it was in Somalia, is frequent and intense. Furthermore, women in exile have a high fertility rate (at least compared with the host communities) and this brings them into continual interaction with the health system. Health centres therefore became important sites of field research in London. One of the health centres in the study area has a weekly African Women's Health Clinic, staffed by a British outreach nurse and Sadiya as a lay health adviser.[5] The clinic has grown out of a recognised need for Somali women requiring special medical treatment due to their severe circumcision type and the lack of awareness and knowledge of this cultural practice among British health personnel, and, in this particular case, the availability of Sadiya as a resource person. 'I could not have run this clinic without Sadiya,' said the British outreach nurse who was in charge. 'She speaks five different languages and is well known and respected within the Somali community'.[6]

Besides the health clinic, I frequented the two refugee advice centres along the high street and got to know the staff, had lunch at the Somali restaurant along the same road, visited friends of Sadiya and went by bus to see Somali women in places located a little bit further away. The contours of a 'field' – locations of empirical focus – slowly emerged as I frequented the different sites. My field – like all fields, I think – was indeed 'practised place' (de Certeau in Hastrup 1995: 57). According to Hastrup, practised place 'incorporates the ethnographer in an important sense, she herself is a ritual context-marker. She does not construct reality ... she is part of the defining consciousness of the space' (1995: 57). My presence established the immediate, active 'field' from which this ethnography is produced.

The 'field' as it emerged in London was not a fixed place, but a room of willed relations and selectively trodden space, or, in the more solemn words of James Clifford, 'discursively mapped and corporeally practiced' space (1997: 186). Sadiya was the main instrument in locating the sites of fieldwork involvement. Even though I sometimes went on my own, she was always present in the sense that people with whom I communicated saw me as a 'friend of Sadiya'. My field was more or less 'wherever I was with Sadiya' in person or by network (Clifford 1997: 189). The 'locality' then, of my anthropological investigation of female circumcision in exile, was not primarily a demarcated spatial field in the suburbs – the creation of a relatively stable cultural setting where persons interact meaningfully – but rather an 'extended site' in lived space and time (Gupta and Ferguson 1997). The transition from 'place' to 'space', from 'locality' to 'location' in fieldwork tradition does not necessarily mean that the field has lost its materiality altogether, but rather that it has become widened so as to incorporate more objects and relations for ethnographic descriptions. Fieldwork on 'female circumcision' in a London suburb setting meant incorporating fields of interaction of many different scales, as these stretched out in social and territorial spaces as well as in time (see Grønhaug 1978). The temporal dimension is a particular methodological challenge when grappling with the construction of this ethnography.

The Relevance of Memory

Sadiya always introduced me to her acquaintances in London as an old friend and colleague from Somalia, and she sometimes recounted experiences from our common past. This information never failed to light up the faces of the women I met. Her introduction 'allowed me into their world' (Hastrup 1995: 70), but not only because I was a friend of Sadiya, a highly respected and well-liked person. More importantly, I think, my knowledge and experience of Somalia before the war was a strong basis for interaction with Somalis in exile. Shared memories of a once treasured but lost country constituted an experiential bonding of sorts: a fieldwork rapport, not of likes or dislikes, personal fit or non-fit, but of a commonality through life biographies. As memory must be evoked in intersubjective relations, meeting again in London created opportunities for remembering Somalia, for recalling places and people. 'It is so nice when you are here,' said Sadiya one day, taking great care in serving me Somali food. 'It is like when we were at home.' It was not a nostalgic comment, I thought, but uttered as if I brought some normalcy to her life. I was certainly not a refugee and did not share the experiences of forced migration, but my person somehow constituted continuity in her life, a link between here and there, now and then. Certainly, I was a member of the majority society (not British, but still European), but also a person to whom Somali women could relate with comparative ease – there were a number of issues that did not have to be explained or unnecessarily detailed, such as, for instance, the circumcision procedure and why it is done. The appreciation of my Somali experiences in the field in London was so striking that I discussed my observations with several Somali friends and colleagues living in exile. The commonality in personal history, one of my friends pondered, offered conversational 'comfort' to many women, living in what they themselves often experienced as an alienating and painful exile condition. As refugees, circumcised Somali women frequently have to deal with others' imaginations and fantasies about their bodies and lives – often having no resonance in their own experiences – and which they are unable to counter.

In London, Somali women risk meeting people, in particular health personnel, who cannot conceal their emotional commotion and disgust when they encounter and see a circumcised woman. To them the circumcised vulva signifies an 'abused' child and a 'primitive' culture. Women naturally take offence at many of these reactions, which some experience as greatly distressing. More importantly, however, the ignorant gazes by significant others on their own bodies make them remember their own circumcision and instigate them to reflect upon their own traditions. For Somali women it is therefore a great relief to meet and speak with women of the majority society who are able to appreciate them beyond the label of a 'mutilated woman'. To me, memory and experiences of visits in Somalia became more than a communicative instrument in the fieldwork situation. It was in fact the basis from which I could engage meaningfully in intersubjective relations with Somali women when I first contacted them in London. Somehow we had a 'common interest' in understanding the exile situation. My informants, of course, also had to live it, which is quite another challenge.

For many Somali women, encounters with uninformed health personnel and others intimidate them and make them ashamed of their own 'culture' – the scar in their genitalia representing a very concrete cultural embodiment. The embarrassment many women experience at the gaze of others evokes memories of a frequently traumatic bodily intervention, which occurred a long time ago, when they were very young girls. Having spoken to numerous women in Somalia and heard the stories of their circumcision operation and its sequel in young life and marriage (Talle 1993), I could easily picture their despair and frustration at the intrusive questioning about a mark that was inscribed in their bodies in order to secure their future lives. My own experiences of intimidation and moments of 'identity loss' (Hastrup 1995) during fieldwork in Somalia in the late 1980s helped me to imagine the helplessness often perceived by Somali women in exile. One particular instance should clarify what I mean.

In an arid area among camel nomads in central Somalia along the Somali–Ethiopian border, my female assistant and I paused at a watering place on our way to some homesteads further away. It was one of those terribly hot days and we sought relief in the shadow of a single tree. While we were sitting there an elderly woman and her young female relative joined us. The women had come to water the family's goats. During the conversation we learnt that the woman was a circumciser and we began to discuss the issue with her. The young girl was tactfully quiet, but curiously followed our conversation. Suddenly, upon having understood that I was not circumcised, she turned to her elder relative in open disbelief and uttered: 'Is she not circumcised?' Upon getting a discreet but confirming nod from a more informed relative, she instantly moved her body away from me in a frightened gesture. She had been sitting next to me – I had been admiring her carefully plaited hair and fine facial features – and I still intensely remember her swift, dragging movement over the sandy soil without standing up. She literally made a physical distance between us. The arid landscape, the overwhelming heat, the drinking livestock herds, the whole setting of foreign scenery added momentum to her bodily rejection and caused a strong feeling of alienation in me. This was certainly not a place for uncircumcised bodies! Her aversion to my 'polluted' status was for a moment also my own. This experiential insight was a moment of clarity in my understanding of the moral force of a bodily inscription. This particular feeling of being different, which I experienced in a nomadic setting in Somalia, has often been evoked in encounters with Somali women in exile.

Every Somali woman carries a circumcision tale of her own and the memory of that pain inscribed in the infibulation scar connects her to a social group, a country and a common identity. Pain and infibulation are one and the same thing for women in Somalia; in fact the link is so obvious that it does not have to be spoken aloud (see Clastres 1987; Summerfield 1993). The memory of the pain is for ever inscribed in a bodily scar of belonging (Clastres 1987). The overpowering pain girls had to endure at the hands of close relatives when the identity mark was made is, many years later in the exile context of London, brought to mind in diffuse and contradictory feelings of shame and otherness. The newly experienced attention to their infibulated genitalia evokes the pain, but also a longing for the place where the scar was initially carved, as it were.

The uncertainty of Somali refugee women in exile and their acute and often painful awakening to being 'different' are embodied in many ways – in clothing, diffuse illness conditions, tense limbs and aching hearts (Tiilikainen 1998; Talle 2007). As refugees, Somali women experience considerable discomfort and lack of confidence from living in what they consider a hostile and incapacitating environment. The sense of 'loss' women experience as refugees in foreign lands is meaningfully located in the shifting context and in the 're-complexification' of a body mark that at its 'point of local consumption' in exile becomes utterly ambivalent (Strathern 1995: 168)

Veiled Identity

It was Sadiya's scarf tightly folded around her head and face in an orthodox Muslim style in a veil-like fashion (*hijab*) that struck me the first time I met her in London. Later I saw many women dressed the same way. The covered body gave Sadiya an alien look, both in respect of how she used to dress in Somalia before the war and now with regard to the surrounding British society: the veiled woman makes a stark contrast to the London city people. Ironically, through the act of concealing and protecting their bodily selves, Somali women make themselves visible to outsiders and in that act they draw boundaries between selves and others.[7] In the political context of contemporary Europe, the veiled woman has in fact become an icon of 'cultural difference'.

Some Somalian women in London claim that they wear the *hijab* because they have become more truly religious in exile. One woman, herself heavily clothed in a dark grey *jellabib* (the loose cloak, covering the body from head to toe), said that after they came to London they had become more religious in a 'deeper sense', and she laid her right hand on her heart. 'Deeper sense' referred not only to an emotional state of belonging, but also to the fact that Somali women had begun to read the Koran and to observe the five pillars of Islam more actively, which she claimed had made them more enlightened in exile than they were back home in Somalia. 'We could leave circumcision, but not the hijab,' declared two elderly women I met at a refugee centre, while eagerly reading aloud to each other from the Koran. The way they put their words convinced me that they spoke the truth. 'Decent' dressing in Muslim style has, in the context of London and in the life of these women, become more important than the cutting and closing of their genitals. It is worth noting that orthodox Islam does not prescribe female circumcision, at least not the severe form practised by the Somalis. On the contrary, many Muslim groups in Europe disparage African Muslims for such non-religious practices.

Female circumcision, in particular infibulation, is a contested issue among Somalis in exile (also recently in many places in Africa).[8] The growing medicalisation (and politicisation) of the circumcised body in London (and other exile contexts in Europe) directs attention to the female body in quite novel ways. The flight to London and hence, the repositioning of Somali bodies rekindle thoughts and sentiments deeply sunk in the consciousness. The surfacing of repressed experiences (the experience of pain, for instance) may lead to 'natural phenomena' being debated, and often to action (Hastrup 1995). 'You just feel you have to, or the other Somalis will look at you as if you were naked', explained Sadiya when I asked why so many Somalia women had changed their style of dress. She was hinting at the pressure of a common morality, but also at the vulnerability of the exile situation. 'Naked' may be taken symbolically to mean nothing but humans without history and culture – without an identity (Arendt in Malkki 1995a). By veiling themselves, Somali women craft an identity as 'accepted' others within the 'national order of things' (Malkki 1995b) and by that act they create a meaningful continuation in their lives. The *hijab* disconnects them from the British surroundings, but simultaneously connects them to a larger world of Islam and to the history of their country. In this context of shifting social and political circumstances, the bodily inscription of female circumcision has lost much of its potency as an identification mark of excellence.

Ethnography and Context

Empirically and analytically, my field research in London became a continuation of earlier fieldwork in Somalia and my knowledge of female circumcision in that context. By ill-fated circumstances, I had shifted the geographical locale for my study just as the women had done for their lives. I had travelled with them, so to say, from where they came to where they went. In her book *A Passage to Anthropology*, Kirsten Hastrup (1995) distinguishes between the ways realist ethnography and reflexive ethnography contextualise social phenomena. Realist ethnography refers to context as a totality in the form of a geographically situated community or a positioned semiotic code (or a 'culture'); reflexive ethnography, which I think my work approximates, sees context as 'fragments of life [which] are connected through reflections of the experiential space of the ethnographer' (Hastrup 1995: 57). Within the latter view, 'context' cannot be formally defined, but is defined through analytical practice. The context is not 'outside' our data, but is integral to them – context is both constituted and constituting (see Dilley 1999).

In writing the ethnography of 'female circumcision in exile', past experiences and memory have been part of my interpretative frame. Field experiences from Somalia helped me imagine Somalis in exile and make room for 'novel connections' (Hastrup 1995: 63). Through women's bodies and the memory of pain, the exile situation resonates deeply with the Somali situation; the bodily pain experienced by women as young girls – a memory from which they cannot escape (Clastres 1987) – is forcefully and ambiguously invoked in exile encounters. Reflection and interpretation of fieldwork observations in London have alternated between two situated contexts, separated in time and space, but connected by memory and the movement of bodies.

The cultural embodiment of infibulation as simultaneously an act of beautification and an act of pain enters the analytical space as a relation of deep relevance. In exile, when the performance of circumcision is no longer 'conventional' (Mackie 1996) – encompassed as it is by a global FGM discourse, by legislative and medical institutions and by the disapproving gaze of others – the embodied pain often instils feelings of identity loss in the women, but also inspires women's articulated protests against their own traditions. Many women (and men) in exile strongly oppose and voice their views against the practice of female circumcision, while, however, remaining firmly Somali. Through heightened observation of religious practices, women in London and elsewhere in diaspora (and also in Somaliland/Somalia after the war) seem to forge and carve out an identity as Somali Muslims. In this process they have come to regard infibulation as a 'bad tradition' (*ado xun*) and unreligious practice.

By 'right' ethnography is not primarily meant getting the details correct, which certainly is important enough, but rather establishing a coherent (and convincing) description of relevant connections (and disconnections). Identifying relevant contexts for ethnographic description will continue, I think, to emanate from intersubjective relations in varied fieldwork settings. The ethnography of 'female circumcision in exile' is a far-reaching and multifaceted story, connecting in multiple ways global forces with pain trajectories in individual lives. Depending upon contextualisation, this experience of human life, where actors and systems of different scales and means of power intersect with great force, potentially opens the way for writing several ethnographies. In the construction of this particular ethnography, memory – embodied pain experienced by women, as well as previous fieldwork experiences – has also been part of the analytical context.

Notes

1. My acknowledgement to Professor Marit Melhuus, who, as one of the editors of this volume, read my chapter thoroughly and offered very useful views. I also want to thank my friend and colleague Inger Altern for her insightful reading of my text.
2. The World Health Organisation (WHO) estimates that as many as 130 million women in the world today have been genitally 'mutilated' (WHO 1998).
3. It is estimated that some 800,000 Somalis were displaced from their homeland and livelihood during the civil war of the 1990s; approximately 200,000 of these have been repatriated to their home territories. In Britain alone, there are some 80,000 Somali refugees; about 34,000 of these live in London (Office for National Statistics 2004), but figures are uncertain (Hopkins 2006). Their numbers in Britain have been steadily increasing with incoming Somalis from other exile countries in Europe.
4. Her mother passed away in January in 2005, seventy-six years of age, and is buried in the Muslim graveyard close to their home.
5. More similar clinics are being established in London. They have also been established in the USA, and in a less organised form in Norway and Sweden.
6. Besides English and, of course, Somali, Sadiya speaks Arabic, Czech and Italian. She learnt Arabic in Cairo, where she went to primary school as a young girl while her father was enrolled as a law student at the university, and she studied medicine in Prague. Italian was the university and hospital language in Mogadishu when she specialised as a gynaecologist and obstetrician.
7. In Somalia after the civil war broke out, women in veils also became a common sight.
8. Most Somalis in exile reject infibulation, but many continue to cherish *sunna* (literally 'in the Prophet's way', a good deed, which in medical terms refers to the excision of the clitoris's prepuce or the clitoris (WHO 1998). This is recognised as a less severe intervention. *Sunna*, however, as regularly practised by the Somalis (and others) today can be quite an extensive operation, often including excision of the clitoris as well as minor stitching.

References

Appadurai, A. 1991. 'Global Ethnoscapes: Notes and Queries for a Transnational Anthropology', in R.G. Fox (ed.), *Interventions: Anthropologies of the Present*. Santa Fe: School of American Research, pp. 191–210.

Carrithers, M. 1992. *Why Humans Have Cultures: Explaining Anthropology and Social Diversity*. Oxford: Oxford University Press.

Cassanelli, L.V. 1982. *The Shaping of Somali Society: Reconstructing the History of a Pastoral People, 1600–1900*. Philadelphia: University of Pennsylvania Press.

Clastres, P. 1987. *Society against the State: Essays in Political Anthropology*. New York: Zone.

Clifford, J. 1997. 'Spatial Practices: Fieldwork, Travel, and the Disciplining of Anthropology', in A. Gupta and J. Ferguson (eds), *Anthropological Locations: Boundaries and Grounds of a Field Science*. Berkeley, Los Angeles and London: University of California Press, pp. 185–222.

Dilley, R. 1999. 'Introduction: the Problem of Context', in R. Dilley (ed.), *The Problem of Context*. Oxford and New York: Berghahn Books, pp. 1–46.

Geertz, C. 1975. *The Interpretation of Cultures*. New York: Basic Books.

Griffiths, D. 1997. 'Somali Refugees in Tower Hamlets: Clanship and New Identities', *New Community* 23 (1): 5–24.

Grønhaug, R. 1978. 'Scale as a Variable in Analysis: Time-spaces in Social Organization in Herat, Northwest Afghanistan', in F. Barth (ed.), *Scale and Social Organization*. Oslo: Universitetsforlaget, pp. 78–121.

Gupta, A. and J. Ferguson. 1997. 'Discipline and Practice: "the Field" as Site, Method, and Location in Anthropology', in A. Gupta and J. Ferguson (eds), *Anthropological Locations: Boundaries and Grounds of a Field Science*. Berkley, Los Angeles and London: University of California Press, pp. 1–46.

Hastrup, K. 1995. *A Passage to Anthropology. Between Experience and Theory*. London: Routledge.

Hastrup, K. and P. Hervik (eds). 1994. *Social Experience and Anthropological Knowledge*. London: Routledge.

Hopkins, G. 2006. 'Somali Community Organizations in London and Toronto: Collaboration and Effectiveness', *Journal of Refugee Studies* 19 (3): 361–80.

IAC – Inter-African Committee on Traditional Practices. 2007. Symposium for Religious Leaders, Abidjan, Ivory Coast. 23–25 October 2007.

Mackie, G. 1996. 'Ending Footbinding and Infibulation: A Convention Account', *American Sociological Review* 61 (6): 999–1017.

Malkki, L. 1995a. *Purity and Exile: Violence, Memory, and National Cosmology among Hutu Refugees in Tanzania*. Chicago and London: University of Chicago Press.

———. 1995b. 'Refugees and Exile: from "Refugee Studies" to the National Order of Things', *Annual Review of Anthropology* 24: 495–523.

Marcus, G.E. 1998. *Ethnography through Thick and Thin*. Princeton: Princeton University Press.

Moore, H. 1999. 'Anthropological Theory at the Turn of the Century', in H. Moore (ed.), *Anthropological Theory of Today*. Cambridge and Oxford: Polity Press, pp. 1–23.

Nussbaum, M. 1999. *Sex and Social Justice*. New York: Oxford University Press.

Office for National Statistics. 2004. '2001 Census Data'. Retrieved from www.statistics.gov.uk/tc.asp.

Sanjek, R. 1990. 'On Ethnographic Validity', in R. Sanjek (ed.), *Fieldnotes. The Makings of Anthropology*. Ithaca and London: Cornell Univerity Press, pp. 385–418.

Shell-Duncan, B. and Y. Hernlund. 2000. 'Female "circumcision" in Africa: Dimensions of the Practice and the Debates', in B. Shell-Duncan and Y. Hernlund (eds), *Female 'Circumcision' in Africa: Culture, Controversy, and Change*. Boulder: Lynne Rienner Publishers, pp. 1–40.

Strathern, M. 1995. 'Foreword' and 'The Nice Thing about Culture is that Everyone Has It', in M. Strathern (ed.), *Shifting Contexts: Transformations in Anthropological knowledge*. London and New York: Routledge, pp. 1–11, 153–85.

Summerfield, H. 1993. 'Patterns of Adaptation: Somali and Bangladeshi Women in Britain', in G. Buijs (ed.), *Migrant Women: Crossing Boundaries and Changing Identities*. (Cross-cultural Perspectives on Women, Vol. 7), Oxford: Berg, pp. 83–98.

Talle, A. 1993. 'Transforming Women into 'Pure' Agnates: Aspects of Female Infibulation in Somalia', in V. Broch-Due, I. Rudie and T. Bleie (eds), *Carved Flesh/Cast Selves: Gendered Symbols and Social Practices*. Oxford: Berg, pp. 83–106.

———. 2007. 'From "Complete" to "Impaired" Body: Female Circumcision in Somalia and London', in B. Ingstad and S.R. Whyte (eds), *Disability in Local and Global Worlds*. Berkeley: University of California Press.

Tiilikainen, M. 1998. 'Suffering and Symptoms: Aspects of Everyday Life of Somali Refugee Women', in M.S. Lilius (ed.), *Variations on the Theme of Somaliness*. Proceedings of the EASS/SSIA International Congress on Somali Studies, Turku: Centre for Continuing Education, pp. 309–317.

Toubia, N. 1995. *Female Genital Mutilation. A Call for Global Action*. New York: Women Inc.

World Health Organization. 1998. 'Female genital mutilation: an overview'. Geneva: World Health Organisation.

9

An Ethnography of Associations?
Translocal Research in the Cross River Region

Ute Röschenthaler

This chapter is inspired by reflections about research carried out in the remote rain forests of the Cross River region of Cameroon and Nigeria.[1] It presents the research project and the mobile method that was applied to realise its objectives: the reconstruction of dissemination histories of the various associations in the region and to understand the driving force behind the process of dissemination. I shall argue that the method of research has an impact on the kind of information that is obtained in the field; the chapter also argues that the imponderabilities of fieldwork have at least as decisive an impact on the results as the method itself. I am also interested in the interplay of the anthropological assumptions and the interests of the local people.

The Cross River region is known for its richness in associations: The groups living there, such as the Ejagham, Banyang and Korup, own numerous women's and men's societies (often termed secret societies) with executive functions; cult agencies to detect individuals with malevolent intentions; and associations of the youth for the staging of competitive performances. The associations existed largely irrespective of language and ethnic identities. Some of them were in only a few villages, while others had spread over the entire region.

In the more recent times, associations have rarely been the subject of anthropological research because of European ideas of old-fashioned male sociality that used to be associated with them. The classical ethnographies suggested that they were part of the culture of a certain ethnic group. Before being able to develop the objective of studying the associations' histories and their dissemination, I needed to discover that, in this region, associations had been developed, acquired and disseminated by purchasing rights in their intellectual property. I had to find out that their dissemination emerged in close connection with the (precolonial) economic development of the region by the trade in slaves and palm oil. In the course of this trade, associations also became commercialised and transactable. During these transactions, the knowledge of their management was taught and the rights in the associations' performances were acquired. Part of the driving force for this process was that they helped to organise the trade and govern the villages better; another was that they became part of the prestige economy and were acquired with the objective of 'having more to eat', i.e. to lead a better life and to participate in economic and symbolic forms of competition.

The realisation of this project needed a methodological approach that was different from the classical approach of carrying out research in one village: the reconstruction of dissemination required the documentation of the histories of associations in many villages; and the method needed to be adapted to the local practices of sharing knowledge. Would the result be an ethnography of the Ejagham ethnic group, of the region or of its associations? Once I had decided that the associations were the unit of study, the focus of the subject of investigation shifted from the study of an ethnic group and its culture to the study of an element of culture, its local uses and its regional context, i.e. from people to things or institutions. This, too, changed the character and the method of the undertaking.

From the Study of People to the Study of 'Things'

My interest in studying dissemination histories appeared to follow a trend in anthropology. With the ongoing processes of globalisation and the growing mobility of people, objects, ideas and techniques, among other things, ethnographic studies began more often to divert their focus of interest to mobility, and this needed a different unit of study. Not only the growing awareness of processes of globalisation but also the developments of the 1980s, especially the literary turn, contributed to the changed perception of ethnographic studies and had an impact on the meaning of ethnography. Ethnography was now also adopted by other disciplines.[2] The changed focus entailed a modified ethnographic approach, which made it necessary to cope with the mobile and multi-sited properties of the research subjects.

The growing interest in global processes of migration and consumption had also revived the discussion about the histories of things and their diffusion. Arjun Appadurai (1986) and Igor Kopytoff (1986) introduced the concepts of biography and social history to the ethnographic study of things. They were among the first to draw the anthropological attention to things being thoroughly socialised and to their study in a world that was perceived to be more mobile than ever. They analysed the social history of things and the meanings different people gave to the same objects in different contexts and phases of their lives. Appadurai (1986: 34) emphasised that it was important to differentiate between the study of individual things which resulted in their 'cultural biography', and the study of types of things, which resulted in their 'social history'. This aspect is of methodological importance for my study of the dissemination histories of associations.

In each village, each association has it individual history, which begins with the foundation of this association in the village. The importance of its introduction as an innovation is acknowledged when the association's chief memorises the name of its founder each time a libation is poured in the name of the association. Associations of the same name usually exist in many villages, but its chief in each village coins 'his' association, makes the number of members increase or reduce, and increases or reduces its performances, popularity and reputation in the region. In being positive, he may persuade other villages to buy the association from him, instead of from somewhere else. Such a purchase includes the knowledge of how the association works and the rights to own it and resell it in exchange for goods, food, animals and money. The objects and insignia involved are not sold. They have to be commissioned separately from a specialist. The transfer is done in a period of training, at the end of which the association is in the village of the buyers and, being intangible property, remains in the hands of the sellers at the same time. Each association, for example, the men's *Ekpe* association, has its history in each individual village that owns it. This individual history is part of the larger history of the *Ekpe* associations in all the different villages who own it, and these taken together make up the history or biography of *Ekpe* in the region. This history of the entire *Ekpe* association, together with all the histories of the other associations of different names in the different villages, make up the landscape of all associations in the Cross River region.

Because they disseminate translocally, the associations are not an exclusive part of a group of people with the same ethnic identity. They are as mobile as the people who own them. They are taken along when people resettle to another place, but, more often, they are disseminated by purchase. Migrations and the transactions of associations are mediated by trade and marriage relations. On their way from village to village, they partly remain the same and are partly altered, given new meanings, and their dancers receive a unique outfit, and sometimes different names, too. This makes the distinction between the ethnography of people and that of things or institutions. The study of people concerns their cultural practices and material objects. In contrast, when things or institutions such as associations are the subject of study, the comprehension of 'their social life' entails following them from place to place as they are owned by different people at different times and in different places. Their owners change them and give them new meanings and use them in different ways.

The Multi-sited Method

In the course of investigating the accelerated movement of people, things and ideas in the process of global mobility (Featherstone 1990) and the need to replace centre–periphery models and the problematic idea of the territoriality of ethnic groups, new methods have been tested. African societies have become more mobile and global in the course of these developments, too, due to better roads, technical means of displacement and access to developments in the electronic domain. African societies have, however, long been much more mobile than previously assumed or realised in ethnography (de Brujn et al. 2001). That institutions such as associations are mobile and should be historicised is nothing new, but has only rarely been realised in practice. This has to do with the history of Western thinking and ethnographic traditions of representation, for which ethnic groups with one culture were good to think with. Their administration, classification and ethnographic description were more feasible with delimited ethnic and cultural units rather than with mobile, identity-switching and flexible groups, which were difficult to define and to pin down. Western ideas on associations have contributed to not perceiving people and parts of culture to be mobile and associations to be purchasable.

In an analogy with the geographical concept of landscapes, Appadurai (1990) had earlier outlined other 'scapes', such as ethnoscapes, technoscapes and ideoscapes, which had emerged from movements of people, things and ideas among others. George Marcus (1995) took up Appadurai's suggestions and proposed to follow not only people and things but also ideas, stories, myths and techniques on their global journeys. To do this, he developed the method of multi-sited ethnography. This multi-sited method was useful, too, in studying the mobility of associations in the Cross River region. These, of course, did not veritably reach global dimensions. Only one of them, the *Ekpe* society, made its way in the course of the slave trade across the Atlantic Ocean to Havana, from where lodges were disseminated further into the hinterland of the island of Cuba (Palmié 2006).

An early version of multi-sited ethnography was practised by Leo Frobenius. Even before Malinowski began to outline his stationary concept of long-term ethnography, the researching traveller Leo Frobenius described his procedure in the field as the 'polygraphic' method, which he explicitly contrasted to the monographic one. He insisted that his intention was not to stay in one place for a long time but to go on travelling and to compare the findings he collected during a short time in one place with those of many other places. The difference between this multilocal procedure and the more modern ones lies in the assumption with which Frobenius went out for data and object collection. Frobenius was aware of Africa having a history, for which Africans are still grateful to him, much more than the Trobrianders were ready to appreciate Malinowski's detailed ethnographies. Frobenius, however, assumed that the mere existence of an object or an association in one or more places was already enough proof for what he called the 'paideumatic relationship' of its owners in different places. He did not verify his assumptions and ask the people where they actually had their objects from and who they sold their associations to, or why they did so. He had different questions at that time (Frobenius 1925: 335–347; Luig 1982: 12; Streck 2001; Röschenthaler 2004c).

It was evident from the beginning that a compromise between the number of places visited and the ethnographic depth had to be made. The strong points of the Malinowskian holistic ethnography – the long-term study and the sound contextualisation of cultural elements – cannot be redeemed by a multi-sited ethnography. Shortness of time simply works against it. Günther Schlee (1985) and James Clifford (1999) in their discussion of interethnic and multilocal research have pointed to this inevitable shortcoming, but did not think it a serious problem. What was decisive was the time spent in the field, they argued, and the moving to many places did not reduce this amount of time. The process of ethnographic reflection and the search for answers continues in several places as it does in one village. A broader overview of the region and the knowledge of many places balance the greater in-depth knowledge about one place. More opinions can be heard, which allow reinterpretation and a process of understanding until, even here, the findings start repeating each other. The contexts differ, but will not be completely different.

Following the Associations in the Cross River Region

After having decided on the mobile method and the associations as a unit of study, I had fifteen months to carry out the project. Between 1998 and 2001, I went with an assistant on a number of excursions to eighty-one Ejagham villages in Cameroon and Nigeria and forty-eight adjacent places of different ethnic identity, taking down the histories of villages and associations. The villages were of different size and socio-political organisation.[3] An earlier, more classically oriented ethnographic study that I had carried out in the same region in 1987 and 1988 had been of great help in giving me a basic understanding of the people.

In the eighty-one Ejagham villages alone, I counted the names of about 140 associations and of seventy cult agencies. Half of the associations were men's societies, a quarter of them women's societies. The remaining quarter was made up of dance associations, in which young people (often of both sexes) were members. Some were of the same category but had different names in each village, while others existed under one name in nearly all the villages (see Röschenthaler 2004b). About fifty of the associations (*akum*) and fifteen of the cult agencies (*ajom*) were widespread, so their history of dissemination could be reconstructed, or, at least, a substantial part of it.

The village of Agborkem, for example, was a middle-sized village of seventy-five compounds and two *Ekpe* halls. It owned eleven functioning associations (*akum*), at least one society for mutual help on the farms and four cult agencies (*ajom*), two of which were no longer functioning. These were active agencies to protect the villagers and reduce their fears of witches, thieves and other malevolent individuals. One of them was *Obasinjom,* who had an entertaining masked performance, during which he divined the problems of clients (Röschenthaler 2004a). Among the associations were four for men, two for women and five for youths and boys. The youth of Agborkem had not yet acquired a dance association, unlike most other villages, which used brilliantly painted face masks in which they combined old warrior performances with modern images and accessories. The women's association was *Ekpa* which was one of the oldest societies and owned by the women only. With *Ekpa* the women ensured the survival of the community and protected their interests. The other association was *Njom Ekpa,* which was a village-owned society, helped to govern the village and performed at funerals of members and when hired for other festivities, with a dancer who balanced a huge carved box on her head. She was accompanied by two girls with mirrors and surrounded by seven to nine, women who performed male roles with weapons. The men's societies, *Ekpe, Obhon* and *Angbu,* served as the executive arm of the village government. *Ekpe* and *Njom Ekpa* were complex graded associations, kept secret knowledge and also acted as courts; *Etokobi* was an ancient warrior society, to which belonged the formerly skin-covered masks of *Nkpe* and *Nchebe* and a number of others that were owned by the landowning families in the village. Agborkem was patrilineally related to one or two other villages, with whom it performed the *Etokobi* ritual dance together.

The taking down of the histories depended in each village anew on the readiness of the communities to assemble and talk about their past and their culture. In most places the village governments readily agreed to our request, while in others the negotiations lasted for hours. People often thought we had come to buy their associations, as representatives of other villages had come before. In every village, my assistant and I started by introducing the project to the village chiefs and to the assembled community to negotiate the conditions under which they would tell us the history. The points of debate were usually the value of their historical knowledge and of their associations. This could lead to heated discussions, shouting and bargaining, until it became clear that they also enacted intra-village power struggles, which focused around the question as to how much they would sell their knowledge to me for. In only a few villages was no agreement possible at all. These were cases in which the various parties in the village were so at odds with each other that they were not able to sit peacefully together and remember the history. When they had solved their problem a year or so later, they told the history in the same way as the others.

After an agreement was reached and the drinks were negotiated, we usually started the interview with the village government, which consisted of lineage heads, big men, as well as women and youth representatives. The actual interviews lasted one or two hours, and were often complemented later on by performances of associations and conversations with individual personalities. At the end, the chief poured the libation with the dregs of the drinks. In his speech, he named his predecessors (the chiefs before him) and summarised the reason for our coming. He also used the occasion to pronounce his wishes for the future: good luck in hunting, many children, enough to eat and also more money, better prices on the world market and, most important, a road to transport their produce.

It was more than a coincidence that those villagers who negotiated in a most distressed way about our interviews were at the same time those who complained most bitterly about their desperate economic situation. In particular, these villages were only accessible on foot. They had to carry their produce, for example, heavy bags of cocoa, often for ten hours to the next passable road on narrow bush paths across hills and rivers. If ever possible, these least developed villages employed Ghanaian or Nigerian workers and carriers, who later on returned to the village on the same footpaths with cushion chairs and roofs of corrugated iron from the markets in town.

In some areas negotiations were difficult, and in other areas people remembered the past more or less easily. Here, frequent migrations had taken place in the recent past, and the villagers often remembered only a short time space because they memorised their history from the last settlement where they had lived together with their ancestor, who was the father of the patrilineally related brothers and sisters in those villages who danced their *Etokobi* together. These villages also did not remember well where their associations came from. Another reason was that few conflicts about resources had prevailed, which made a detailed argumentation dispensable. The

Nigerian historian Okon Uya called such areas 'corridors of forgetting' (personal communication). Finally, economic instability not only contributed to heated disputes about our research but also to the preoccupation of the villagers with the more existential necessities of their immediate survival.

The histories that I collected represent official versions accepted by the village governments.[4] The family heads, who made up the male part of the village government, claimed rights to the village history (see d'Azvedo 1961; Murphy 1980), while the owners of the associations did the same. The women had no right to talk about the men's associations, and the men respected the women's rights to exclusively talk about theirs. Associations, particularly, were understood as a means to 'provide their members with something additional to eat', and therefore, no individual member had the right to talk about matters of their association alone. Laws forbade individuals to profit from them. This implied the assumption that talking included the transmission of knowledge, and this was not given for nothing, because knowledge reduced in value the more people shared it (Barth 2002). Simple conversation with people could therefore easily raise the suspicion that these had conveyed information to me. Therefore, people always preferred to talk in groups and not alone. To regard historical knowledge as property and a valuable resource had, of course, implications for the handing down of historical and associational knowledge and the possibility of its being memorised.

From the Data to the 'Landscape' of Associations

In the course of this mobile multi-sited research several types of data emerged:

1. Some of the data were quantifiable, such as the number of houses or of associations. The method had some properties of a regional survey but did not restrict itself to this. The experience of having been in so many villages enabled me to compare the associations' uses and performances. The data were comparable and paradigmatic. The main objective of the project, however, was not comparison but to follow the associations along the ways they had taken and to put these pieces of history metonymically together into larger histories. More information came from qualitative interviews. In classical monolocal field research, some of these would certainly have remained qualitative. In the different villages, however, after some time, some of them gained weight and became to a certain extent quantifiable. This is not so far from Malinowski's notion (1922: note 6) when he described ethnography as a mixture of different methods and as the process of an oscillation between data collection, interviewing and analysis of abstract rules, which the people could not give.

2. The most rewarding part of the project was to cross-check the data on the dissemination history of associations – the many details of who had bought an association from whom – and fitting them together like a jigsaw puzzle on the dissemination maps of the individual associations. This made it possible to reconstruct the biography of a specific association, such as that of the men's *Ekpe* society, for example. Only the cross-

checking of these data revealed that, despite of the politics of remembering, their large majority was reliable. They allowed me to put the puzzle together and define ideally one place (occasionally it was several) or area from where an association had started to be disseminated and from where the villages claimed that they had acquired it, and a cultural frontier (Kopytoff 1987) where it had ended so far.

In Calabar, a former slave port, this method of cross-checking did not lead to any good results because of the highly competitive history production by the chiefs of the several ethnic groups, who each claimed to be the first owners (first-comers) of the place. The active history production did not necessarily lead to more reliable results (see Röschenthaler 2002). This means that, in 'corridors of forgetting' and in places that had a severe dispute, the method did not work well.

3. Other information was more personal and explorative, and its richness depended on the skills of individual personalities to express their thoughts in more detail than others. Some local personalities developed far-reaching reflections and interpretations of associations. However, I could not expect them to produce the type of analysis that would be my own job and be in my own handwriting: to make sense of my findings, translate these ideas into an academic language and make them comprehensible to an international audience.

All this was much more than participant observation, and therefore Bourdieu (2003), alluding to these tasks, preferred the term 'participant objectification' for the procedure in the field.

4. The reconstruction of the association's dissemination was not obtainable by a classical ethnography of one place and time and a few key informants. It needed travel to many places to find out why people had acquired their institutions and from where, in each place anew. The people at one place would not supply the information for another place for reasons of not being informed or feeling they had no right to talk. Covering an extensive area made the method similar to the early polygraphic method outlined by the diffusionist Frobenius. The difference lies mainly in the verification of the dissemination routes that the associations have taken, and the consideration of the motivations and objectives of the associations' owners to have them. Associations do not simply diffuse. The process is based on individuals' decisions to have them and to spend considerable sums on this.

The dilemma of lacking time to explore the changing contexts of associations in each locality was obvious, in many cases. It was impossible to watch performances in every village and fully check the extent to which their owners had changed them.[5] But the advantage of the multilocal project was clear. It lay in the experience of having been to many places, knowing what they looked like, and having talked to their chiefs about their associations and why they had or did not have them. This knowledge completely changes the relevance of all the other data, too.

After having followed the ways the associations had taken and put together the individual local histories, the biographies of the associations could emerge. These were usually unfinished biographies and contained those parts the people remembered. Their exact beginnings and ends were only rarely determinable with certainty, as the invention of an association was often mythified and after its death a society could still be revived. These biographies taken together produced, in the words of Appadurai, the social history of the associations or, with emphasis on their dissemination, a landscape of associations in the region.

This landscape or social history of associations was in its entirety not known to the local people. They had never spent the time getting to know it, and, in addition to this, the information was no freer for them than for me. These histories had first to be remembered, which was hard work, as I was told, then taken down, collected and put together to make this landscape of associations, which extended trans-ethnically across the region. And the ethnographic part of it was to understand why it had evolved in this way as the creation of the associations' owners, who continued to trade them along the established trade routes and thus kept this landscape not only alive but constantly changing.

Ethnography and the Dissemination of Associations

In the predominantly rural Cross River region, the most common mode of dissemination of associations was by purchase and sale. In this way, *Ekpe* became the most important and widespread of all associations in the region. Often *Ekpe* was at first presented to me as the 'traditional government'. Soon, however, it became clear that it was acquired by the individual villages not too long before colonial times. It was a 'bought tradition'. Its dissemination history shows that it was most probably invented near the Atlantic coast and disseminated from there far into the hinterland along the trade routes in the same direction as the European commodities moved. Altogether, *Ekpe* was bought and sold many hundred times. It is still bought these days. If its knowledge happened to be forgotten, it could be re-bought (Röschenthaler 2006).

Associations were also disseminated by being taken along when a village migrated. A few associations spread by branching from a centre and forming lodges in other villages. One of the women's associations was disseminated when its members married into another village. Dance associations whose performances entailed hardly any secret knowledge could be bought but were more often simply imitated or copied. Only the powerful *Ekpe* society had developed means to protect its dances against copying. Because people traded the knowledge of the associations' management and rights in performances as immaterial property, associations remained with the owner and at the same time became the property of the buyer. In this way, associations were infinitely reproducible. Yet their owners did not trade them like commodities on the market. They carefully decided about a sale according to the status and the family history of the potential buyers.

Other associations were less widespread, such as the women's *Njom Ekpa* association, with its huge carved headdress, and the cult agency *Obasinjom*, which had allegedly been invented near the Cameroon/Nigerian border around the beginning of the twentieth century. From the Cross River region, it even reached the Bakwiri at Mount Cameroon, where Edwin Ardener came across it in the 1950s (Ardener 1970; Geschiere 2001; Röschenthaler 2004a). On their journey, the associations spread from one place to the next, across ethnic or language units and administrative and national borders – which during the classical time of ethnography formed the normal units of study (Schlee 1985). Owning the same association endowed their owners with a supplementary identity and, in some cases such as *Ekpe*, committed them to economic and social relations with other owners of the same association.

That a biography could be documented implies that the identity of an association remained the same in the different villages despite the many changes it underwent on its way. Its structure was often modified according to the size of a village and the numbers of possible members for the various grades and posts. Performances were altered and specific tasks and rules added according to its chief's management. Some also used sign languages with which to verify the membership of traders who came from faraway villages. The existence of such a sign language comprehensible by members of a certain association across the region shows the mobility of members and the care taken in the transfer of this part of the knowledge which was not to be altered. The comprehension of the sign language of the *Ekpe* society enabled traders who were members to travel with their trade goods across a larger area and receive free food and lodging from the association. Beyond its core area of dissemination, associations often lost their regulating functions and were subsumed under other more important societies or transformed into dance associations.

At the outer margins of their dissemination frontier, they tended to change in such a way that individual pieces such as songs, dances, masks or names disseminated on their own, as happened with the *Ekpe* society among the Igbo (see Bentor 2002). At such a point, the identity of an association dissolved and copying and 'stealing' of performances prevailed, as easily happened with the dance associations (Röschenthaler 2004b). The owners of dance associations did not intend to build up a network like that of *Ekpe* and could not enforce their rights in performances. The youth's desire for independence reflected a general tendency also of communities with a minimal degree of political hierarchies, who opted for equal positions and attempted to evade any subordination to others (see Fisiy and Geschiere 1996). The villages united in the *Ekpe* network only because it facilitated trade.

This economy of culture implies that something like the spirit of the association that made it work is supposed to be transmitted by the purchase, and the individual owners had to activate this with their joint powers. They spent considerable sums of money on this, and expected to acquire something powerful that also brought them additional food and drinks. This spirit was not an external entity coming from the forest. It was rather the *esprit de corps* its members developed (Kramer 2005). The association would only work according to the members' ability to develop its 'spirit' or its agency with the acquired knowledge. This associational spirit was thought to be attached to the association like a brand to a product and also determined the price or value of the association at a certain time in a particular place. The *Ekpe* society became particularly powerful and managed to build up an influential network across a large area. Parts of this 'community' of *Ekpe* owners were able to unite and defend their interests. All *Ekpe* members could never meet, and nobody knew all of them. Only some of them met, for different purposes, and so it was an imagined (Anderson 1983) and translocal community.

Conclusion

How much the research I had undertaken depended on the specific circumstances and the people I worked with became visible only when I compared the details collected in the various villages. This possibility opened up new perspectives and had an impact on the meaning of the data in other places. Had I carried out research in only one area, I would probably have drawn different conclusions on historical knowledge, remembering and forgetting. Had I started research in one of those 'corridors of forgetting', perhaps it would never have occurred to me to reconstruct the dissemination history of associations at all.

Reflection about the ethnographic method, the modes of data generation and the implications of writing ethnography is essential to understand the undertaking of fieldwork and the production of anthropological theory.[6] The entire process is based on a number of premises and presumptions that are part of the ethnographic undertaking itself, shifting to and fro an involved perspective from within and a reflective perspective from outside. Participant observation entails these two perspectives and the impossibility of realising the two at the same time: learning to see and act from the local point of view in daily exchange and critically resuming reflection upon what has been gathered from this endeavour – participant objectification. This same procedure is resumed in the method of ethnographic presentation: the experience of the field needs to a certain extent to be retold and shared (to enable the reader to produce an image of the life in the place over there). The information collected needs to be interpreted and analysed. This involves personal interest, which often has to do with the extent to which othering is undertaken and whether difference or sameness to the people described is emphasised. Decisions on the subject of study (conscious or unconscious personal and political interests) and how this is delimited also greatly influence ethnography. Rather than being two different steps, these are as inseparable as the two sides of a coin. Their separation is an academic exercise a posteriori, inasmuch as ethnographical convention implies that the material presented must serve as a mere example to demonstrate a certain theoretical argument.

These are some of the implications that are part of the academic baggage carried along to the field, and they are influenced by personal decisions, by the individual context and by specific academic traditions. There are other factors that have far less to do with the individual context of the researcher: the local contexts in the field that have great impact on the way ethnographies develop. Ethnographies easily give the impression that it is clear what they entail.[7] They suggest that the careful selection of a topic and a method and their scrupulous realisation necessarily lead to the desired result. They do lead to a result and this is the only possible result that was obtainable. The extent, however, to which the factors can be known that lead to this and not to another ethnography remains debatable.

Notes

1. The project on the dissemination history of associations and cult agencies in the Cross River area of south-west Cameroon and south-east Nigeria was supported between 1987 and 1988 by the German Academic Exchange Service and the Graduiertenförderung des Landes Berlin. Between 1998 and 2001 the project was hosted at the Institut für Historische Ethnologie, University of Frankfurt am Main and supported by the Deutsche Forschungsgemeinschaft (German Research Council). I am particularly grateful to Mike Rowlands, to whom I owe the inspiration for the project, and to Carola Lentz, for her persistent encouragement for me to realise the project. For their critical comments on the draft of this chapter I am grateful to Richard Kuba and Matthias Gruber.

2. These understand ethnography mainly as a method of data generation (according to Bryman 2001). He also argues that ethnographic research has to face economic constraints. It has to be carried out in less time, due to the argument that it is too costly and time-wasting. Ethnography as a descriptive or literary endeavour, I would argue, had always represented only a part of the whole of a life world in time.

3. Of these surrounding ethnic groups, only a few are better known for classical ethnographies of the 1960s, such as the Yakö, from the works of Daryll Forde (1964), the Mbembe, from Rosemary Harris (1965), or the Banyang, from Malcom Ruel (1969).

4. They do not represent the view of former slaves or other members of the community. However, we also did additional interviews with individual knowledgeable persons. For this project, an official version was acceptable because for me the relation to the histories of other villages was important. The owners of the associations and cult agencies each had the right to talk about their own institutions. Apart from wonderful stories, men never talked about women's associations without the owners' official permission, and in the same way women did not talk about men's institutions. Not for nothing were the associations acquired at high expense and they explicitly served to generate wealth and bring their owners (as a group) additional food and drink.

5. *Ekpe*, for example, was changed greatly on its way from the coast at Isangele and Calabar to the hinterland. The number of grades and the names of masks and posts differed again and again, and I have the impression that the resulting confusion was not completely unintended by the society's owners. One of the reasons for this lay in the fact that candidates for initiation did not always know for sure whether they were admitted to a certain grade. They had first to pay a sort of application fee and were later told whether the amount given was high enough or not. Former slaves and their children were not allowed to enter the higher grades, which had different names in different villages.

6. The meaning of ethnography has been thoroughly transformed during the history of the term and has gone far from its literal or original meaning. Right from the beginning, the idea of ethnography entailed both the descriptive product and the method of data generation/collection. During its history, ethnography assumed different meanings in different anthropological traditions. When the term was first used in 1770 – at least in Germany (Fischer 1988) – it designated above all the discipline. This meaning is kept in the former socialist countries up until today. In Western Europe ethnography was replaced by the terms ethnology and anthropology, and ethnography was associated more with the written product. During the twentieth century, anglophone anthropology took the lead in greatly developing ethnography as a method.

7. 'What exactly is required of it today is by no means clear', argues van Maanen (1995: 2; see Wax 2001). In some of the present ethnographies, the people have disappeared from the titles. Similarly to the classical generalising ethnographies, they are present and non-present at the same time; ethnic groups have become imaginations of the profession and ethnographic writing has been largely demystified as a subjective self-realisation (Marcus and Fischer 1986). Only the 'ethnographer's magic' (Stocking 2001), the famous ethnographic gaze and the 'miracle of empathetic understanding' (van Maanen 1995) remain of the method. The term ethnography has become empty and calls for replacement, though it continues to serve as the essential part of our academic identity.

References

Anderson, B. 1983. *Imagined Communities*. London: Verso.

Appadurai, A. (ed.). 1986. *The Social Life of Things*. Cambridge: Cambridge University Press.

———. 1990. 'Disjuncture and Difference in the Global Cultural Economy', in M. Featherstone (ed.), *Global Culture. Nationalism, Globalization and Modernity*. London: Sage, pp. 295–309.

Ardener, E. 1970. 'Witchcraft, Economics, and the Continuity of Belief', in M. Douglas (ed.), *Witchcraft. Confessions and Accusations*. London: Tavistock, pp. 141–60. Also in: Ardener, E. 1996. *Kingdom on Mount Cameroon*, edited by Shirley Ardener. New York and Oxford: Berghahn Books, pp. 243–60.

Barth, F. 2002. 'An Anthropology of Knowledge', *Current Anthropology* 43 (1): 1–18.

Bentor, E. 2002. 'Spatial Continuities: Masks and Cultural Interactions between the Delta and Southeastern Nigeria', *African Arts* 35 (1): 26–41, 93.

Bourdieu, P. 2003. 'Participant Objectification', *Journal of the Royal Anthropological Institute* (ns) 9: 281–94.

Bryman, A. 2001. 'Introduction', in A. Bryman (ed.), *Ethnography*. London: Sage, pp. ix–xxxi.

Clifford, J. 1999. 'Kulturen auf der Reise', in K. Hörning and R. Winter (eds), *Widerspenstige Kulturen: Cultural Studies als Herausforderung*. Frankfurt: Suhrkamp, pp. 476–513.

D'Azvedo, W. 1961. 'Uses of the Past in Gola Discourse', *Journal of African History* 3 (1): 11–34.

de Brujn, M., R. van Dijk and D. Foeken. 2001. *Mobile Africa. Changing Patterns of Movement in Africa and Beyond*. Leiden: Brill.

Featherstone, M. (ed.). 1990. *Global Culture. Nationalism, Globalization and Modernity*. London: Sage.

Fischer, H. 1988. 'Ethnographie', in W. Hirschberg (ed.), *Neues Wörterbuch der Völkerkunde*. Berlin: Reimer, p. 129.

Fisiy, C. and P. Geschiere. 1996. 'Witchcraft, Violence and Identity. Different Trajectories in Postcolonial Cameroon', in R. Werbner and T. Ranger (eds), *Postcolonial Identities in Africa*. London and New York: Zed Books, pp. 193–221.

Forde, D. 1964. *Yakö Studies*. Oxford: Oxford University Press.

Frobenius, L. 1925 (1910). 'Betrachtungsweisen reisender Kulturforscher', in his *Erlebte Erdteile*, Vol. 3. Frankfurt: Frankfurter Societäts-Druckerei, pp. 335–347.

Geschiere, P. 2001. 'Witchcraft and New Forms of Wealth: Regional Variations in South and West Cameroon', in P. Clough and J.P. Mitchell (eds), *Powers of Good and Evil: Moralities, Commodities and Popular Belief*. Oxford: Berghahn, pp. 43–76.

Harris, R. 1965. *The Political Organisation of the Mbembe*. London: HMSO.

Kopytoff, I. 1986. 'The Cultural Biography of Things: Commoditization as Process', in A. Appadurai (ed.), *The Social Life of Things*. Cambridge: Cambridge University Press, pp. 64–91.

———. (ed.). 1987. *The African Frontier. The Reproduction of Traditional African Societies*. Bloomington: Indiana University Press.

Kramer, F. 2005. *Schriften*, edited by T. Rees. Frankfurt: Suhrkamp.

Luig, U. 1982. 'Einleitung', in U. Luig (ed.), *Leo Frobenius: Vom Schreibtisch zum Äquator*. Frankfurt: Societäts-Verlag, pp. 7–43.

Malinowski, B. 1922. *Argonauts of the Western Pacific*. London and New York: Routledge and Dulton.

Marcus, G. 1995. 'Ethnography in/of the World System: the Emergence of Multisited Ethnography', *Annual Review of Anthropology* 24: 95–117.

Marcus, G. and M. Fischer (eds). 1986. *Anthropology as Cultural Critique*. Chicago: University of Chicago Press.

Murphy, W. 1980. 'Secret Knowledge as Property and Power in Kpelle Society: Elders versus Youth', *Africa* 50 (2): 193–207.

Palmié, S. 2006. 'A View from Itia Ororó Kande', *Social Anthropology* 14 (1): 99–118.

Röschenthaler, U. 2002. 'A New York City of Ibibioland? Local Historiography and Power Conflict in Calabar', in A. Harneit-Sievers (ed.), *A Place in the World. New Local Historiographies from Africa and South-Asia*. Leiden: Brill, pp. 87–109.

———. 2004a. 'Transacting Obasinjom. The Dissemination of a Cult Agency in the Cross River Area', *Africa* 74 (2): 241–76.

———. 2004b. 'Neuheit, Bricolage oder Plagiat? Zur Entstehung neuer Tanzbünde im Cross River-Gebiet (im Südwesten Kameruns und Südosten Nigerias)', *Paideuma* 50: 193–223.

———. 2004c. 'Der Weg der Bünde. Transethnische Forschung im Cross River-Gebiet', *Afrika Spektrum* 39 (3): 427–48.

———. 2006. 'Translocal Cultures. The Slave Trade and Cultural Transfer in the Cross River Region', *Social Anthropology* 14 (1): 71–91.

Ruel, M. 1969. *Leopards and Leaders: Constitutional Politics among a Cross River People*. London: Tavistock.

Schlee, G. 1985. 'Mobile Forschung bei mehreren Ethnien', in H. Fischer (ed.), *Feldforschungen*. Berlin: Reimer, pp. 203–18.

Stocking, G. 2001. 'The Ethnographer's Magic', in A. Bryman (ed.), *Ethnography*, vol. 1. London: Sage, pp. 3–46.

Streck, B. 2001. 'Leo Frobenius: Erlebte Erdteile', in C. Feest and K.-H. Kohl (eds), *Hauptwerke der Ethnologie*. Stuttgart: Kröner, pp. 118–22.

van Maanen, J. 1995. 'An End to Innocence. The Ethnography of Ethnography', in J. van Maanen (ed.), *Representation in Ethnography*. London: Sage, pp. 1–35.

Wax, M. 2001. 'Tenting with Malinowski', in A. Bryman (ed.), *Ethnography*. London: Sage, vol. 1, pp. 82–100.

10

Tracking Global Flows and Still Moving

The Ethnography of Responses to AIDS

Cristiana Bastos

Contrary to some grim predictions regarding its future as a branch of knowledge associated with vanishing worlds and with colonialism, anthropology is alive, well and perhaps more politically engaged and theoretically vibrant than ever. Furthermore, ethnography and fieldwork remain its core and method. They had to adjust to the novelties, to new settings, new spatial definitions, new research agendas, new forms of interaction with the subjects, new sources of data. But, rather than succumbing to or being submerged by the methods of other disciplines, fieldwork and ethnography evolved and often became tools for other social sciences as well.

How did anthropologists respond so efficiently to change? Not by planning survival strategies ahead but, as in the old days of the discipline, by daring to leave for the field with an open-ended plan, by getting enough involvement with their research subjects to the point of restructuring their original questions, by addressing issues that might not match the conventional tools of neighbouring disciplines – by taking some risks and using creative skills, just like in the old days. As in the past, we were basically trying to conduct fieldwork, hoping that the chaotic mass of information around us might be turned into data, subjected to analysis, maybe systematised into a monograph, eventually contributing to theory and, maybe, re-intervening in society with appropriately informed tools.

At least, that was how I felt during fieldwork in Rio de Janeiro, Brazil, trying to track the use and production of knowledge about AIDS in the early 1990s. That was a time when there were hardly any appropriate medicines for AIDS, when most of those affected died, when health professionals felt powerless and when scientists were pressured from above and below to move fast and produce. For once, knowledge mattered more than money, bringing together, in deprivation, rich and poor, First and Third World. Knowledge was scarce and precious. New knowledge was waited for and scrutinised. New knowledge was also what I was after. Looking for it in a place like Rio could bring up some new perspectives and insights.

Ethnography and fieldwork had to be rearranged accordingly. The field site was not confined to any particular setting in Rio, or, should I say, to Rio. Research was about a number of groups and social actors that could be found in the city, that sometimes left the city, and yet others that could eventually be found in the city, plus some that had an impact on life in the city while never actually being there. They were based in Brasília, or in North American or European cities and places. They often went from one to the other and belonged to several at once: transnationalism, we would say later to conceptualise such a state of being, but at that time the term was uncommon, at least in this particular subject.

To make things more intricate, my field observation had started earlier in New York, a city where I had moved a few years before in order to attend graduate school. New York had provided me with the research problem, the interest, the theoretical background; it was not just the academic reference, like an imaginary audience for the discussion of field results; it was also the empirical setting with which the daily reflection interacted. It had been in New York that I had drafted the question that had evolved into the one that brought me to the 'field' in Rio. The complex universe of behaviours, interactions, symbols, feelings and meanings from where I had captured the early version of the problem kept evolving in new directions, and I could not stop following them as well. In a way, I was engaging in multi-sited fieldwork before the term became popular. To meet the prevailing methodological standards, I had to subordinate one site to the other, so that one of them (Rio) was 'the field' and the other (New York) was 'background information'.

I had a central interest in the relation between science and society, between knowledge and politics, and in medical anthropology in general. AIDS brought all of them together. Grass-roots movements emerged in response to the epidemic, governments were lobbied for money, laboratories and research centres were lobbied for results, scientists were lobbied to act faster and more efficiently. International organisations adopted the cause and lobbied all over the world for action and responses. Either spontaneously or as a result of these actions, local responses emerged throughout the globe. New York seemed to be the place where it all started.

The presence of the epidemic in the late 1980s in New York was inescapable, visible in public demonstrations and lived in private distress. It invaded medical anthropology classes as well, not without raising among some of us the feeling that the cognitive tools we had to address the phenomenon were insufficient. We could go out counting bodies and accounting for distress, measuring anxiety, scaling behavioural acts, evaluating prevention, coping, organising, charting representations, linking ideas and behaviours. All of that anthropologists were doing, most often following directions and reproducing styles of enquiry defined elsewhere, somewhere in between epidemiology, public health, biomedicine and a pragmatic understanding of what social sciences are for. Some anthropologists went further and addressed key problems of society via the study of AIDS. They mapped the lines of gender, class, race and social exclusion through the extension of the epidemic. Anthropologists were also to address international aspects of AIDS and focus on the interactions between society and science, but that would come later.[1]

While admiring the research that was going on about AIDS in the late 1980s, I still aimed at something else. My interest in the interaction of science and society was extended to a concern about the world dimensions of the politics of knowledge. AIDS brought the two lines together. Since the early years, it was assumed that there was also an epidemic outside the US, but it might appear to be different: framed differently, social constructionists would say. How would the world asymmetries influence the shape of the pandemic, and vice versa? Would a global epidemic diminish the gaps in the world, or increase them? What would the diverse local responses to AIDS be throughout a socially and economically divided world, one whose contrasts were doubled in the health patterns of rich and poor? Would there be any input from the peripheries into the production of meaningful knowledge in the context of this epidemic? Would social variables be accounted for in the understanding the distribution of the pandemic?

In my first contact with data from Africa, for instance, the distribution of HIV reporting by nations resounded with the geopolitics of colonialism, even though colonial rule had been gone for decades. But it was nearly impossible to articulate that as a problem at a time when 'African AIDS' was presented under the blanket notion of a pattern 2 (heterosexual transmission), in contrast to the pattern 1 identified in the US and Europe (related to gays and drugs).[2] The focus was on individual behaviour, not on the social variables that might better account for the spread of the epidemic in Africa. Social scientists were called in to investigate these behaviours, to enlighten their fellow medical scientists about the obscure rituals of scarification and genital mutilation that were blamed for the extension of AIDS in Africa, plus African hypersexuality and resistance to change. Social scientists were caught in the search for individual behavioural variables: if not gay sex and drug injecting, as in the US, then bloody rituals, promiscuous sex, eating monkeys or even sex between humans and lower primates. Racism and prejudice pervaded these hypotheses. Not surprisingly, much of the African response, including from scholars and political leaders, took the form of AIDS denial.[3] There was hardly any space to formulate a truly social science strategy, such as looking for the social variables associated with the distribution of AIDS in Africa – war, colonialism, social violence, gender, power, displacements, accumulated misery.

As years passed, research on African data would show how social variables shaped the actual distribution of reported cases. In the background, the social and economic distresses of the colonial rule and its aftermath politics were key variables. They correspond to social phenomena like wars, urbanisation, displacement, migration or ideologies of denial regarding the epidemic. But only later would this become clear.[4]

Getting in touch with African AIDS data was probably what led me to try to account for world variables in the research problem. How could there be such diverging perceptions of its epidemiology? Could local societies give some input in the global production of knowledge? And how should one anchor the question – both theory- and field-wise?

My theoretical interests were shaped by interaction with recent literature in fields like the new sociology of knowledge and the social studies of science. A few authors had started addressing the production of scientific knowledge as a legitimate subject for sociological and anthropological study.[5] Rather than the vague Foucauldian associations of power and knowledge or Bourdieu's theoretical frames, the new, empirically based studies might provide a reference for what I wanted to do. And yet none of them addressed the social variable I was most concerned with – the global scale and world asymmetries. A couple of decades earlier these issues had raised some interest among development and dependency theorists,[6] who argued against common-sense ideas of modernisation and backwardness. But the world seemed to have changed. The talk of the day in the late 1980s was globalisation, not dependency. It remained to be seen how social scientists would address this. From within anthropology and sociology, there were some signs of interest about mapping world connections and developing a global framework, suggesting the possibility of a macro-anthropology.[7] And yet including these concerns in the agenda of the social studies of science was still a long way ahead.

In my understanding, AIDS was an issue particularly prone to address both the questions regarding globalisation/dependency and the interactions of science/society. That meant introducing variables regarding the big fracture of the world into the study of science and society or, more specifically, of the politics of scientific knowledge production. But it was still a challenge to design the methodology for such a broad issue, to define what to hold on to and even where to go.

I started from evidence regarding the interaction of social movements and the making of science. AIDS-related grass-roots movements in the United States had had an impact at least on the release of new drugs, speeding up some bureaucratic delays and eventually influencing the development of clinical research protocols. Some of the clinical procedures developed in that context had helped to improve the conditions for people with AIDS and saved lives. Community action had also induced important changes in prevention and in ways of coping with the disease.[8]

There was something new and factual in the way knowledge was produced and used, at least in the clinical area. It was not clear whether the social movements would also influence the framing and pace of biomedical research, besides specific clinical approaches. Would they lobby successfully towards the creation of antiviral drugs? Towards less toxic treatments? Vaccine development? More prevention devices? A better understanding of the transmission routes? Of the disease pathogenesis?

In the coming years, there would be pressure on the part of AIDS activists into all these research directions, some of them achieving more success than others. Activists created expert groups for monitoring research and ended up in advisory committees of public and private pharmaceutical labs.[9] In sum, some among the most affected within society, either by being ill themselves or close enough to the epidemic, talked back to the core of scientific research and, at least in some instances, were heard and, in the end, had a meaningful impact.

This was my point of departure. Where to go next should be a place suitable for understanding what was happening in a wider, world setting regarding the issues of science and society, narrowing my focus to ways of creating, distributing, using, adapting and negotiating knowledge about AIDS. That is how Rio de Janeiro, Brazil, came into the picture.

Rio de Janeiro in the early 1990s was the closest to the 'big fracture' that in my understanding depicts the contemporary world. Rio is a totally fractured city, where First and Third world are in intimate interdependency. Slums grow alongside the luxury and middle-class areas, and the economic interdependency between them is not a theoretical model conceptualised by social scientists: it is outstandingly visible and part of the *carioca* self-image.

The spatial proximity of the rich and the poor in Rio may shock northern visitors, unprepared to face such a concentrated version of the world, but for *cariocas* from either side of the social fence it is a fact of life. It was ironically depicted as a distinguishing mark of Rio, as some would note while I was in the field: 'In São Paulo you will not find this, poverty is hidden in the far suburbs, here in Rio it is everywhere, the poor are next to the rich, downtown, at the business centre, in Zona Norte, in the beach neighbourhoods of Zona Sul as well.'

And, in spite of the intimacy depicted, the '*asfalto*', inhabited by the middle classes, and the '*morro*', inhabited by the poorer ones, are separated by spatial and symbolic boundaries. There are easily identifiable micro-neighbourhoods, there are devices of class, speech, language skills, jobs, cultural references. Also, the slum hills are often subject to unofficial rules and governance by drug lords, who try to control and, when possible, expand their areas of influence. To make sure that the local population of each *morro* abides by their power, drug lords use a variety of means, from inducing terror to handing out gifts, including expensive sports grounds or support for widows and orphans.

Life in the *morro* is most of the time like that of any working-class or poor neighbourhood, with low-quality housing and chaotic urbanism on the high slopes, which are, although often beautiful and with spectacular views, unsuitable for appropriate construction. However, the wars related to the drug traffic for the control of territories and flows of commerce produce moments of terror and danger for everyone in the *morro*. While the drug war might better be depicted as an ongoing process that produces an undermining, permanent fear, those highly visible periods of 'war' might better be depicted as battles, which are either related to the takeover of one *favela* by another drug lord, by a war response, by conflicts between rival factions, or by confrontations with the police. In these moments, gunshots can be heard around the neighbourhood and they affect the middle-class buildings of the nearby *asfalto* as well. Occasional deaths from stray bullets occur. These events raise the fears of the middle classes, who also raise their defence devices – higher gates, bulletproof walls, security windows, therapy, eventually moving their residence to a safer building. As for the distressed inhabitants of the *morro*, when possible, they head out to seek temporary or permanent housing with kin or friends in other neighbourhoods.

Social movements and community initiatives tried to reduce the effects of the violence and stereotypes of marginality associated with *favelas* while working towards improving community empowerment and the material life of the *favela* inhabitants in general. In the 1970s, many *favelas* were provided with the basics of urban infrastructure, like running water and electricity. In the 1980s-1990s, programmes of education, health improvement and social integration targeted those communities and had positive effects. Progressive churches, NGOs and sometimes the state or city departments helped towards the integration of the *favela* population into full citizenship.

The proximity of the social worlds represented by the *favelas* and *asfalto* in Rio de Janeiro was not just about fears, bullets, inconveniences and displacement. It affected life in many other ways. It affected the production of knowledge, including the production of science. It affected the social sciences, naturally, but it affected the biomedical sciences as well. It affected them in the traditional way of inconveniences, like the bullets in the classroom walls of the School of Public Health, neighbour to a big *favela* that was periodically involved in wars, or like the interrupted lab experience caused by a power failure after an innocent swim in the lab reservoir by the neighbourhood children.

The intimacy between these two worlds affected the range of research interests as well: misery and deprivation were right there, and their role in the development of diseases was not a theoretical hypothesis for epidemiologists. Diseases of poverty filled hospital beds, not as a curiosity of clinical medicine textbooks, but as pathological entities that were eating up patients' bodies and their lives. The 'exotic', 'tropical' diseases, far removed from bioscience research labs in the developed world, were a priority on the research agenda of Brazilian biomedical scientists. Class, social exclusion, segregation, underdevelopment, in sum, the tensions and fractures of the world were not theoretical hypotheses. They were right there.

The vital Brazilian scientific community, familiar with both sides of the world divide, had been a main inspirer for my attempts to follow the complexities of the way knowledge flows in our day. Would I find there, instead of the traditional one-way transfer of knowledge from centres to peripheries, some sort of answer back from 'peripheries' to the 'centres', some sort of multilateral participation in the process of knowledge making? Analogous to what happened between science labs and activists in New York, would I find here any negotiation and some proactivity towards influencing mainstream research on AIDS – for instance, in the development of locally adapted therapies, tests, strategies for prevention and clinical intervention and, eventually, conceptual developments meaningful for basic biomedical research?

And so I arrived in the city of Rio envisaging fieldwork, trying to understand the ways in which the agents and subjects of biomedicine perceived, used, enacted, performed and produced medical knowledge. I was aiming at capturing the social and cultural factors involved in the shaping of that knowledge. At an earlier moment, I had drafted a rough scenario where the social actors relevant for the final analysis, like 'Brazilian research' as a whole or 'responses to AIDS in Brazil' as a block, might have an empirical counterpart.

It did not take much time to realise that things were different. There were many interrelated groups and individuals identifiable by their involvement in the responses to AIDS. There were governmental bureaus, federal-, state- and city-based. There were NGOs that had either been born as a response to AIDS or adopted the fight against AIDS as a central line of intervention. There were clinical settings that had developed special AIDS services. There were lines of research within laboratories and research centres. There were a lot of people working with AIDS, living with AIDS, treating AIDS and trying to implement medical and prevention campaigns. But they seemed to go in different directions and hardly composed a communicating whole. Factions and dissension marked their interactions, dissension being probably at its highest moment when I started fieldwork in the early 1990s.

I had to juggle, then, with several interacting groups and social actors, from clinicians and patients to laboratory scientists and epidemiologists, from activists and community organisers to journalists and academics; they were not always on good terms with one another. Like ethnographers dealing with different and sometimes opposing factions, I had to manage all sorts of multiplicity – in space, in socialising, eventually in loyalties, in political choices and in views of the world. Sometimes that meant a quasi-cognitive divide among versions incompatible among themselves, all of them claiming true, none of them being false. Traditionally conservative and progressive social actors might be mixed and matched; AIDS, action, epidemics, policies, prevention, treatment meant different things to different social actors, even though they appeared to deal with the same thing. Cognitive maps and the nuances of signification had to be readjusted from group to group. Naturally, mistakes and faux pas occurred, just as in any other field site.

Adding to the complexity and multiplicity of groups, there was also the matter of expansion; in order to understand the scope of action and attached meanings, I had to follow them and their external routes, sometimes literally, sometimes via their narratives. That meant travelling to some meetings abroad, either in other Brazilian cities or further away, like the big international AIDS conferences in Europe or the US.[10] In all of this, besides the traditional methods of hearing, talking back, interacting, collecting narratives, observing in a participant mode, taking notes, and reflecting, there was a lot of reading involved: documents, leaflets, newspapers, scientific articles, conference proceedings, drafts to present at future conferences. There was video-watching and content analysis of media messages, from ads on posters and TV spots to more elaborate educational booklets and videos. And there was also writing and participating in the meetings, giving back interpretation while in the process. Participant observation meant being co-opted, in some instances, as an informal and sometimes formal consultant on projects, a participating social scientist in research meetings and events, or being taken as a colleague in the process.

The quickest and easiest sphere to get familiar with was the NGO world, filled with fellow social scientists, the 'organic intellectuals' in the Gramscian sense. They had academic training, some of them held or were about to obtain their PhDs and MAs, they had enough contact with the university world, but they had chosen a life of direct action and intervention in society. Universities, like the opposition to dictatorship in the 1960s and the religious-inspired social movements that had emerged in the previous decade and remained a support for social causes, had been a supplier of people, creative energy and know-how to NGOs, which would later become the synonym for civil society.[11]

The presence of social scientists from abroad like myself within the daily life of some NGOs did not cause much disruption or even curiosity – it was something most people were familiar with, either because they were themselves in the social sciences or because they were familiar with 'gringo' visitors from international agencies.[12] For the same reasons, ethnographers did not need to explain what they were doing – they were either very welcome or resented. I had the good fortune to experience a long period of grace and felt welcome most of the time, particularly with the NGOs that dealt with the provision of knowledge about AIDS in Brazil. A strong involvement with some of them, however, also meant exclusion from some others, who felt difference as dissension.[13]

There were NGOs of all sizes and styles. There were big and well-endowed NGOs, there were umbrella NGOs, there were small neighbourhood NGOs, religious-based groups, special-interest groups.[14] AIDS NGOs reflected this variety. ABIA was a large, cosmopolitan, well-connected group that addressed intervention on the circulation and provision of knowledge about AIDS in Brazil as a task. GAPAs were action groups that gathered volunteers to work on many aspects of the epidemic, including direct support for people in need. After the birth of the first GAPA, in São Paulo (1985), a few others were spontaneously formed in other cities – not a franchising process, but an informal network style and a parallel response to similar needs in different places.

The importance, visibility and intervention capacity of NGOs were a relatively new phenomenon, something in which Latin America was a front of innovation. And at the time there was mot much social theory on NGOs. One of the few early works on the topic (Landim 1988) analysed their emergence in Latin America as an effect of the styles of aid on the part of Northern donors. NGOs had become semi-professional local agencies shaped to suit international demands, where there had once been spontaneous social movements or community-based groups.

Landim's work helped me to see through the local scene: although AIDS NGOs were the local social actors, they were also the local expression of something wider, transnational, the other end of which was somewhere else, not present, not talked about, somehow ignored. It could be a Norwegian progressive church, a Canadian charity, a London-based international NGO dedicated to distributing funds for AIDS worldwide, the Global AIDS Programme of the WHO based in Geneva, a USAID agency in Washington. Not all the NGOs in Rio were funded, however, and the issue was not exempted from resentment, sometimes generating negative synergies. Small NGOs might be self-funded, live on members' volunteer services or combine both these strategies.

There were a few meetings and attempts to structure the generality of Brazilian AIDS NGOs; while I was in the field, there was also some analysis, on the part of AIDS activists, of the reasons for the failure of these attempts. They pointed out the heterogeneity, the differences in goals, the styles of action and such circumstances as the obstacle to the achievement of unitarian, consistent action.[15] In my analysis, the international flows of funding and the rise and fall of international enthusiasm for the role of NGOs in the world action against AIDS, which peaked in 1989 and 1990, with the support of Jonathan Mann's leadership in WHO's Global Programme on AIDS, were as important as the internal factors might have been.

The one thing that all NGOs shared was the fact of not being a part of the government. That, as they often made explicit, did not equate to be anti-government, even though sometimes it looked as if it were the case. Many times during the period of my fieldwork and before that (roughly 1985–91), in spite of sharing the fight against AIDS in Brazil, NGOs and the government emerged as opponents rather than partners. Underlying this dissension was a long history of opposition between social activists and authoritarian governments. On the surface, things took the form of opposition between medical and social perspectives – the government, recruiting medical experts, used a conventional public health approach, giving a secondary role to social aspects, and while some smaller NGOs had good contact with the government (e.g. the *Grupo Gay da Bahia*), some of the most vocal NGOs, backed by international organisations and by their own political and social science knowledge, insisted on the centrality of the social dimensions of AIDS and called for socially informed policies. They created their expert knowledge, challenged government statistics and their use of naturalised epidemiological concepts, including that of 'risk groups', which they considered culturally inadequate, prejudiced and misleading.[16] They created media messages, while rejecting those sponsored by the government as inadequate or offensive.[17]

For an observer like me, who had also witnessed how US activists wrote to their representatives in the legitimate expectation of their support, the dissension between NGOs and government found in Brazil appeared extreme. The tensions seemed stronger than the motives – something that could only be understood in the context of Brazilian political history, marked by long periods of authoritarian regimes.

The transition towards more democratic forms of government in Brazil in the 1990s would eventually blur the boundaries between them and diminish the tensions. Indeed, the government would even recruit NGO specialists, adopt their views, publish their catalogues, fund them. This was a curious turn of events in what at times was experienced as a failure of the NGO movement to create an articulated, consistent and national agenda.

Again, it was a transnational move that influenced the change: a big grant from the World Bank, matched by the Brazilian government, helped to develop an intense and ultimately successful AIDS programme which, among other things, revitalised the world of NGOs while restructuring them. In that context, the government passed funds to NGOs through cooperation projects. Some NGOs felt tied down and limited in their new role, in the move that Reilly (1995) describes as the 'journey from protest to proposal', which was increasingly bureaucratic, and slowly replacing the partisan mode.

NGOs and the government were the visible social actors regarding policymaking, and they were central in the role of diffusing knowledge about the epidemic. In some instances, both were involved in producing and negotiating knowledge about AIDS, which was reused at a global level. The government had suggested some adaptation to the international criteria used for the definition of what counted as an AIDS case. The NGOs had tried to influence the whole understanding of the epidemic towards a more relevant role for its social and human dimensions. Some NGOs challenged some of the prevailing assumptions that stigmatised the disease. They worked towards de-stigmatisation,[18] replacing the assumption that a person infected with HIV was one of the walking dead, carrying a timebomb – something that, by provoking fears, led to denial and clandestinity and therefore multiplied the spread of the infection in society. They also challenged the notion of risk groups – another step to denial – and implemented more inclusive messages. A whole line of research on sexuality emerged from this standpoint. In several instances, knowledge produced in this context flowed back to the mainstream.[19]

But this was just a fragment of the whole picture. To study the use, production and negotiation of biomedical knowledge – something that was mostly ignored by NGOs and by the government – I had to focus on other social actors, something I also tried to do from the very beginning. Searching for clinical settings and research labs was not as easy as getting into the world of NGOs, but it ended up being feasible. I was able to observe, interact and interview in places as different as a special AIDS unit of the most highly considered university hospital in the city, Fundão, part of the Federal University of Rio de Janeiro; the outpatients clinic and inpatients services in the more deprived university hospital António Pedro (Niterói),[20] and briefly in the old Hospital Gaffrée e Guinle (Tijuca, Rio); the outpatients health centre in Rua do Resende, a hustling spot for prostitutes and transvestites; and the complex of FIOCRUZ,[21] a large campus on Avenida Brasil that housed the Oswaldo Cruz Institute for biomedical research, other research facilities, the National School of Public Health and the landmark Hospital Evandro Chagas, created in the 1910s as a research hospital to study tropical infections while treating patients with them. I also included brief visits to some of the medical care and research centres of São Paulo, Bahia and Belo Horizonte. No matter where and even though I made it very explicit that I was focusing on the health personnel's use of knowledge about AIDS, physicians and nurses always expected me to focus on the patients – whom, while in hospital and other vulnerable situations, I would not subject to any extra voyeurism. Also expected from me was ethnographic interest in alternative treatments or magical-religious-superstitious interpretations and responses to the new disease. That an anthropologist focused on the making of mainstream knowledge and science, rather than on the usual exotica, was harder to take.

Among these medical sites, the AIDS unit of Fundão was my first reference. It had an exceptional endowment, due to a fortunate coincidence of political factors at a given time, as a director portrayed it. Such an endowment avoided the chronic deprivation experienced in other units. It had better means, and a multidisciplinary team that fought for a careful, multi-perspective understanding of something entirely new for heath providers and patients. This included regular meetings with detailed discussions on each case. New knowledge was at stake. New knowledge was being used and produced every-day. This was, at least in theory, an exceptional observing point.

While the unit had been created in order to provide high-quality medical care, research became part of the daily procedure; the possibility of channelling new knowledge to the mainstream was not out of question. As often happens in Rio, this unit was, in the words of a few of my interviewees from that service, 'an island of First-worldness surrounded by an ocean of Third-worldness'. The removal of chronic, Third-world-like deprivation had helped to build some patient self-empowerment, noted the health personnel. Those outside the unit, sharing the alleys with other infectious-disease patients and not subject to the particularities of the AIDS unit, were not so empowered to deal with their condition as those within.

Everyone there knew that they were in a small artificial universe and that right outside the door things were not as easy. Pressure was felt all the time, when going outside, when closing the door, when rejecting patients that the small number of beds could not accommodate, when, as some summed up, facing the real world out there. And yet, while in that little universe, things were special, not only for the patients but for the health personnel as well. Their routine had a different pace and logic from the routine in the infectious-disease wards, where knowledge was stable in textbooks and medical classes and where elderly doctors could be consulted for difficult questions. Knowledge about AIDS was in the making at every moment and at a fast pace. Unexpected things mattered. There were social dimensions. There were too many unknown elements. There was pressure from above for the creation of trans-disciplinary teams, themselves a novelty.

The members of the newly created multidisciplinary team were not used to the proximity and constant interaction between different health professions, or to the horizontal interactions that challenged the established hierarchies.[22] They had regular meetings to process the impact of the new epidemic, discussing not only the clinical aspects but also the social and psychological aspects of each case. In those early times, they even reflected collectively on their own feelings regarding each case and on the overall impact of AIDS in several aspects of their lives.[23]

Knowledge was in the making, not in books, and what came in articles and xeroxes did not cover the variety of issues they faced on a daily basis. The project resounded with the trans-disciplinary utopia that at some point marked a moment of responses to AIDS in some places of the world – a utopia that was backed by the style of intervention of WHO's Global Programme on AIDS under Jonathan Mann's leadership in the late 1980s.

But by the time I observed the unit and interviewed the team workers, in 1991, its fourth year, the epidemic had settled into its routines and had created patterns of personal and collective response. Professional territories and hierarchies regained shape and what had been an arena for fully interactive discussion of new knowledge gave place to independent fields, fractured by profession, where physicians, nurses, psychotherapists or social workers, who constantly used and created original knowledge, something that contrasted with their previous professional experience at the hospital.

To sum up, new things were happening all the time, new knowledge was being created and used on the spot. But how would it articulate back to the mainstream production of knowledge? That was my question, and here was my ethnographic setting. Seen from afar, these could be the local actors in a plot of interaction where the peripheries talked back to the centres. In theory, they could and should be talking to the main research sites, they could help scientists and physicians in Europe and the US to see through some of the intricacies of multiple infections in immune-deprived bodies; they could and should be sharing what was their taken-for-granted (but not everyone's) knowledge about the intimate connection between social vulnerability and health vulnerability; they could and should be sharing with the entire world some of their expertise on handling difficult cases with minimal resources; in some instances, like some of the basic research scientists I interviewed, they could be sharing a more complex understanding of the immune functions, going beyond the mechanistic views of aggression and therapeutic responses. But this epistemologically revolutionary shift was not to happen this time around. What was to happen was perhaps more modest than a scientific revolution, but interesting enough in terms of how peripheries talk back to the centres.

When I ended the formal ethnographic observation, such a South-North counterflow of knowledge was bound to happen, but could not be detected or proved, even if expected. In clinical settings, teamwork had retreated to specialised work. The routine had absorbed some cross-professional interaction, but things got back to what they had always been in hospitals – doctors were doctors, nurses were nurses, social workers were social workers, each group moving through their speciality, their way of interacting with and acting upon patients and problems, and through their own international networks. They participated in international meetings, they made modest contributions to the mainstream growth of knowledge and they were, by and large, a long way from publishing in the major medical journals. Keeping to the long-established order of things, knowledge flowed from centres to peripheries, from North to South.

As for the world of NGOs, they too had absorbed a routine of either supplying services to people with AIDS or producing specialised knowledge on issues of prevention. They moved towards a combined action with the government, partly as an effect of the World Bank mega-loan (as the government created a platform for the NGO's work and was responsible for the distribution of funds), partly as an effect of democratisation within the government and partly as an effect of mutual growth and learning form one another, as the government had absorbed part of the critical mass of NGO activists and clinical and public health experts.

In 1996, when I had not only returned from the field but also written the dissertation that had been at the root of everything, what I had envisaged as a hypothesis, but could not find empirically, had finally taken shape: there was a sphere of responses to AIDS that brought together activists, clinicians and government officers consistently, as 'Brazilian responses', a local AIDS culture.

Was this an illusion, an effect from the perspective of distance, feeding into the thesis that ethnography is only achievable at a later stage, not during observation? It might have been, but there is something else besides methodological indulgence. The year 1996 was also a turning point in the history of AIDS. It was the year when the effective cocktail of anti-HIV treatments (combining anti-protease- and anti-transcriptase-specific drugs) was released and announced to the world as the cure for AIDS. These medical developments had partly resulted from the interaction between the multiple actors involved in the responses to AIDS: the research laboratories and their scientists, the activist expert organisations, the funding agencies, the pharmaceutical labs, the public health agencies, the universities, the bureaucracies, the public.

The responses to AIDS had thereby obtained a structure among the different possibilities sketched – not yet vaccines, not universal prevention, not a utopian scientific revolution, but sophisticated, efficient antiviral drugs. Also, expensive drugs. Predictably, this would bring the world of AIDS back to the bipolar health patterns – treatments for those who could afford them, multiplied vulnerability for those who could not.

This is when Brazil – now as a block, 'Brazil' – comes into the picture and to leadership. During the years when responses to AIDS were mounting as I observed them, different groups and different social actors were going in different directions and were not always on good terms; heterogeneity and dissent made it impossible to speak of a 'Brazilian response'. By the mid-1990s, however, some consistency had been achieved; clinicians, activists and government worked together. So, when the first legal actions were promoted by São Paulo AIDS activists towards guaranteeing free treatment for AIDS patients in the public systems, including the new, expensive antivirals, they were favourably backed by the courts, by public opinion, by the health services, and by the government. After years of building up a culture of AIDS across different specialities, Brazilian society had achieved unique conditions to supply AIDS patients with the best possible treatment, if one was to be found. Once this happened, there was no way back – and, if the price was the problem, it also became the locus for Brazilian protagonism on the international scene. Now, other unexpected things happened: empowered peripheries were talking back to the centres, arguing that patent laws could not be an obstacle to the provision of health care for AIDS patients. Brazilian leaders challenged the International Trade Organisation regarding patents and royalties on AIDS treatments, threatening to produce them on the side. The technology was available, through a South-South axis, which involved Brazil, India and Southern Africa.

None of this was predictable while I was in the field, and my efforts to update my observations do not bring any certainty regarding the future. The moment brings some optimism, at least for some: a South–South engagement in the production of treatments at affordable prices seems a promising alternative to the re-emergence of economically generated world partitions, where North means safe and South means vulnerable. The AIDS epidemic may have brought a change to the world patterns of health, of responses, of empowerment; and yet we do not, and cannot, know what is going to come next.

What has ethnography taught us regarding this case, and how has this case helped in thinking about ethnography? Thinking about the first half of the question, I realise that, as in the old days, ethnography helps by going beyond the mystifications, simplifications and mechanistic views that either social disciplines or politicians suggest as accounting for social phenomena; now that Brazil has became an international star in the world of responses to AIDS – for it has indeed curbed the epidemic predictions as a result of coordinated action, part of it being the provision of AIDS treatments in the public system – other nations look there for magic formulas ready to import.[24] Those formulas are not a given nor can they be exported or imported – the difficult task of ethnography and ethnographically informed history is to show the idiosyncrasies of each case. That may help to reduce damage; in no circumstances should it work as an obstacle to action – as the study of particulars can always help in the understanding of new and different situations.[25]

Focusing now on the second half of the question – what do ethnography and anthropology learn from this – I return to the beginning: the world may have changed, in connectivity, in pace of interactions, in the complexity of arrangements that are present in every aspect of local action, but that does not bring an end to ethnography. Instead, it brings new challenges and restores it to its very principles, asking for imagination, for multiple cognitive resources, for ability to follow the field subjects in challenging ways, for time in the field, for the freedom to indulge in detail and for the driving passion to produce an interpretive synthesis.

Acknowledgements

The time and actions recalled in this chapter report to the period when I was a graduate student at the CUNY Graduate Center doctoral program in Anthropology, in New York, and affiliated with the PPGAS of the Museu Nacional, UFRJ, and the Instituto de Medicina Social, UERJ, both in Rio de Janeiro. I thank the Wenner Gren Foundation for Anthropological Research for the grant that supported fieldwork. I am indebted to an extraordinary number of people for support, insights and pieces of information; just to mention some, my thanks to Shirley Lindenbaum, Vincent Crapanzano, Sergio Luis Carrara, Antonio Souza Lima, Richard Parker, Veriano Terto, Silvia Ramos and many others. I also thank Helena Wulff for the invitation to the EASA session where this reflections were represented, and to Jon Mitchell for editorial support.

Notes

1. For an exemplary study of the interaction between AIDS activists and the making of science, see Epstein (1996) and, quite recently, Lachenal (2004). For global aspects of AIDS issues, see Farmer (2001) and Hahn et al. (2004).
2. I explored this issue in more detail in the monograph *Global Responses to AIDS* (Bastos 1999) and the article 'Behavior as a Social Variable' (Bastos 2001).
3. E.g. Chirimuuta and Chirimuuta (1989) and the consistent denial of the existence of a major epidemic on the part of Southern African political leaders.
4. Only late in the epidemic was there any literature attempting to identify the social variables behind the spread of AIDS in Africa (e.g. Packard and Epstein 1991; Schoepf 1991), and even today the implications of those hypotheses are explored timidly and often left behind when something more spectacular and more suited to the chain of positivist thinking comes up. See, for instance, how difficult it has been to evaluate the impact of war and colonialism in the spread of AIDS – although some iatrogenic hypotheses focusing on vaccination campaigns have been raised – and how easy it has been to jump at hypotheses that blame the epidemic patterns on monkey-eating and promiscuous sex, as has recently happened regarding HIV subtypes and bushmeat-eating in Cameroon (see Lachenal 2004).
5. Early works on the new sociology of science or social study of scientific knowledge included Latour and Wolgar (1979), Mulkay (1979), Knorr-Cetina (1981); in the 1990s, the interest was expanded into anthropology (e.g. Heath and Rabinow, 1993).
6. E.g. Shils (1968), Sagasti (1971), Cooper (1973), Morazé (1979), Polanco (1985), Gaillard (1991), Mogadham (1991), Goonatilake (1993).
7. E.g. Hannerz (1992).

8. Except for Epstein (1991) and a journalistic report (Nussbaum 1990), not many works portrayed the process at the time. For a later, major and comprehensive monograph, see Epstein (1996).

9. That process happened rapidly in a few short years; I witnessed the shift in both social actors from year to year at international conferences (for more detail, see Bastos 1999: chapter 2).

10. After the 1990 conference in San Francisco was boycotted by many activists due to the US customs rules prohibiting admittance of travellers that are HIV-positive, most conferences were held outside the US, including the one in 1992, which was transferred from Cambridge, Massachusetts, to Amsterdam. Occasionally supporting my trips as a science journalist for a Lisbon weekly, I participated in some of these conferences (Florence, 1991, Amsterdam, 1992, Berlin, 1993). In 1994, as a result of a team project with Hospital Evandro Chagas (Rio), I had a paper approved for the Yokohama (Japan) conference, which I ended up not attending as part of a process of closing what seemed an interminable field experience. But withdrawing from international conferences and from living in Rio was not enough to put a closure to the field, which remained around me for much longer, as the AIDS epidemic kept being top news everywhere. Later, years after I really put an end to the research and moved on to other subjects, Brazilian international protagonism in the fight again made it all come back.

11. For an accurate report on the genesis of NGOs as a movement, see Landim (1988). During the field period, I myself witnessed the public changes in the perception of NGOs as an entity. While in the early 1990s I had often to translate the concept as 'non-profit' for US or European colleagues and I could still detect some caution among other Brazilian social actors regarding NGOs (ONGs), after the Rio 1992 world meetings for the environment there was a shift in public perception, as NGOs had a prominent role at that forum. After that event, the media adopted the term NGO as if it had always been there; slowly, it spread through the international media as well.

12. To my surprise, any Northern visitor, not just those from the US, could be a gringo. One could be a Dutch gringo, for instance, and even I could be referred to as gringa, in spite of my nationality (Portuguese), which is associated in Rio with the backwardness of European peasants who migrated to the New World and kept their old ways. Only for the convenience of an argument would the idea of having been former colonisers come up – for instance, to blame the Portuguese for Brazilian underdevelopment. The coloniser/colonised trope, as found in Spanish-speaking Latin America or former British colonies, is almost inverted in Brazil.

13. For example, the leader of GGB (Grupo Gay da Bahia), who had received me very generously in Salvador, explicitly despised my choice of being too close to Rio's ABIA, therefore an 'abiana', and made it clear that we would no longer have any business, not even basic sociability.

14. I describe this world at length in the monograph Global Reponses to AIDS (Bastos, 1999), whose chapter 4 (on Brazilian AIDS/NGOs) is available at http://www.vibrant.org.br/downloads/a1v1_raidsb.pdf.

15. See Galvão (1992), Solano Vianna (1992).

16. In this area alone, a vast sub-field of research on local sexual cultures, drawing from the constructivist view on the local sexual ways (e.g. ABIA 1988c, 1989; Guimarães et al.1988; Ramos 1989) and was developed into an interpretive anthropology model by Parker (1991).

17. See ABIA (1988a, b).

18. The most remarkable of these efforts were from the *Pela VIDDA* groups, aimed at self-empowering people with AIDS, mostly inspired by the life and work of Brazilian activist and writer Herbert Daniel.

19. The World Health Organisation's Global Programme on AIDS, particularly under the leadership of Jonathan Mann, absorbed much of Herbert Daniel's views on PWAs' rights (he was a keynote speaker in the International AIDS Conference in Amsterdam, 1992) and included some of Parker's analysis on sexuality into their policies.

20. In Niterói I followed an outpatients service for a low-income population, and was temporarily integrated into a team that provided medical care as part of medical training This part of the research was accomplished due to the generous invitation of Doctor Rosa Soares, also a professor of clinical medicine, whom I met at a training course in tropical medicine in FIOCRUZ. For a brief period I was part of her large team, which included residents and medical students under training, as well as occasional specialists.

21. In FIOCRUZ, after following a course on tropical medicine, participating in public conferences and seminars and interviewing scientists in different research laboratories, I became (after fieldwork) involved with a research team as a consultant at the epidemiology unit at the Evandro Chagas hospital when the team tried to have an interface with community organisations for the purpose of evaluating a prevention programme – and needed the consultancy of a social scientist. This programme was included as an ethical requirement within a larger multi-centre project for a cohort study and epidemiological surveillance, funded by WHO, with the purpose of having indicators and instruments for future studies of efficacy in preventive vaccines. This was not a part of my own research.

22. This team had been created according to the notion of integrated assistance, with the aim of better addressing the multidimensional aspects of AIDS. It was a multi-professional team, which included full-time infectious-disease specialists and residents, nurses and nurse aids, social workers, psychotherapists, psychiatrists, nutritionists. Other specialists from the hospital staff, such as dentists, ophthalmologists, gastroenterologists, dermatologists, pathologists and pneumologists, served regularly in the unit.

23. Those early moments were captured in an unpublished monograph produced as a result of participant observation for an MA thesis in psychiatry (Souza 1988).

24. As part of the prolongations of my ethnography, I recently (2005) watched a major representative of China asking the former president of Brazil, Fernando Henrique Cardoso, what the formula was and what China could learn in order to act upon AIDS. It had been under Fernando Henrique Cardoso, a sociologist, and his wife Ruth Cardoso, an anthropologist, that the visible AIDS Programme had been launched. The synthetic official response focused on the empowerment of Brazilian civil society – something that my ethnography shows is not a given, but the result of a long, complex process of interactions, which also experienced some odd and almost despairing moments. For a development of this point, see Bastos 2008.

25. So China, with no history of civil society involvement in the responses to AIDS comparable to that of Brazil, may look at other aspects of their public health system and public culture to see what might be their optimal response to the epidemic.

References

ABIA (Associação Brasileira Interdisciplinar de AIDS). 1988a. 'Quem semeia pânico, colhe epidemia: Caras e máscaras de uma campanha equivocada', *Boletim Abia* 2: 1.

———.1988b. 'Onze críticas a uma campanha desgovernada, *Boletim Abia* 2: 2.

———. 1988c. 'AIDS: O número de casos e o caso dos números', *Boletim Abia* 3: 1.

———. 1989. '… E se o Presidente?', *Boletim Abia* 8: 1–2.

Bastos, C. 1999. *Global Responses to AIDS: Science in Emergency*. Bloomington: Indiana University Press.

———. 2001. 'Behavior as Social Variable and Social Variables as Behavior: Lessons from the AIDS Epidemic', *AIDS and Anthropology Bulletin* 13 (3): 10–11.

———. 2008. 'From Global to Local and Back to Global: the Articulation of Politics, Knowledge and Assistance in Brazilian Responses to AIDS', in M.-L. Follér and H. Thörn (eds) *The Politics of AIDS: Globalization, the State and Civil Society.* New York: Palgrave Macmillan, pp. 225–41.

Chirimuuta, R.C. and R.J. Chirimuuta. 1989. *AIDS, Africa, and Racism,* new and revised edition. London: Free Association Books.

Cooper, C. 1973. *Science, Technology and Development: The Political Economy of Technological Advance in Underdeveloped Countries.* London: Frank Cass.

Epstein, S. 1991. 'Democratic Science: AIDS Activism and the Contested Construction of Knowledge', *Socialist Review* 21(2): 35–64.

———. 1996. *Impure Science.* Berkeley: University of California Press.

Farmer, P. 2001. *Infections and Inequalities.* Berkeley: University of California Press.

Gaillard, J. 1991. *Chercheurs des Pays en Développement. Scientists in the Third World.* Lexington, KY: University Press of Kentucky.

Galvão, J. 1992. 'AIDS e ativismo: O surgimento e a construção de novas formas de solidariedade. Seminar', in AIDS e Ativismo Social e Político IMS/UERJ, Rio de Janeiro.

Goonatilake, S. 1993. 'Modern Science and the Periphery: the Characteristics of Dependent Knowledge', in S. Harding (ed.), *The 'Racial' Economy of Science.* Bloomington: Indiana University Press, pp. 259–67.

Guimarães, C.D., H. Daniel and J. Galvão.1988. 'A questão do preconceito', *Boletim Abia* 3: 2–3.

Hahn, R., M. Singer and I. Susser. 2004. *HIV.*

Hannerz, U. 1992. *Cultural Complexity: Studies in the Social Organization of Meaning.* New York: Columbia University Press.

Heath, D. and P. Rabinow (eds). 1993. 'Bio-politics: the Anthropology of the New Genetics and Immunology', *Culture Medicine and Psychiatry* 17 (1): 1–2.

Knorr-Cetina, K. 1981. *The Manufacture of Knowledge: an Essay in the Constructivist and Contextual Nature of Science.* Oxford: Pergamon Press.

Lachenal, G. 2004. 'Monkeys, Butchers, Virologists and HIV Emergence in Post-colonial Cameroon', paper presented at *EASST-4S Meetings.* Paris: Ecole des Mines.

Landim, L. (ed.). 1988. *Sem fins lucrativos.* Rio de Janeiro: ISER.

Latour, B. and S. Woolgar. 1979. *Laboratory Life: The Construction of Scientific Facts.* Princeton: Princeton University Press.

Mogadham, A.A. 1991. *The North–South Science and Technology Gap.* New York: Garland Publishing.

Morazé, C. 1979. *Science and the Factors of Inequality.* Paris: UNESCO.

Mulkay, M. 1979. *Science and the Sociology of Knowledge.* London: Allen and Unwin.

Nussbaum, B. 1990. *Good Intentions: How Big Business and the Medical Establishment are Corrupting the Fight Against AIDS.* New York: Atlantic Monthly Press.

Packard, R. and P. Epstein.1991. 'Epidemiologists, Social Scientists, and the Structure of Medical Research in Africa', *Social Science and Medicine* 33 (7): 771–82.

Parker, R.G. 1991. *Bodies, Passions and Pleasures: Sexual Culture in Contemporary Brazil.* Boston: Beacon Press.

Polanco, X. 1985. 'Science in the Developing Countries: an Epistemological Approach on the Theory of Science in Context', *Quipu* 2 (2): 303–18.

Ramos, S. 1989. 'Sex, drugs, AIDS e Sarney (a pior AIDS do mundo)', *Boletim ABIA* 6: 8–9.

Reilly, C. (ed.). 1995. *New Paths to Democratic Development in Latin America: the Rise of NGO-Municipal Collaboration.* Boulder, CO: Lynne Rienner.

Sagasti, F. 1971. 'Underdevelopment, Science and Technology: the Point of View of the Underdeveloped Countries', *Science Studies* 3 (1): 47–59.

Schoepf, B.G. 1991. 'Ethical, Methodological and Political Issues of AIDS Research in Central Africa', *Social Science and Medicine* 33 (7): 749–64.

Shils, E. (ed.). 1968. *Criteria for Scientific Development.* Boston: MIT Press

Solano Vianna, N. 1992. 'AIDS no Brasil: Avaliando o passado e planejando o futuro', in Seminar AIDS e Ativism Político, 11–13 May 1992. Social Medicine Institute, State University of Rio de Janeiro.

11

Ethnography in Motion
Shifting Fields on Airport Grounds

Dimitra Gefou-Madianou

Ethnography today is changing fast from its traditional forms, both from within the discipline and through the appropriation of fieldwork by other social sciences. Both developments have forced us to rethink of our methodology and find new ways to capture the present. And this is a present that moves, that makes itself felt in shifting grounds that host floating images and fragmented realities. To follow these movements ethnographers have to devise flexible forms of fieldwork that generate 'openness' and reflection on their informants' part, and which may take them to the mobile grounds of their action wherever it takes place, in my case to an airport.

The new Athens international airport has been built in the grounds of a closed community of Arvanites, whose cultural and linguistic past have been traditionally looked down upon by the neighbouring Athenians, stigmatising them even in their own eyes. Despite the first negative reactions to the airport, which took their fields and vineyards, thus disrupting their sense of identity, the locals are now appropriating the airport's cosmopolitan and polyglot environment and see afresh their own bilingual past. For an ethnographer with a long history of involvement in the area, airport allusions and intimations show new ways of interpreting local identities.

The Community, the Airport and its Appropriation

It is an undeniable fact that the new Athens airport Eleftherios Venizelos in the Messogia area of Attica constitutes a major technical feat and a great stride on Greece's way to modernisation. The more so, if we consider that the new airport is part of a huge set of technical projects that took place mainly in and around the capital, with the aim of modernising the infrastructure for the successful organisation of the 2004 Olympic Games. In fact, seven major projects were completed in the area, such as

Athens's expressway known as Attiki Odos, the construction of the new Lavrion port, which will eventually replace that of Piraeus, the new Marathon highway, the new horse-racing and shooting grounds of Athens, and several new major international hotels and business centres.

From another point of view, the construction and operation of such a big project, like the new airport and its adjuncts, has tremendous repercussions for the entire region of Messogia. First, it has irreparably upset the Messogitic culture of vine cultivation and wine production, which was the area's most central cultural and economic characteristic[1] since 'for ever' – from the time of Dionysus as my informants characteristically maintain and Greek mythology ascertains. Secondly, it has transformed beyond recognition the population composition and image, from an endogamous, marginal(ised) and inward-looking Arvanitic-speaking community, which at times has been looked down upon by the neighbouring Athenian elite,[2] into a 'suburb' of the capital populated by increasing numbers of Athenian urbanites, who enjoy better access to their businesses and the airport, as well as by legal and illegal economic migrants (from inside the country and abroad), who work in the area. Thirdly, it has changed the uses of land from agricultural into residential (*oikopeda*)[3] and industrial, as well as service-providing, and has set apart great chunks of it for the construction of condominiums and other urban housing projects. The same is true for the character of the roads, which from rural, provincial by- and throughways are fast becoming suburban lanes and highways. Lastly, it has endangered the few patches of green and forest that have survived from fires, arsons and the illegal building of houses.

Such great changes in the area operate at many different levels concurrently and affect the social and economic life of the people in manifold ways. Clearly a lot of money has been made by several people, including locals. The price of land has increased tremendously and the new businesses, as well as the flourishing of those already established, have absorbed a sizeable part of the local workforce. At the same time, though, there seems to have been a darker side in this development, which, having conducted extensive fieldwork for more than fifteen years, I have been able to experience in my interaction with the locals.

It is a case of 'shifting grounds', loss and confusion. As an informant, Mr Nikolos, told me, the topography of the area has changed so radically with the airport and the other building projects that it has become fairly difficult to locate his own vineyards. In relation to the community, Mr Nikolos's vineyard is situated at the other side of the airport, which means that he is now obliged to use the newly built highway in order to cross to his land. It is not a matter of distance only that is involved here. Due to his relatively old age, Mr Nikolos does not really know how to use the highway and its exits and he is getting confused. Moreover, he cannot visit his land driving his motor cultivator, as he used to, but has to take a bus – or use the newly built suburban railway – to a neighbouring village and then walk from there to the fields. But even this stage of his itinerary is far from simple.

Traditionally, fields in the area of Messogia were not clearly demarcated with fences and hedgerows, but each farmer knew exactly which individual vine plant belonged to whom.[4] In their place, villagers had developed a quite intricate system of topographical signs, which included a twisted olive tree here, a rock there or a small out-church further down the hill. Now most of these signs have gone and Mr Nikolos is lost in the middle of fields that he simply knew better than the back of his hand. Lastly, to complete the picture, I have to stress that a great number of subsidiary building projects are still in process in the area, while those already in place are occasionally extended. This means that, whatever new topographical signs Mr Nikolos may presently devise, he will pretty soon have to review them. Understandably, Mr Nikolos gets annoyed and, in order to avoid all the fuss, asks his son to drive him to the fields in his private car, something he manages to arrange not as often as he would like and definitely not at all as he used to. All in all, the lifelong relationship of Mr Nikolos with his vineyard has changed dramatically.

Such a situation is very common among the older generations of Arvanites in the Messogia region, especially those of middle to lower income. The fact that they do not have titles of the land (*ktimatologio*) makes them worry. 'Our children will not be able to find our own fields' as they characteristically maintain. For them, the airport and the other projects that surround it have somehow stolen their land and vineyards; the airport has complicated their relationships among themselves and with their ancestral fields, and has opened the door to 'legions of foreigners'. That is why right from the beginning they fought against the implementation of the airport plans for more than four years. When the project was finally approved by parliament in 1994, reactions and legal representations continued as local action groups lodged complaint after complaint in order to delay the actual works. It was only after the official opening of the airport early in 2001 and with the Olympic Games only four years away that it became clear to all parties that the situation was irreversible; the airport could not be wished away and they had somehow to live with it.

For more affluent people, who have always had connections with the capital, the new airport was perceived right from its inception as a challenge that could be translated into money. They, too, had second thoughts, even serious objections, against its building, as they had always been identified with the wine culture of the Messogia area due to their substantial expanses of vineyards. A clear proof of all these was the launching of the 'Wine Roads', a sightseeing trip in the Messogitic plains (*kambos*) passing through famous Messogitic vineyards, well-established and widely known wineries, from remote caves, picturesque out-churches and ancient temples.[5] Materially and culturally, wine production added to their cultural and economic capital and reproduced their ambivalent relationship with the hegemonic Athenian elites and the Greek state:[6] on the one hand, the affluent Messogites enjoyed a particularly exalted position in the traditionally endogamous and marginal Arvanitic communities, while on the other they could escape to the capital, where they could indulge in luxury goods consumption – something that in its turn reinforced their status back in the community.

Still, the building of the new airport, imagined as it was within the parameters of an entirely new game, an environment of structural changes, a milieu of new dangers and new opportunities, firmly bypassed the realities of a Messogitic community locked in a pre-existing and, in many respects, static and antagonistic relationship to the neighbouring capital of Athens. Everything was shifting around the new airport and the atmosphere of modernity that engulfed it: grounds, relations, laws, money.

I have already mentioned the changes in the uses of land and the construction boom that has been taking place in the area. Here, I would like to add the existence of considerable lacunae in the relevant legislation, a fact that complicates practically many business activities connected with land transactions, such as the transfer of land and inheritance rights. At the same time, this legal confusion has allowed a number of private individuals and members of municipal bodies to make quick money or to take loans from the banks and the EU for occasionally ill-conceived and equally ill-assessed commercial projects.[7]

All in all, most local inhabitants of Messogia agree that the airport and the surrounding projects have utterly transformed their area for good. Like it or not, they have opened it up to influences and structural changes from without, with positive and negative consequences. The scene is set, then, for the Arvanites of Messogia to take part in the transformation of their community and the entire Messogia region into – as they themselves half-jokingly assert – the centre of the capital (*giname to kendro*), the Attica region and the Balkans. 'We have got our own back on them [the Athenians] for all the years they have looked down upon us as provincials; from a province we have become the centre, the new business hub of Athens and Greece, the communication and transportation centre of the country, South-Eastern Europe and what not'. Metonymically, that is, they appropriate the properties of the airport as their own and apply them to the very structures of their community.

In the present chapter I do not intend to analyse all these changes and the ways they have affected the everyday life of the local community. Rather, I shall concentrate on how people reflect on their identity and how this has affected the way fieldwork can be conducted in the region.

The picture presented in the previous pages may give the impression of an invasion of a traditional community by modernity and the subsequent destruction of its sociocultural and economic underpinnings. However, this has proved to be only one reading of the situation, which the construction of the airport and the surrounding projects helped to amend in a most curious but sociologically explainable way. Until the building of the airport, the evolving relationship between the community and the outside world, mainly the nearby capital, appeared to be experienced in a dichotomous and antagonistic manner that presumed inward-looking and stereotypical icons of both the self and the other. With the construction of the airport – in other words, the building of modernity into the 'traditional' structures and on the actual grounds of the community – we encounter a qualitatively different approach to identity construction and to the very process of social transformation itself.

For, as I have slowly realised, both my informants and myself were somehow forced to adopt a reflective approach of our own identity and of the identity of the community itself, the more so when visiting the airport for a variety of social activities. They started talking to me in a specific way that was quite different from before, and they appeared to be ready to understand themselves in different and more open ways.

In the polyglot and multicultural environment that the airport and other Olympic Games-related projects have created, an environment where tourists, passengers and migrant workers from all over the world meet, my informants have started to change their attitude towards their identity as Arvanites and the way this relates to the hegemonic ethnic and national Greek identity. In other words, I am going to describe briefly the manner in which the new airport has been appropriated by the Messogitic communities and the way in which this appropriation has affected the concept and the very logic of my fieldwork amongst them.

From this perspective, then, the paper could be read in three different though inter-related ways: first, as a methodological exercise of how the dramatic changes occurring in a place do alter the ways in which anthropologists do ethnography; second, as a process of how identities may change through creative appropriations of the 'place' and its transformations; and third, as a contrapuntal critique to the notion of 'non-places' as introduced by Marc Augé (1995).

Let's Go to the Airport: or How 'the Ancient, the Modern and the Foreigners All Speak Foreign Languages'

As we have seen, the airport seems to operate as a catalyst. In many ways, visiting its grounds works as an alternative to older forms of social gatherings in 'traditional' cafes or in the village square. It has not supplanted them at all, but it has added a new dimension in the social life of the community. It would not be far-fetched to argue that for many the airport grounds are seen as a promenade, as the place where activities that organised social relations in the past can now take place. For example, the highway to and from the airport gives younger people the possibility to ride their cars or motorcycles in style. To spend an hour or two riding around and drinking coffee in the airport with friends and acquaintances is enjoyable and relatively low-cost. Even sitting on the benches and watching the planes coming and going while eating an ice cream or popcorn is entertaining in a manner that sitting in the local cafes of the community never was. More than that, other activities include shopping in the airport arcades and constructing stands in designated areas where major local wine producers advertise their products. In that sense, it is interesting to see that 'the airport' and the tropes of existence associated with it themselves become an object of consumption.

Although the Arvanites were traditionally an endogamous community, there have always been people who opted out for a number of reasons. For example, young unmarried couples preferred to meet outside the community in order to avoid gossip, as dating was discouraged. Then, young married couples also preferred to entertain themselves outside the community, as, even in their case, too, mixed-gender public gatherings were open to gossip and thus avoided. One has to remember here that the traditional cafes of the community were patronised exclusively by men and that there were no other public places, except the church and the relatively recently introduced supermarket, where men and women could be seen together.[8]

Lastly, more affluent families, which nonetheless shared the community's 'traditional' values, elected to entertain themselves outside the community and to spend their disposable income on luxury goods offered in the posh areas of the nearby capital. That was part of their strategy to accumulate status and to reinforce their position in the local social hierarchy. Spending time and money outside the community relativised their provincial identity and, at least in their eyes, transformed them into part of the city and the bourgeois scene of the capital.

This is not so any more. As an icon of modernity and as a vista for consumption that has been built on their forefathers' land and vineyards, the airport enables wider social categories of locals to appropriate modernity without crossing the municipality borders. In this way, from an object of intrusion and an agent of perpetual occupation of their homes and of their way of life that had to be resisted, the airport has become incorporated in their vision of things. While drinking coffee in one of the airport cafes, a middle-aged informant retorted sagely: 'And you should not forget that the place where we are sitting right now is on top of my father's vineyards.' Consuming cappuccino freddo rather than Greek coffee or the more ubiquitous Nescafé frappé on top of the recently uprooted family vineyards can be seen as an act of symbolic appropriation, perhaps even as an attempt to cast away the black spells of cultural confusion that had dominated community members throughout the long and acrimonious period of the airport's construction.

But, on top of this, there is an additional form of consumption that operates here. It is the consumption of 'the airport' itself and everything that it stands for. I have suggested earlier that even sitting on the benches and watching the air traffic is enjoyable. It is, as it were, the consumption of the scene that exhilarates, a scene that is so close to home and so different from what it used to be that only if it is massively consumed at all levels, with all the senses, can it be appropriated and lose its intrusive value.

Becoming part of the airport scene by inflection, locals become members of the travelling crowd, of the tourists: they leave behind their grounded selves and 'travel' to the airport world. They rank just a bit lower than the airport staff with their sleek uniforms and identity cards, but from another point of view they are above them, if not above the travellers themselves. After all, the latter only use the airport temporarily and, from all points of view, they are always in transit. Indeed, the Arvanites of the local communities can portray themselves as owners of the place, as hosts and proprietors: they knew the place when it was deeply wounded by digging machines and bulldozers, when it was merely naked, with all its contours, the hills and the lowlands. In other words, they knew the place when it was not, in its prehistory as an airport to be -which, significantly, coincided with their history as a community.

They were there before, in other words they were there all along, that is, before it was even conceived as an idea in the mind of the Athens technocrats, and they have followed its construction in all its phases until the present – many local farmers have a deep knowledge of the by-laws that governed the compulsory expropriation of land that went to build the airport.

Secondly, they can come and go to the airport whenever they choose as they are not locked into a time-structured relationship with the place and its operations like the staff and the travellers – at the level of social rhetoric, some informants joked that when they travel (which they rarely do) they do not have to check in; 'it is the planes themselves, you see, that pick us up from our front door ... you know, just like minicabs'.

Thirdly, they can park their cars wherever they want, as the local police staff are usually friends or relatives – in the unlikely event of receiving a ticket, this can be cancelled through the local mayor and his staff, for the airport territory administratively belongs there.

Lastly, they can use restricted throughways accessed through loose fences and removable traffic barriers to move from one place to another or from one village to another, at least now while parts of the airport are still under construction.[9]

If these are not reasons for claiming a proprietary relationship, then nothing is. The airport, then, stands as an 'interpositional place' consisting of 'an instantaneous configuration of positions' (de Certeau 1984: 94).[10]

In all respects, the airport itself has passed through a process of accommodation: from a cause of serious apprehension first, it progressively became an object of curiosity, and more recently of celebratory appropriation. It exists as a place in its own right, but also as an added layer of meaning that pervades the quotidian discourse of the Arvanitic communities with its aura of cosmopolitanism and modernity. If a further proof of this were needed, this could be found in the recent decision of the community to use the airport as the starting point of their pilgrimage to their ancestors' villages of origin in south Albania (northern Epirus as they prefer to call it). This year their trip will take place by plane instead of the much cheaper tourist couches they used before; and they will arrive in the bilingual (Albanian- and Greek-speaking) villages via Tirana, a much longer trip. In this capacity the airport is becoming the emblem of the area, something they are very proud of.

In this capacity, the airport is also becoming an attraction, something of their own, part of the sightseeing locals may offer to visitors, including the anthropologist. In my recent visits to the field I was often taken to the airport for coffee, pizza, shopping or window-shopping, or simply for a ride in the car. It was a shock to me that, after the baptismal rites of an informant's grandson and the traditional customary feast in the house, some of the guests were invited to the ultra-modern spaces of the airport cafes for early evening refreshments.

I noticed that other informants of mine often invited me to the airport as well. The invitation 'Let's go to the airport' became a favourite among my informants, especially female ones, who felt more restricted in the community.

From the high windows of the airport buildings, one could contemplate the remaining vineyards and the distant mountain, the barrier that traditionally separated them physically from the capital city of Athens and formed the geographical dimension of a much more comprehensive cultural discrimination. Yet, from another angle, the coffee shops near the cargo area offer a view that is much more homely and moving. In the reflection of these windows, they could see the village itself, their own houses, the trees and the gardens. It is here that everything comes together. The airport loosens up, it loses its exclusivity as it is embraced by the community and the surrounding Mt. Hymettus's slopes. In the reflections trembling in the breeze of the rolling hills and the plain on the shiny façade of the tall cargo building – which my informants jokingly called 'horse-cart square' (*karoplateia*), paraphrasing the word cargo in Greek – the village and even my informants looked so close and so distant, at least to my own eyes, it was as if I were in a different place.

Even for people who do not really visit the airport, like my very good informant the elderly cooper Mr Fanis, the situation can hardly be different from this. His warehouse is three minutes away from the new super-modern Attiki Odos highway sign, 'Exit 21: to Messogia North', written only in English. It is a modest construction in bad repair, with a tin roof and concrete brick walls that stands in stark contrast to the nearby highway and the airport buildings, including two international hotels. In the past, Mr Fanis was indeed a very talented cooper, one of the major coopers in the area, but now, for the last fifteen years or so, he only repairs old barrels, usually before the period of grape harvest. Sitting outside his shop, which is an extension of his house, he sees the planes passing above his head as they are preparing for landing and comments on the origin of their passengers: 'Are they English? French? Italian? Perhaps they are Germans or Americans. They all have to pass from here [his community] before going anywhere else; they have to step on this soil of ours first.' Staring at the aeroplanes flying over his place, Mr Fanis often recognises their country of origin and imagines the foreign language their passengers would speak. It is the same with the passing tourists who stay in nearby hotels and jog outside his front door, or ask for cigarettes at the local kiosk in their 'broken Greek' or in their foreign tongues.

Mr Fanis likes all this; it makes him excited. It somehow reminds him, by association, one might say, of the only time he found himself away from his community. It was during the Second World War, when Fanis fought against the Italians in south Albania, or northern Epirus – depending on which side you are with. His officer had asked him to help with the language, as his own idiom was so close to that of the Albanian locals. He was proud of it at that time, despite the fact that he was ridiculed because of this same idiom when he first joined the army, for Arvanitika was considered – even by the Greek state – a sign of his ambivalent Greekness. He felt special in a period when Arvanitika was banished as a potential threat to Greece's ethnic and national integrity.

All these unknown (but not strange to him) sounds, those of the tourists that he hears and those of the air passengers that he imagines, also remind him of another polyglot environment: the old days when his grandparents on his mother's side were alive and spoke Arvanitika to each other – his grandmother could actually only speak Arvanitika – and when most people in the community were bilingual. Sometimes he also reflects on his father who spoke in the sing-song idiom of the Cycladic island of Santorini,[11] where he came from, but not a word of Arvanitika. That language Mr Fanis took from his grandparents and his mother. Even today, he is unable to tell you a joke in Greek, only in Arvanitika. 'Otherwise, nobody will laugh,' he says.

Indeed, Mr Fanis was brought up in an environment where many idioms coexisted for a while, until political developments banished Arvanitika from the public arena. The airport wakes memories from the past, his own and the community's, memories that are not always pleasant, often painful but always desirable. The airport has brought back some of this aroma of polyglot cosmopolitanism. Even Mr Fanis, an erstwhile enemy of the airport project and the process of globalisation, understands this very well. 'Now, everybody speaks in his foreign tongue; we can do the same, nobody will say a word.' As he, sitting outside his shop sunning himself, characteristically maintains: 'The ancients who are buried in this earth spoke ancient [Greek]; I know it from my daughter who went to the university; we 'modernised' people living here now speak differently; and the foreigners (*xenoi*) above us [pointing at the passing airplanes] speak differently as well; we all speak [in] foreign languages now.'

At the same time, people like Mr Fanis feel the downside of this late surge of polyglot cosmopolitanism, however liberating it may feel occasionally. In his own words: 'In a few years there will be no vineyards and no wine. Barrels will not be needed then. I will be shown to the passing tourists, exhibited like in a museum.' Even now, tourists step into his workshop, see him working and ask about the lost art of barrel making. He enjoys their presence, and he is proud to show them that he also knows a 'foreign language', using some Arvanitic phrases and words in his speech.

Ethnography in Motion:
Reflections, Confessions, Free Associations

It is not only Mr Fanis who experiences this different attitude. Many of my informants had denied their Arvanitic (Albanian, that is) origin in the past and (like the Athenian elite) had looked down on less well-off and uneducated co-villagers speaking the idiom; now even these people started to change their attitude. It was much to my amazement that, during the visit to the airport after the baptism of his grandson, Mr Christos Profis, a successful wine-producer and owner of a big winery in the area, started telling jokes to his invited guests – including the anthropologist and her family – in Arvanitika, and in very good spirits he made fun of himself, his guests and Messogites-Arvanites in a way I had never seen before in the long period of knowing him; he jokingly compared Arvanites of Messogia to the Athenians; he recalled Arvanitic stories and forgotten phrases of past songs, inviting other men, relatives and friends to join him; even his wife Tasia and other women participated in this 'memory exercise'. It was a rare scene and I strongly doubt whether it could have taken place anywhere else. The links, the free associations with the airport uttered and expressed in various clear or insinuating ways by many of the people participating in the feast, left few doubts. Light like the aeroplanes, the thoughts of my informants flew to the open horizons and in the spaces free associations inhabit. It was as if the movement, the atmosphere, the noise in the airport area all assisted in what was taking place: they were definitely in a state of transcendence, liberated from the shackles of their Arvanitic past.[12]

As the occasions of visiting the airport with my informants became more frequent, it became clear to me that in the airport these people felt much freer to express their otherness. My informants were stepping out of the specific 'otherness', an otherness that the anthropologist, in this case myself, took for granted. It was a place where by definition the concept of identity became even more fluid and open. I cannot overstate the difficulties I encountered with some of the very same people throughout the first years of my fieldwork in the area, especially in relation to the Arvanitic identity and idiom.[13] Until the closing years of the 1990s some of my informants refrained from speaking even a word of Arvanitika among themselves – at least in front of me – and refused to admit that they even understood a word of the idiom. Even my poor knowledge of Albanian acquired by taking private lessons was roundly condemned; they identified themselves as people from northern Epirus – 'Voreio-Epirotes' – a term much more amenable to the sensitivities of the Greek hegemonic nationalist discourse of the times. In the new environment of the international airport, which the government has been at pains to portray as a cultural icon of modern cosmopolitan Greece, a country at the crossroads of the Eastern Mediterranean, a bridge between Europe and the Middle East, the rigidity of 'traditional' identification props, like the language idiom, are fast losing their grip.

However, the shifts in my informants' attitudes did not concern only their Arvanitic origin and language. It also concerned other aspects of their lives. They talked to me in a different, more open way, and about more personal things. It was as if the airport milieu provoked some forgotten, 'lost', silenced aspect of their past, even those suppressed into their unconscious. I could not imagine that such a crowded, noisy environment, with shiny lights and a great mobility of people and goods, an environment that seemed so familiar and close to home, but at the same time distant and unknown, a neutral and faceless place at first sight, could become a place of confession, a place where my good informant Antonia (a married woman with three grown-up children) revealed to me 'the story of her life'. This narration of hers has changed our relations since, making us much closer; we are not just 'an anthropologist' and 'an informant' any more, but good friends.

Antonia's Story

During our visits to the airport, the conversations that took place there with Antonia were more sincere, intimate, friendly and confessional. The airport bench where we have often sat and talked since then (and I have to admit that I myself hope for such visits to the airport), seems to loosen up her feelings; she becomes more relaxed and animated, expressive and communicative, 'open' and emotional. It was during one of the airport outings to visit her brother's newly opened and luxurious wine stand when Antonia talked to me about the way she had got married, a story she had talked about to me many times in the past. She definitely liked talking about it to me; it was a 'special' marriage, as she used to call it, a mixture of a marriage arrangement (*proxenio*) and a love affair all at once. I had the opportunity to hear about this wedding arrangement in my long stay in the community from almost all people concerned, Antonia's parents and younger sister, and also from her husband's side. Yet the story I heard from her was quite different this time, and I could tell the difference before she even started to talk to me, from the expression of her eyes, the movements of her hands, the whole body language and most of all the tone of her voice. There, sitting on an airport bench Antonia revealed to me the 'secret of her life', as she later called it, 'the most real part of myself which was a lie', a lie that she kept very well hidden even from her own self. The story was that her marriage to Spyros was merely a marriage prearranged by both her own parents and her husband's father, since her childhood.[14] It was something she had felt uneasy and embarrassed about since she was a little girl; she would get annoyed and angry when her parents and especially her grandparents, talked to her about it. She did not want to even hear about it. That's why she finished high school and the lyceum and persuaded her father (who had a soft spot for her, because she was his firstborn child and was baptised after his father's name[15]) to allow her to take English language lessons in Athens (something not very common for young women of her times, especially for firstborn girls in well-off families like her own – her destiny in life was to get married to a man of her social and economic rank and have children when still young)[16]; she wanted to be someone, to travel and see the world, or at least to get married outside her community if possible. For Antonia's family, Spyros was the right man for her: young, educated (he had finished high school and a technical school), tall and strong, and most importantly the only child, and a male one, in his family (*monahoyios*), since his mother had died at his birth. As such, he would inherit all his father's fortune, which was big. And Gikas, Antonia's father, was counting on that, as was her mother. On the other hand, Spyros's father knew Antonia's family well, rich and respected (*archondes*), as I have heard him say about them. His son was brought up in the same neighbourhood with Gikas's children ('they were brought up together'). He knew them well and he liked Antonia, also tall with a strong body for good births, a chaste girl, good-looking, and with a very good dowry; and their vineyards were close, meaning that if these were put together they would make a very large land entity.

Antonia maintained that she hardly 'knew' Spyros until that day in June. She had been responding negatively to the whole situation until then; she could not even remember Spyros's face that day, as she later told me, 'a neighbour but a stranger (*xenos*)'. Antonia was almost twenty-four when she took her decision:

> It was an afternoon in June; I was returning to Messogia from Athens by the local bus after my English lesson. It was hot, the bus was crowded; I was feeling tired. I had gained weight and I was feeling bad about it; I though people were looking at me … and all of a sudden I felt old. I opened the window. There, sitting at the window seat, looking outside at the vineyards and hills and feeling the early summer breeze on my face, I decided I would get married to Spyros. When I returned home, I talked to my mother and father about it and the engagement ceremony (*aravones*) was arranged that very day.

She told her sister and cousins 'she was in love with Spyros' and the same to her friends; she wanted everybody to know that she got married for love, not because of a marriage arrangement, and that's what I knew from her until then:

> Only my first cousin Roula – we were very close – married now and living in another village, knew the truth. That I had been in love with someone else for years, since high school; he was two years older than me. He left Messogia after my engagement; and migrated to a country in South America, I think, I do not remember the name. He is married with children, and has become rich … He waited for me for a long time; I do not blame him; the situation was difficult; and we both knew it.

And it was indeed difficult since it had to do with social class differences and, most importantly, with the civil war and its repercussions, which were still 'fresh' at this time. Antonia's boyfriend, her 'secret', came from a poor family who lived on the outskirts of the community; his father was a shepherd, a profession that ranks low in a community of farmers and vineyard cultivators like Messogia. He was also a partisan during the Second World War and the civil war that followed, thus making him an enemy by definition; he belonged to the opposite side from Antonia's family. What is more, during the very first year of the civil war and the atrocities that took place in the area, and in her particular village -which was the most right-wing village in the area – it is said that this partisan had killed Antonia's uncle; her father's younger brother. It was during the difficult year of 1947. Antonia had a lot of memories of her grandparents and her close relatives talking about this event during her childhood and adolescence. Her memories were coming thick and fast as she was recalling all this: half-spoken words at home about killings between close kin came to her mind; even semi-forgotten scenes of cut-throats, arson and then informing against old comrades, the secret police coming from Athens to arrest people and send them into exile. But the scenes she remembered vividly were her grandmother cursing the 'murderer's' family on her uncle's grave in the cemetery, and her mother grabbing her from her wrist and hastily changing their route when meeting with her 'secret boyfriend's' mother in church or in the street. Nobody from her family talked to the other family ever. That's why her parents would never have allowed her to marry that boy. She knew it from the beginning: her affair was doomed.

Listening to Antonia's confessions and entangled memories I thought for a moment that the scene resembled more to a psychoanalytic bench rather than an airport one, despite the sharp difference of the places. The stillness and quietness of the first and the movement and the noise of the latter seemed to lose their sharpness.

The Airport, the Informants and the Anthropologist: a Changing Relationship

Since the airport inauguration in early 2001, I have had the opportunity to listen to other informants of mine talking to me about more personal things or matters that had not been discussed before. And I can say now, as I look back and recall these instances, that all the shifts in attitudes were somehow connected with the airport. It was as if the airport were helping my informants to express themselves more freely, to free their inner thoughts and to open up their souls. The concept of time was operating in a different way: past and present memories were inextricably enmeshed.

Gazing at the Messogitic plains (*kambos*) and landscape from the square on the small hill near the cargo area, a land that was only vineyards until 1990 but now contains the oblong hulk of the new airport, my informants remember, relive, experience a variety of states and emotions. For instance, another informant, Mr Nikos Goulas, who has worked in Christos Profi's winery since he was a young boy, remembers the old winery of Pappas, which the community had legally fought to get from its owner and turn it into a community cooperative. There were a lot of fights in the community: between poor and rich land-owners; left- and right-wing believers during the 'troubled times of the war and the civil war that followed' – 'a lot of fights and blood are buried in this land'. For Nikos and other people of the community, this land was the lived history of their families, the vivid presence of their long-gone ancestors, whose names had been given to the vineyards.[17] Their identity was enmeshed with the vines and infused in the wine; it was their land. Now all this has been lost for ever. The land, much of it, has become cement, asphalt, hotels and aeroplanes.

There was no doubt, therefore, the influence of the airport was a fact; my informants had certainly started to change their attitude towards their past and their identities, and towards me. But this change concerned me as well. On the one hand, being acquainted with the airport and its services, I was more natural and confident of myself. I felt at ease when moving around, especially in the main buildings where the departure and arrival jalls were situated. I could occasionally be of help to my informants there.[18] On the other hand, I have to admit that communicating with my informants in the airport environment has changed my attitude towards them as well. Little by little and without it being a conscious act, I realised that I was seeing, responding, interpreting and even accepting my informants differently; as if they were different people. It was as if the boundness and the rigidity of the relation between the anthropologist and her informants were removed. Both my informants and myself came closer to each other in a way that we had never experienced before. The well-defined and clearly separating line between my place of belonging (Athens) and theirs (Messogia), where I have been doing fieldwork for the last sixteen years, was washed away there; it felt as if I were starting fieldwork in a new 'field'. My informants and myself were both 'out of place', each outside our own places.[19]

To put it in another way, both my informants and myself have been involved in a process of 'place making'[20] (Basso 1996: 58; Gupta and Ferguson 1997: 6–12; see also Bloch 1995, 1998). We were transforming airport spaces (spaces of my own analytical description) into 'places' (places of my informants' everyday life worlds, as well as my own when I was interacting with them),[21] and this seemed to facilitate and to smooth out our way of communication. It loosened the tongues, allowed emotions to come to the surface and let loose our free associations; it made me consider more analytically the ways my informants have encountered the airport, perceived it and invested it with significance (Feld and Basso 1996: 8–9; Marcus 1998a). I myself had also become more open to them; I caught myself talking about more personal things to my informants, and taking political stands, something that I had consciously avoided when I was doing fieldwork inside the community – I was definitely more cautious there. I even somehow revealed my political ideas and beliefs and I identified with my informants' feelings and attitudes when it came to the civil war accounts. And by doing so, by showing my sensitivities and emotional stands to my informants, I had a very positive feedback; they became even more open to me. Both of us being liberated from the conventions of 'classic fieldwork' seemed to work out very positively, at least for the anthropologist.

It was also at the airport that I realised my own preconceptions about the community when I heard my informants complaining about how the Athenians 'still call us "Arvanites"', although so many years have passed since our ancestors inhabited this land, and '"Arvanitika" [idiom] is dying out and not really spoken any more', and since so many changes have taken place in the area, especially in the last decade, that their community has become a 'suburb of Athens'. I had heard their complaints many times in the past, but it was the first time that I really understood what they meant. I occasionally caught myself thinking and acting like an Athenian.

And now, by looking at them from afar (by reading my field notes and interrogating my memory), reliving airport experiences, I often come face to face with a deep and unconscious internalising process.

But there is something more that can be said about this curious game of identities revealed and intertwined in and through the airport. Temporarily withdrawing our attention from the actors themselves, both the local/localised subjects and the anthropologist, and redirecting it towards the airport itself, we may perceive the latter as a 'place' endowed with a biography and history, which should not necessarily be so; at least not if we were to follow Augé's anthropology of 'non-places'. More specifically, Augé introduces the notion of 'non-place' to describe constructions such as airports, shopping malls and highways in the age of supermodernity. In this manner, Augé draws a distinction between 'places', which are rendered meaningful through embedded history and are thus capable of bearing social life, and 'non-places', which are removed from lived historical experience and wherein subjects, barely connected to each other, interact at a level of surface homogeneity. In the case of the Athens international airport at Messogia things are markedly different. As we saw, though unsettling local structures and identities rooted into the very soil of the region, the building and operation of the airport also enriched and promoted social life for the local community. It evoked memories, (re-)connected the community with its marginalised past, reinvigorated the hitherto muted Arvanitic language and stimulated new ways of dealing with both the Athenians and the state. In a curious manner, then, through its appropriation by the locals, the airport acquired qualities akin to more traditional socialising places.

Concluding Remarks: 'Shifting' the Ethnographic Practice

As I mentioned before, various levels of shifting are nowadays taking place in the Messogia community concurrently. First, there is the concept of land and its uses, which from uncultivated grassland, pastures and wild forests since antiquity, which nymphs and other *exotika* creatures used to inhabit (as my informants maintain[22]), or from vineyards and olive tree fields, has been transformed into international industrial grounds where aluminium and other metal creatures reside, move and fly. Secondly, there has also been a shift in how people feel about these changes, about the 'shifting grounds' of their social life and their own identity. For, on the one hand, the airport and its surroundings have disrupted the bounded character of their community and diluted their sense of location, while on the other promoted new understandings of themselves and of the place they live in – airport and all.

Finally, there is a major shift in ethnographic practice. For, as I began to realise, I had to be there to capture all these visible and invisible shiftings. I had to accommodate myself and be 'there' when people thought, reflected, identified with, and associated all these feelings and emotions with their past, present and future lives. I had to possibly experience myself similar feelings and emotions; to bring myself in a similar state than my informants; to be able to possibly identify with them and their experiences (Lacan 1977, Gefou-Madianou 2003a). I had to be there, but where? The 'when', 'how' and 'why' had to be taken into consideration, but all these concepts were very fluid; These shiftings have forced me to look for new ways to understand the community's present. And this was a present that moved, that made itself felt in shifting grounds that hosted floating images and fragmented realities. To follow these movements I had to move with them. I had to discover new, flexible forms of fieldwork which generate 'openness' and reflection on my informants' part, and which would (and could) take me to the mobile grounds of their action wherever it takes place. If anything, anthropological fieldwork is not about grounding oneself anymore in the middle of action; it is to follow the action wherever it takes place; to 'follow the thing' in George Marcus's words (1998b: 91). But the place was not the same as it used to be, for both my informants and myself. Ethnography was, and had to be, in motion following the transformations of the 'place'.

Notes

1. See Gefou-Madianou (1992b, c).
2. See Gefou-Madianou (1999a).
3. Oikopeda: legal and mostly illegal 'transformation' of forest or pasture into residential land, by dividing the land into small pieces, selling it and building unlicensed houses. This has been a very common practice in Greece for the last fifty years. The fact that the government(s), in order to gain votes, has legalised most of these projects by providing them with electricity and running water, thus including them in the existing 'city plan', has reinforced these practices even more.
4. For an extensive description of these practices, see Gefou-Madianou (1992a, b).
5. In this way, the 'Wine Roads' programme connected the community's present with the glorious past, leaving out all Arvanitic elements.
6. See Gefou-Madianou (1999).
7. See Gefou-Madianou (1992c).
8. See Gefou-Madianou (2003b).
9. 'Now' is 2003. Since the 2004 Athens Olympic Games, airport security has become stricter to the degree that certain practices described in the chapter, such as trespassing and parking in restricted areas, cannot take place any more with impunity.
10. I am using de Certeau's term 'interpositional place' (1984) in order to frame the main issue here. However, I am not using the terms 'space' and 'place' the way he does (see also note 20).
11. That is why Mr Fanis's father remained a 'foreigner' in the community's eyes, all his life: 'a foreigner in his own home', as Fanis told me many times.
12. My interpretation of the scene was that the polyglot and multicultural environment of the airport had somehow liberated them.
13. See Gefou-Madianou (1998).
14. This practice of infant betrothal was common among the Arvanitic populations of Greece and the Balkans, but it is not so common any more.
15. His younger son was also named after Mr Giorgos's father, Antonis. It is common among Messogitic populations to give to their firstborn child (irrespective of sex) his/her paternal grandfather's name to secure it; if a male child was born later on, he would also take his grandfather's name and he would be the real heir. See also Gefou-Madianou (2003b).

16. Even today women after twenty-five years old are considered relatively 'old' for marriage. Especially firstborn daughters had to get married soon in order for younger sisters to have their turn; older brothers had to wait for all their sisters (older and younger) to get married first before they were allowed to get married themselves.
17. See Gefou-Madianou (1999).
18. There is no doubt that my informants felt more at ease in the cargo square rather than in the main building of the airport. When they had to be there, they seemed rather awkward and insecure. For instance, when first visiting the airport's main Hall for the opening of her brother's VQPRD (*Vins de Qualité Produits dans une Région Déterminée*) wine stand, Antonia almost got lost, and during our next visits she made sure that, either we started the trip from the village together or we met outside the main hall before entering.
19. For interesting connections or even freeassociations with the term, see also Augé's 'non-place' (1995), Bhabha's 'third space' (1994) and Lacan's 'hybrid space' (1988). They all suggest, though each through quite different modes of analysis, that cultural systems and symbolic discourses of human history are constructed in a highly contradictory and ambivalent space, a space where past or present, inside or outside, public or private, conscious or unconscious are all tightly entangled and result in a profound alteration of awareness: something we perceive in a partial and incoherent manner.
20. I follow the terminology of Heidegger (1971) when referring to the concepts of 'place' and 'space', which is the opposite to de Certeau's. It is the terminology also used by contemporary ethnographers and geographers cited in the text. (See also note 10).
21. By this, I do not mean that my informants and myself, as social agents, enter this process of 'place making' on the same conditions.
22. It is worth noting that, in South-East Attica symposiums organised yearly by local committees, a great number of papers refer to a romanticised and exoticised attitude of Messogia people towards their land.

References

Augé, M. 1995. *Non-Places: Introduction to an Anthropology of Supermodernity*, translated by John Howe. London and New York: Verso.

Basso, K.H. 1996. *Wisdom Sits in Places: Landscape and Language among the Western Apache*. Albuquerque: University of New Mexico Press.

Bhabha, H. 1994. *The Location of Culture*. London and New York: Routledge.

Bloch, M. 1995. 'People into Places: Zafimaniry Concepts of Clarity', in E. Hirsch and M. O'Hanlon (eds), *The Anthropology of Landscape: Perspectives on Place and Space*. Oxford: Clarendon Press, pp. 63–77.

———. 1998. 'Time, Narrations and the Multiplicity of Representations of the Past', in D. Gefou-Madianou (ed.), *Theory of Anthropology and Ethnography. Recent Trends*. Anthropological Horizons Series. Athens: Greek Letters, pp. 207–33.

de Certeau, M. 1984. *The Practice of Everyday Life*. Berkeley: University of California Press.

Feld, S. and K.H. Basso. 1996. 'Introduction', in S. Feld and K.H. Basso (eds), *Senses of Place*. Santa Fe, NM: School of American Research Press, pp. 3–12.

Gefou-Madianou, D. (ed.), 1992a. *Alcohol, Gender and Culture*. London and New York: Routledge.

———. 1992b. 'Exclusion and Unity, Retsina and Sweet Wine: Commensality and Gender in a Greek Agrotown', in D. Gefou-Madianou (ed.) *Alcohol, Gender and Culture*. London and New York: Routledge, pp. 108–36.

———.1992c. 'Retsina and EC: Identity in Messogia, Greece', Paper presented in 'Towards an Anthropology of Europe' at the Second EASA Conference, Prague, August 29–31.

―――. 1998. 'Reflexivity, Otherness and Anthropology at Home. Dilemmas and Juxtapositions', in D. Gefou-Madianou (ed.), *Anthropological Theory and Ethnography. Recent Trends*. Anthropological Horizons Series. Athens: Greek Letters, pp. 365–435.

―――. 1999. 'Cultural Polyphony and Identity Formation: Negotiating Tradition in Attica', *American Ethnologist* 26 (2): 412–39.

―――. 2003a. 'Conceptualisations of the Self and "the Other": Issues of Identity in Current Anthropological Theory', in D. Gefou-Madianou (ed.), *The Self And 'the Other'. Conceptualizations, Identities and Practices in Greece and Cyprus*. Athens: Gutenberg, pp. 15–110.

―――. 2003b. '"On the face of my husband they see me". Public and private as loci of gender identity construction', in D. Gefou-Madianou (ed.), *The Self And 'the Other'. Conceptualizations, Identities and Practices in Greece and Cyprus*. Athens: Gutenberg, pp. 111–181

Gupta, A. and J. Ferguson. 1997. 'Culture, Power, Place: Ethnography at the End of an Era', in A. Gupta and J. Ferguson (eds), *Culture, Power, Place: Explorations in Critical Anthropology*. Durham, NY: Duke University Press, pp. 1–32.

Heidegger, M. 1971. 'Building, Dwelling, Thinking', in his *Poetry, Language, Thought*. New York: Harper and Row: 143–62.

Lacan, J. 1977. 'The Field of the Other', in his *Écrits*. London: Tavistock: 671–702.

―――. 1988. *'Where is Speech? Where is Language?' The Seminars of Jacques Lacan, 1954–55*, edited by J.A. Miller. Cambridge: Cambridge University Press.

Marcus, G. 1998a. 'After Cultural Critique', in D. Gefou-Madianou (ed.), *Theory of Anthropology and Ethnography. Recent Trends*. Anthropological Horizons Series. Athens: Greek Letters, pp. 67–108.

―――. 1998b. *Ethnography Through Thick and Thin*. Princeton: Princeton University Press.

Epilogue 1

Re-presenting Anthropology

Simon Coleman

A few years ago, I wandered into the anthropology department at the University of Chicago and found my attention grabbed by the contents of a glass case that was standing in the entrance hall. It was a display of field notes made, as far as I remember, by past Chicago anthropologists, and I spent a happy twenty minutes deciphering the often dog-eared texts dotted around the case. What made this display so alluring – much more intriguing than displays of finished monographs – was the window it afforded on to a normally hidden practice of ethnography: the notes represented fragments from 'the field', providing apparently intimate connections not only with places but also with the private consciousnesses of ethnographers in action; and of course they had that particularly poignant immediacy of notes written for a present that is now long past.

This image of field notes converted into museum (and altar?) pieces came back to me as I read the contributions to this volume. Authors are asking some hard questions about the current impact and practice of anthropology, about its ability to avoid becoming an intellectual anachronism by responding to a world that is both changing and demanding new dimensions of and justifications for our discipline. Reading these pieces, we are encouraged to reflect on whether we can discern continuities of approach across varied projects, and invited to examine our discipline's sometimes fetishised assertion of the centrality of 'a practice' (participant observation) whose precise elements have tended to be ill-defined. It may be that we are facing the development of forms of 'adjectival ethnography', by which I mean a situation wherein not only scholars outside our discipline, but also many within, react to shifting, increasingly hard-to-encapsulate 'fields' by deploying practices that evoke some of the elements of ethnographically oriented fieldwork but strategically diffuse and fragment its physical intensity, moral density and temporal depth: the fieldwork 'gaze' replaced, in effect, by a 'glance'. Such work may seem to be more ethnograph*ic* than ethnograph*y*. And these issues force us to ask what is actually meant by ethnographic 'presence' in a world where the temporal and spatial coordinates of cultural practices shift before our very eyes.

So contributors have provided us with some uncomfortable and yet necessary concerns about the future of our discipline – concerns that have methodological, epistemological but also political dimensions. In particular, we are faced with challenges that revolve around questions of fragmentation – not only of older notions of holism and cultural boundaries, but also of the idea of the author as coherent ethnographic authority, and indeed of a discipline that increasingly accommodates numerous sub-branches of expertise. The apparent deconstruction of our discipline can lead to challenges both in how we define our fields to ourselves and in how we define the worth and distinctiveness of anthropological versions of ethnography to multidisciplinary grant-giving bodies or ethics committees. However, we can surely make fragmentation work for us, enriching the subtlety and application of what we do. In the following, I want to explore some of the ways in which chapters do so. I group authors in terms of how they explore those two key, if troubled, constituents of the field: time and space.

Time

Following Johannes Fabian's *Time and the Other* (1983), much anthropology written since the 1980s has become aware of the need to situate fields in historical flows that show the connections (and not merely the disjunctions) between field and home. However, two chapters in this volume problematise the links not of history as such, but of memory, between fieldworker and field. Fabian himself explores how past fieldwork should be regarded as research whose recall to what one might call the 'authorial present' (the time of writing) cannot be taken for granted. With apologies to L.P. Hartley, it is as if one's own fieldwork past has become 'a foreign country'. For Fabian, the involuntary nature of individual memorising means that a part of ethnographic enquiry is out of control: positivism, one might say, defeated by Proust. He shows how memory seeps into ethnography's manifold forms of inscription and experience, but he also deploys memory as a means of questioning what is actually meant by 'presence' 'in' the field. If 'being there' is so important to us (see Geertz 1988), we need to understand what the grounds of such being consist of. We need also to appreciate how constructing ethnographic knowledge involves forms of forgetting: the myriad decisions Fabian takes in transcribing texts involve exclusions as well as inclusions, through choices that are not always conscious.

For me, Fabian's piece evoked David Parkin's (2000: 93) reference to the biography of remembered events and concern with how they fare in the long passage from initial experience to theoretical – and, one might add, textual – placement. Parkin argues (ibid.: 90ff.) that field notes and what the writer remembers about the events to which they refer may sometimes take on the character of a template, providing a generative model on which subsequent data are collected and interpreted; or they may take on new meaning in the light of more recent theories and interpretations. In a curious way, both Fabian and Parkin also remind me of Peter Stromberg's (1993) study of evangelical Christian conversion narratives, and his point that such narratives themselves are performative means of bringing an original 'event' back into the present – and indeed into presence. Anthropologists, like evangelicals, are accustomed to recalling, reframing, reconstituting original experiences through narratives; but rather more than religious practitioners they need to be aware of memory's ability either to contain hidden fluidities or, alternatively, to become comfortingly but misleadingly hardened.

Judith Okely's depiction of the 'un-innocent' anthropologist entering the field draws on a vision of memory as contained by 'the flotsam of prior representations' – perhaps an anthropological depiction of original sin, in the sense that as fieldworkers we can never become blank pages on which a new culture can be inscribed. But Okely shows how memory can be fertile as well as treacherous, as free associations allow easy movements between past sites of fieldwork and beyond. She demonstrates how other forms of freedom permeate our work as well. Her survey of fieldworkers reveals that one area of predictability is precisely that the unexpected will happen, leading to serendipitous – and revealing – encounters. One question I have here adapts Parkin's template idea: can we say that an anthropologist who returns to the same field is less likely to encounter serendipity, precisely because models of behaviour and expectation have been established between the fieldworker and – to use Okely's term – her 'associates'? Does the charisma of unpredictability itself become routinised? More broadly, Okely's argument provides an intriguing counterpart to Sharon Macdonald's account in this volume of the encounter between anthropology and ethics boards, where one of the problematic features of such an interface is precisely the inherently responsive, indeterminate nature of anthropological planning, as opposed to hypothetico-deductive claims to capture the future through prediction and experiment.

Of course our informants may themselves be living lives where prediction and planning are key to cultural expression: Christina Garsten's tracking of corporate social responsibility, itself a form of ethical practice, is a fascinating example of a kind of anthropology by appointment, where the conference becomes a venue for the crystallisation of a dispersed field (perhaps there are shades of Durkheim here after all). In Garsten's case a certain serendipity occurs through the constitution and reconstitution of a field that is not located in any particular place for any length of time. Part of the interest of her work involves tracing the continual coming into 'presence' (and going into absence) of the field, so that the continuity or regularity sought by anthropologists is embodied in social rather than spatial relations.

Garsten's informants provide a prime example of informants who thrive on planning of their precious time and considerable travel. A poignant contrast is provided by Aud Talle's account of female circumcision in exile, where the stretching out of Somalian women's lives is pernicious rather than serendipitous. Yet notice how Talle's approach as an ethnographer evokes some striking parallels with other pieces in the volume. Talle's field, like that of Garsten, is vulnerable to coming in and out of focus, in and out of presence, since it emerges wherever inscription takes place on the bodies of informants. Or, in another sense, it is located wherever Talle's gatekeeper, Sadiya, decides to take the fieldworker. But such displacement, shared by fieldworker and informant, also creates an important tie between the two: memory now becomes a new kind of resource for the ethnographer, a key link between her and her informants, as both experience a new national context in the light of shared experience of an old one.

The chapters I have been discussing all encourage us to rethink models of ethnography from within a Western, anthropological perspective. Two other contributions to the volume take us away from this 'template', and both have temporal referents. Thomas Widlok's argument that anthropology can gain inspiration from ways in which language documentation redefines the linguistic 'corpus' is not only a plea for us to accept that we can learn from other disciplines, but also an implicit exploration of the technology of the ethnographic intellect, offering a certain domestication of its 'savage' mind. After all, a good linguistic corpus has the potential, argues Widlok, to feed more than one researcher, to provide forms of ethnographic knowledge that can be accumulated over time. With such accumulation also comes a challenge to the assumption that ethnography emerges from the lone, serendipitously wandering fieldworker.

Elfimov also challenges the Western model of participant observation but from a very different angle. He examines an Eastern European model of research; and moreover is interested in memories of past ethnographic practice in Russia. Contemporary Russian researchers seem to face a dilemma in considering whether ethnography should be influenced by its own history, let alone whether it should primarily be interested in retrieving the traditions of disappearing cultures. One irony of Elfimov's account is that classic participant observation is being valorised by contemporary Russian researchers just when it is being questioned in other anthropological traditions. He provides more than disciplinary history, however: a key issue for him – and perhaps also for us – is whether 'in the era of cultural globalisation' it would be better to avoid Western models of participant observation, and instead adapt older, Eastern models of 'multiple case studies'. In making his case Elfimov reveals another, implicit irony: the deep parochialism of Western models of ethnography, and the problematic assumption that Anglo-American methods are the only ones worth considering. Notice also that, like Widlok, he provides an alternative to ethnography as solitary activity.

Space

Anthropology's origin myth is expressed in temporal and geographical coordinates that are both precisely located and yet deeply generic in application. As heirs to Malinowski, we are meant to 'imagine ourselves set down' in a place that allows us to isolate the time and space of fieldwork from other parts of our lives, and in the process to seek repetitive patterns of behaviour and belief that add up to 'a culture' (see Coleman and Collins 2006; Robbins 2007). But, of course, the problem is that the myth has hardened into a template, that we have rooted ourselves in a falsely static and holistic image of fieldwork that was based on intellectual and cultural grounds that were already always shifting. After all, some of the force of Malinowski's work is based on his rhetorical construction of a supposedly isolated field in contrast to a decidedly unsettled West.

Issues of movement, migration and urbanism are hardly new to anthropology, while fleeting access to many informants has probably been fairly common in so-called traditional fieldwork localities (Eriksen 2003: 7). And, if in contemporary anthropology we emphasise metaphors of movement and displacement, we still need to recognise that our emphasis is itself a theoretical choice, serving its own rhetorical function – a form of methodological iconoclasm shattering narrative images of boundedness and continuity. Where I think this volume helps is in the ways in which, as with temporality, it gives us clues as to how to use spatial fragmentation and movement to our own advantage. Dimitra Gefou-Madianou depicts both the ethnographer and her informants going to (and being taken over by) a place of literal motion, that of an airport. One part of Gefou-Madianou's account embodies standard, respected ethnographic practice, as she shows how the 'locals' appropriate certain properties of the airport as their own. Yet something surprising – serendipitous – is also revealed. The ethnographer finds that she and her informants become newly reflective as the airport becomes more than a 'non-place' (*pace* Augé 1995) and is transformed into a place of a certain kind of freedom and even revelation. The new space/place allows time to operate in a new kind of way, and informants participate in 'memory exercises' that would not have taken place elsewhere in the Messogian landscape. As with many pilgrimage sites, movement to a place of movement prompts new forms of confession. While Gefou-Madianou shares with her informants a sense of displacement that has a certain parallel with that described by Talle, a key difference is that this displacement comes to have positive associations: hyper-modernity seems enchanted and liberating – for the time being. Thinking of the Messogian case through Malinowskian tropes, it is almost as if going back on to the veranda, on to a place of semi-distanced reflection away from what looked originally like 'the field', has become a powerful methodological tool.

Time and space are also intertwined in Ute Röschenthaler's discussion of carrying out fieldwork on associations within the Cross River region of Cameroon and Nigeria. Here, Röschenthaler reveals a kind of double displacement from conventional Western ethnography and from her informants: like Elfimov, she invokes earlier modes of multi-sitedness, this time in describing a fieldwork method that moves from the idea of focusing on an 'ethnic group' towards the examination of 'an element of culture' in its regional context. One result of her method is that her reconstructions of history provide her with a perspective that transcends what any single informant would know. The 'holistic' view of the history of associations that she derives can only be gained by moving between places, tracking paths of dissemination and tracing the past as it leaches variably into the present. In this respect, she resembles Cristiana Bastos, who follows global flows in examining a very different element of culture, that of responses to AIDS. Bastos's informants are traced in cities around the world and so her field is also dynamic, but the 'site' she traces, in common with all the best ethnography, contains its own counter-intuitive element of surprise. In tracking movements of knowledge and cooperation, she notes traffic not only between Northern and Southern nations (as expected) but also the possibility of 'South-South' engagements, as the forms of mobility that constitute global relations may themselves show at least some changes in orientation.

The chapters in this volume complement many of George Marcus's reflections on the reinvention of anthropological method, while illustrating a move from critiques of ethnography as writing into a focus on ethnography as fieldwork method. Marcus helps us to look more closely at another anthropological icon of the Malinowskian school, that of the 'situated native point of view', in fieldwork contexts not only of reflexive modernisation, but also where the fieldworker and colleagues at home are only a phone call or, more likely, an email away. We are facing new 'ecologies of knowledge' that require new – and self-conscious – choices of where to focus our work, and new recognitions of the partialities and connections entailed in any given project.

Warnings and Opportunities

The first footnote in Marcus's contribution to this volume provides anthropologists with a salutary warning: 'Conventional ethnography has much to say to others … but there is very little room for intellectual growth in the discipline itself in repetitively fulfilling this worthy function in different domains.' Marcus depicts here a methodological version of Leach's famous 'butterfly collecting', and one where anthropology runs the risk of reducing itself to a somewhat static, 'adjectival' significance across the academy. However, chapters in this volume show how a sophisticated fragmentation of both 'the ethnographic present' and 'the holistic field' can reveal the opportunities inherent in exploring the multiple temporalities and spatialities inherent in ethnography as both fieldwork practice and the process of writing. Fragmentation initially implies gaps: between the fieldworker's own past and present; between historical and contemporary versions of our discipline; between one 'site' and another, and so on. But the recognition of gaps means that we can use them productively, seeing opportunities for new forms of self-awareness and fieldwork strategy rather than threatening attacks on a fixed 'template' of doing research. In one sense, as Marcus implies in his piece, we often work within domains of modern knowledge that are 'already known'. But, of course, it remains the job of anthropology to make the strange 'familiar' and the familiar strange. In doing so, we retain ideals of depth, context and induction, but we operate these ideals across landscapes of time and space that have hugely expanded both physically and intellectually, rendering anthropology more, not less, important in coming years.

References

Augé, M. 1995. *Non-places: Introduction to an Anthropology of Super-modernity*. London: Verso.
Coleman, S. and P. Collins. 2006. 'Being … Where? Performing Fields on Shifting Grounds', in S. Coleman and P. Collins (eds), *Locating the Field: Space, Place and Context in Anthropology*. Oxford: Berg, pp. 1–22.
Eriksen, T. 2003. *Globalisation: Studies in Anthropology*. London: Pluto Press.

Fabian, J. 1983. *Time and the Other: How Anthropology Makes its Object.* New York: Columbia University Press.

Geertz, C. 1988. *Works and Lives: the Anthropologist as Author.* Cambridge: Polity.

Parkin, D. 2000. 'Templates, Evocations and the Long-term Fieldworker', in P. Dresch, W. James and D. Parkin (eds), *Anthropologists in a Wider World: Essays on Field Research.* Oxford: Berghahn, pp. 91–108.

Robbins, J. 2007. 'Continuity Thinking and the Problem of Christian Culture', *Current Anthropology* 48 (1): 5–38.

Stromberg, P. 1993. *Language and Self-transformation: a Study of the Christian Conversion Narrative.* Cambridge: Cambridge University Press.

Epilogue 2

Prelude to a Re-functioned Ethnography

Douglas R. Holmes and George E. Marcus

The challenges for contemporary ethnography are remarkable and compelling, as the contributions to this book attest. Rather than offering a reflection on what these pieces accomplish, we shall focus in these closing remarks on what they anticipate: specifically, what kind of emerging ethnographic practices they prefigure. Indeed, we think each of the contributions in this text, in its fashion is gesturing towards what we have termed a 're-functioning of ethnography'

Jon Mitchell in his introductory chapter (echoing Marcus) acknowledges 'provisionality' in the state of play of contemporary ethnographic practices reverberating in one way or another through each of the chapters to this volume. We think this provisionality is symptomatic of a deeper shift in the nature of ethnographic authority. Both implicitly and explicitly, the authors express an anxiety and uncertainty about the means by which we convey or impart an intellectual authority to our ethnographic practices. Rather than addressing these reflexive preoccupations in the abstract we have chosen to engage them through a brief research scenario in which we re-function the way we pose an ethnographic question and the way we conceptualise an ethnographic project.

The Experiment

We have chosen to develop the first part of this very foreshortened methodological discussion in relation to the anthropology of Europe, primarily because the issues we are concerned with are revealed most acutely in relationship to the institutional trajectories of liberal projects of globalisation, notably those evoked by advanced European integration. Broadly, the re-functioning of ethnography correlates with the emerging cultural ethos of supranationalism and the eclipsing of the intellectual priorities of the Westphalian nation state. We sketch out schematically how contemporary transformations in political economy create reflexive subjects who enliven the conceptual space of what we have termed the 'para-ethnographic.' We are specifically interested in those forces recasting the ideas and sensibilities that can (and cannot) be mediated ethnographically; and, hence, we are preoccupied with the redrawing of the boundaries of what is knowable and unknowable ethnographically. We arrived at the threshold of a re-functioned ethnography by working through unusual challenges operating within a series of ethnographic studies and scenarios and through this labour we have been working out the full implications of multi-sited ethnography (Greverus et al. 2003).

In this piece we start from the standpoint of a particular challenge: the predicament of doing fieldwork within an experiment, a manifold historical experiment that encompasses just about every aspect of our lives together. One shift underwrites the emergence of this experimental ethos. Put simply, under the conditions encompassed by European integration and the liberal dynamics of globalisation more generally, culture is no longer merely or solely contingent on convention, tradition and the past; rather, it has assumed a future-oriented purview and trajectory. We, as anthropologists, are implicated fully in this emerging scene of fieldwork and we are compelled to align our research around its experimental dynamics. This realignment is well under way, notably in the efforts to draw on the intellectual acumen of the social studies of science and technology and the sociology of knowledge more generally, and recasting them to address those communities of practice creating and managing the institutional dynamics of globalisation. Thus, an experimental ethos has come, as it were, to be built into the structure of the contemporary, establishing the premise of and priorities for a re-functioned ethnography.

The experimental ethos of the EU demands of its citizens that they participate in a series of shared endeavours. In the broadest sense (on the macro-level), they are compelled to negotiate continually the nature of affinity and difference as they participate in the continual and unrelenting creation of a vast multiracial and multicultural polity. They are further obliged to narrate this creative undertaking and thereby fashion for themselves a European consciousness. The challenge for the ethnography of Europe is, in the first instance, to candidly acknowledge that emerging configurations of consciousness and practice are inherently ambiguous and, at times, vexatious issues, not just for us as observers but also for our subjects (Holmes 2009).

'Post-modern' Technocrats

On a warm evening in 2006 we (Doug was present in person and George was present in spirit) were sitting on a bench in San Jose, California, talking with Andre Gingrich while a Christmas display was being erected across from the convention hotels. Doug was commenting on a paper by Cristina Grasseni that examined the consequences of EU directives for the lives of herders in the alpine redoubts of Lombardy. Specifically, Grasseni's account examined how the introduction of EU regulations disrupt traditional social practices in an alpine community, creating what the outside observer and the people themselves characterise as 'havoc'. This is, of course, a very common, if not paradigmatic, theme in the current anthropology of Europe. Yet what was curious about the analysis was how this chaotic condition seemed to be instrumental in so far as it established the terms by which the people themselves mediate the processes of Europeanisation. Their responses to the disruptions introduced by the EU regulatory regime became the means by which these alpine communities of practice assimilated over time the sentiments and expectations that constitute the basis of a European identity and European values (Borneman and Fowler 1997; Grasseni 2003; 2006).

We discussed how the formulation of and compliance with EU laws and directives differ in important ways from the administrative practices of state bureaucracies. In the classical bureaucratic tradition, laws were propagated in national capitals and transmitted to various administrative levels and jurisdictions of the state, where they were enforced (more or less) uniformly and (more or less) to the letter. Often various categories of officialdom were physically present in local settings to oversee and ensure accountability with these legal standards and administrative provisions.[1] In contrast, the EU interventions are perhaps more ambitious, aimed at recasting incentives and accountabilities across various social, economic, environmental, political, cultural and educational spheres and not merely compelling conformity to particular rules and regulations.

Then Andre made an intriguing aside. He noted that one of a group of EU officials that he worked with had confided that he and his colleagues were 'post-modernists'. This wry assertion foregrounded a well-known aspect of EU governmentality; it regime of 'discipline and punishment'. We know that Jean Monnet (1978) sought to establish a federal architecture for the European project, underwritten by a progressive ethos. Within one of the most 'conservative' bastions of modern social life – bureaucracy – he sought to fashion distinctive, forward-looking institutional exigencies by drawing on and adapting the French 'social modernist' tradition of planning and development (Rabinow 1999). The question that occurred to us on the bench in San Jose centred on the consequences of displacing Monnet's innovations out of the circumscribed domains of technocracy. What happens when this experimental ethos is imparted to the public at large and assimilated within enormously diverse communities of practice across Europe?

Narrowly, what makes these technocratic interventions 'postmodern' is that the 'chaos' incited by these directives is assumed to be resolved over time by the citizens themselves as they are recruited to perform the labour of integration. People, rather than being compelled or coerced to follow new sets of rules and regulations, will instead embrace the incentives and disincentives inherent in these directives, adapting them to countless situations and contexts. EU citizens in innumerable settings will thus accomplish the social and cultural labour of integration themselves, and, over the medium term, the chaos, as Grasseni pointed out, is mastered in relationship to local practices and a European consciousness of sorts is ingrained in the lives of these citizens through a gradual and almost imperceptible process (Ferguson 1990; Rose 1996; 1999; Ferguson and Gupta 2002).

This basic story recapitulates contemporary 'tales from the field' told about countless upland locales and metropolitan districts stretching from the highland and islands of Scotland to the urban and suburban neighbourhoods of Vilnius. What these stories have in common is that they represent and reiterate the problem of doing fieldwork within a vast, open-ended experiment in which the design is obscure and the goal is uncertain. Experimentation here is not about a formal testing of a particular proposition or hypothesis; rather it is about the continuous evolution of a set of social practices and the critical labour by which Europeans bring to bear new insights and knowledge to modify and refine the assumptions that inform these practices (Beck 2004; Welz and Andilios 2004; Welz 2006).

A re-functioned ethnography addresses the predicament of doing fieldwork within an experiment in which we are all both participants and observers. In a profound way, however, the current European experiment was designed to undo or to resolve a prior experiment put into motion in 1919. This earlier episode of experimentation established, among other things, a calculus of cultural affinity and difference that informed the deepest assumptions guiding ethnographic enquiry in Europe and elsewhere. The current dilemma for anthropologists revolves around untethering our methods from the urgencies of this prior experimental era.

Through the Looking Glass

Woodrow Wilson's ill-fated interventions in the aftermath of the First World War and in the wake of the collapse of the Romanov, Turkish and Habsburg empires sanctioned a volatile era of cultural innovation. By inscribing in the Versailles Treaty the right of 'self-determination' and conferring this right on loosely constituted collectivities – nations, peoples and minorities – radical experiments with culture and particularly with cultural identities were set in motion. The Treaty legitimised various collective ideals – enshrined in fraught historical claims of loss and injury – inspiring communal aspirations and political activisms that were played out across new and contested borderlands (Cowan 2003a; 2003b; 2006; 2007a; 2007b).

The Wilsonian formula – particularly V–VI and IX–XIV of his fourteen points – was crafted from an admixture of illiberal ideas drawn from the Romantic tradition to define human collective identities with liberal ideas of democratic self-determination to establish legally enforceable rights and protections. The result was a tragic reification of 'culture' and 'history' by which peoples and nations could be constituted or reconstituted in relationship to what were believed to be fundamental affinities and irreconcilable differences. As Michael Herzfeld has argued, through much of the twentieth century ethnography was practised through the historical lens that aligned or misaligned our analytical categories with this very particular intellectual history, a history he traces back to heart of the humanist and Romantic traditions (Herzfeld 1987; Holmes 2000).

The violent enthusiasms spawned by the Versailles agreements – legitimising political collectivities by means of volatile narratives of history, tradition, and the past – contributed to the most horrific episodes in the history of twentieth-century

Europe. This earlier era of experimentation is, however, linked inextricably to the current situation in so far as the project of European integration has sought explicitly and implicitly to extinguish or otherwise circumvent this legacy. Much like the Treaty of Versailles, the European treaties impel an equally radical era of experimentation: the trajectory of these experiments is, however, reversed.

As a young man, Jean Monnet served as Chief of Staff to the General Secretary of the League of Nations, a position that provided a critical perspective on this ill-fated project of supranationalism (Monnet 1978). Given this experience, it is hardly a surprise that he and the other architects of the European Union would embrace an institutional stance that was progressive and forward-looking, embracing strategies of cultural mediation and political reform aimed at escaping history (Judt 2005).

The 'escape from history' agenda sought, as we know, to circumvent the traditional antagonisms between and among the nation states of Europe, notably those between France and Germany, and substituted, ideally, a pragmatic institutional practice in the service of a particular expression of liberal governmentality. The history of the EU has, of course, been punctuated by numerous episodes when these old antagonisms reasserted themselves; however, by the adoption of the Maastricht Treaty in the early 1990s the main goal of this agenda had been accomplished. Germany was fully integrated in Europe and this was achieved by means of pragmatic experimentation informed by liberal principles of political reform and economic restructuring. The institutional hold of a blighted history was renounced, and a pragmatic and progressive narrative was embraced. Under this regime, the EU imparts to its citizens the challenge and the burden to negotiate continually the cognitive meanings and political exigencies of a pluralist Europe. The dilemmas this poses for the people of Europe in their daily lives as well as for the ethnographers who seek to study them, are unexpected and daunting (Bowen 2007; Holmes 2009).

Re-functioning

At the outset of the twenty-first century, countless experiments regarding the nature of society and culture are unfolding across Europe, almost all of them in some way related to European integration, though not necessarily the outcome of any EU policy initiative per se. Experimentation here is about the evolution of innovative social practices as well as the critical labour by which Europeans refine the assumptions that inform these practices. Under the sway of an economic liberalism that is both comprehensive and progressive – in the temporal sense – the individual must engage in a self-conscious intellectual task of narrating the contemporary, a continuous delineation of the contemporary by which we all become 'ethnographers unto ourselves'. They and we are preoccupied with the nature of thought and action, the practical and the ethical contingencies that mediate our sentiments, our expectations and our lives together. These are the circumstances that have inspired and enliven the intellectual space of the para-ethnographic and have introduced on to the scene of fieldwork an unruly reflexive subject, a figure that both challenges the authority of our expertise and radically broadens the scope of our *métier*.

The appearance of the figure of the para-ethnographer poses questions for anthropologists that are both destabilising and flattering. How do we pursue our enquiry when our 'subjects' are themselves engaged in intellectual labours that resemble, approximate or are entirely indistinguishable from our own engagements as ethnographers (Hannerz 2004)? What is our role when our subjects are continually questioning the nature of information, the creation of social facts and the framing of cultural knowledge? How has what is essentially an 'ethnographic consciousness' come to shape key intellectual practices of our time?

We have argued that, as our analytical strategies, strategies that have been refined within the discipline of anthropology over the last century or so, gain currency as key intellectual modalities of our time, extremely productive challenges are posed for anthropological ethnography. In the first instance, we have proposed that we must treat these individuals as 'epistemic partners' with whom we collaborate in the production of anthropological knowledge (Knorr-Cetina 1999; Boyer 2005). Our analytical interests and theirs can be pursued simultaneously and we can share insights with them, whether they are software engineers, alpine guides or central bankers, and thus develop a common analytical exchange. We can pursue this kind of alliance even if the ultimate aims of our analyses are different, if not opposed (Holmes and Marcus 2006; 2009; Holmes et al. 2006).

Our relationship with these epistemic partners is the creative nexus of collaboration within the scene of ethnography. We believe that there are vast creative phenomena unfolding just about everywhere you look, and we can engage them by means of this kind of intellectual relationship manifested in ongoing exchanges between ethnographers and para-ethnographers. We close with a very brief, again schematic, example of how we might pose an ethnographic question in a manner that elicits the full creative potential of these exchanges.

Posing the Ethnographic Question

We are alluding here to a collaborative project under the direction of Marc Abélès that is at the moment in the planning phases. Hence our thoughts on this project are still notional and tentative. The project that Abélès is designing seeks to investigate the World Trade Organisation (WTO) ethnographically. We proposed framing our contribution to the project around an idea that would immediately cast the enquiry in terms that are recognisable and compelling to the senior personnel of the WTO. It needed to be an idea, a hook, that in one way or another is alive in their imagination but may be largely implicit and/or unmarked; it had to address the most fundamental aspects of WTO institutional practice while, at the same time, establishing an intellectual purview that exceeds its organisational remit. In other words, we had to create a vehicle for linking our ethnographic questions to their para-ethnographic preoccupations, thus creating a discourse that can be sustained in multiple sites and multiple intellectual contexts.

What we came up with was a statement that conceptualised the WTO's activities as, again, an 'experiment': an experiment in which the economic theory of 'comparative advantage' is being mobilised as the architecture of globalization, serving as the theoretical foundation for comprehensive programmes of liberal reform and restructuring. This locates the current era of market liberalisation within a very specific intellectual tradition and institutional history, which begins with the writings of David Ricardo in the early nineteenth century and is endowed with a global institutional expression by the work of J. M. Keynes and Harry D. White in the mid-twentieth century as the General Agreement on Tariffs and Trade (GATT), the organisational predecessor of the WTO. By exploring this intellectual tradition, we begin to give the notoriously slippery concept of globalisation a very particular ethnographic status.

Comparative advantage thus gestures to specific communities of interlocutors with whom we can investigate the economic principles and intrigues of our time. Within the WTO's culture of expertise, we can engage those technocrats and diplomats who in their daily practices negotiate trade agreements and adjudicate trade disputes. We can glean their critical insights and reflexive narratives about a global regime that they participate in creating and in regulating. There are also cadres of journalists, academics, politicians, policymakers, business people, bankers, lawyers (lots of lawyers), union leaders and representatives of the public at large who create diverse narratives that can both establish critical perspectives and deepen our understanding of the dynamics of the contemporary trade regime.

We then proposed a shift in the analysis, as we suggested in the earlier example, by moving beyond the boundaries of a technocratic milieu and intellectual preoccupations of a particular culture of expertise. We achieve this by restating the question temporally in terms that are consistent with Ricardo's original formulation and congruent with the manner in which Keynes and White instituted them, endowing the question with a progressive trajectory and putting the question, as it were, in motion.

We could ask how comparative advantage gains expression as a continuous unfolding skein of ideas, sensibilities and social practices by which the cultural architecture of globalisation is manifested as moral framework, analytical construct and empirical facts. We thereby open the enquiry to countless interconnected settings, ranging from factories in northern Germany or southern China, forests of Indonesia or Brazil, to middle-class neighbourhoods in São Paulo or Mumbai, gesturing to other communities of interlocutors and anticipating the intellectual labour of para-ethnographers.

Indeed, the design of the project presupposes collaborations with these actors, who are translating the logics of comparative advantage into elite idioms and subaltern argots that exceed mere 'economic' formulas and that are, perhaps, unintelligible from the offices of the WTO in Geneva. These figures, our potential epistemic partners, are experimenting with the cultural exigencies that can underwrite modalities of ethnographic thinking that are forward-looking, informed by sensibilities that we don't, as yet, fully grasp.

What we have suggested in these very brief remarks is that it behoves us to align our research with these epistemic figures, these para-ethnographers, and draw on their intellectual proficiency, not just to inform, but also to frame our enquiry analytically.

We think they can guide us in how to re-function ethnography around the key intellectual ideas and sensibilities of our time.

Notes

1. EU legislation pertaining, for example, to health and safety or environmental standards continues to follow the earlier bureaucratic model of precise and uniform compliance with regulatory norms.

References

Beck, S. 2004. 'Fryst altruism, varm solidaritet och kall etik. Om en biobank på Cypern', in S. Lundin (ed.), *En ny kropp. Essäer om medicinska visioner och personliga val.* Lund: Nordic Academic Press: 43–76.

Borneman, J. and N. Fowler. 1997. 'Europeanization', *Annual Reviews of Anthropology* 26: 487–514.

Bowen, J.R. 2007. *Why the French Don't Like Headscarves: Islam, the State, and Public Space.* Princeton: Princeton University Press.

Boyer, D. 2005. *Spirit and System: Media, Intellectuals, and the Dialectic in Modern German Culture.* Chicago: University of Chicago Press.

Cowan, J. 2003a. 'Who's Afraid of Violent Language? Honour, Sovereignty and Claims-making in the League of Nations', Special Issue on 'Violence and Language', *Anthropological Theory* 3 (3): 271–91.

———. 2003b. 'The Uncertain Political Limits of Cultural Claims: Minority Rights Politics in Southeast Europe', in R.A. Wilson and J.P. Mitchell (eds), *Human Rights in Global Perspective: Anthropological Studies of Rights, Claims and Entitlements.* Routledge: London: 140–62.

———. 2006. 'Culture and Rights after Culture and Rights', *American Anthropologist* 108 (1): 9–24.

———. 2007a. 'The Success of Failure? Minority Supervision at the League of Nations', in M.-B. Dembour and T. Kelly (eds), *Paths to International Justice.* Cambridge: Cambridge University Press, pp. 29–56.

———. 2007b. 'The Supervised State', *Identities: Global Studies in Culture and Power* 14 (5): 545–78.

Ferguson, J. 1990. *The Anti-politics Machine: 'Development,' Depoliticization, and Bureaucratic Power in Lesotho.* Cambridge: Cambridge University Press.

Ferguson, J. and A. Gupta. 2002. 'Spatializing States: Toward an Ethnography of Neoliberal Governmentality', *American Ethnologist* 29 (4): 981–1002.

Grasseni, C. 2003. *Lo Sguardo della Mano: Patricche della località e antropologia della visone in una comunità montana lombarda.* Bergamo: Sestante.

———. 2006. 'Conservation, Development and Self-commodification: Doing Ethnography in the Italian Alps', Paper presented at the 105th Annual Meeting of the American Anthropological Association, San Jose, CA. November 15–19, 2006.

Greverus, I.-M., S. Macdonald, R. Römhild and G. Welz. 2003. 'Introduction', in 'Shifting Grounds: Experiments in Doing Ethnography' (Special Issue), *Anthropological Journal on European Cultures* 11: 1–8.

Hannerz, U. 2004. *Foreign News: Exploring the World of Foreign Correspondents.* Chicago: University of Chicago Press.

Herzfeld, M. 1987. *Anthropology through the Looking-Glass: Critical Ethnography in the Margins of Europe.* Cambridge: Cambridge University Press.

Holmes, D.R. 2000. *Integral Europe: Fast-capitalism, Multiculturalism, Neofascism.* Princeton: Princeton University Press.

————. 2009. "Experimental Identities (After Maastricht)," in *European* Identity. Peter Katzenstein and Jeffery Checkel (eds.) Cambridge: Cambridge University Press: 52–80.

Holmes, D.R., G.E. Marcus and D. Westbrook. 2006. 'Intellectual Vocations in the City of Gold', *PoLAR: Political and Legal Anthropology Review* 29 (1): 154–79.

Holmes, D.R. and G.E. Marcus. 2006. 'Fast-Capitalism: Paraethnography and the Rise of the Symbolic Analyst', in M. Fisher and G. Downey (eds), *Frontiers of Capital: Ethnographic Perspectives on the New Economy.* Durham: Duke University Press: 33–57.

————. 'Collaboration Today and the Re-Imagination of the Classic Scene of Fieldwork Encounter', *Collaborative Anthropologies* 1: 136–70.

Judt, T. 2005. *Postwar: A History of Europe Since 1945.* New York: Penguin.

Knorr-Cetina, K. 1999. *Epistemic Cultures: How the Sciences Make Knowledge.* Cambridge: Harvard University Press.

Monnet, J. 1978. *Memoirs.* Translated by R. Mayne. New York: Doubleday.

Rabinow, P. 1999. *French Modern: Norms and Forms of the Social Environment.* Chicago: University of Chicago Press.

Rose, N. 1996. *Inventing Our Selves.* Cambridge: Cambridge University Press.

————. 1999. *Powers of Freedom: Reframing Political Thought.* Cambridge: Cambridge University Press.

Welz, G. and N. Andilios. 2004. 'Modern Methods for Producing the Traditional: the Case of Making *Halloumi* Cheese in Cyprus', in P. Lysaght and C. Burckhardt-Seebass (eds), in *Changing Tastes: Food Culture and the Processes of Industrialization.* Basel and Dublin: Schweizerische Gesellschaft für Volkskunde Basel/The Department of Irish Folklore, University College Dublin, pp. 217–30.

Welz, G. 2006. '"Contested Natures": An environmental conflict in Cyprus', in Y. Papadakis, N. Peristianis and G. Welz (eds) *Divided Cyprus: Modernity, History, and an Island in Conflict.* Bloomington: University of Indiana Press.

Index

doctoral projects 10. *See also* graduate
  dissertation research as
  methodological laboratories;
  laboratories for the reinvention of
  anthropological method
Dolgikh, Boris 98
Durkheim, Emile 171

E
Ekpe (society) 123–5, 127, 129–30,
  132n5. *See also* association
Elfimov, Alexei 10, 12, 172–73
emotion 8, 35, 39, 65, 114, 116, 161,
  163–64, 166
empathy 12. See also 12, 37, 99, 109,
  111, 113–14, 161. *See also*
  anthropologist and informant,
  relationship between; friendship
  between anthropologist and
  informant; rapport; trust
Endangered Languages Documentation
  Programme (ELDP) 44
epistemic partners 181–82. *See also*
  informants; para-ethnography
ethical guidelines 10, 57, 61, 80, 86, 88,
  91, 92n1. *See also* code of conduct;
  code of ethics; ethics code
ethics 1, 10, 53, 80–92, 92, 92n1, 92n3,
  92n4, 93n9. *See also* ethnography
  and ethics
  and academic freedom 90, 93n14
  code 86, 88, 92n1. *See also* code of
    conduct; code of ethics; ethical
    guidelines
  codification of 80, 81
  committees 10, 83, 86, 91–92, 93n9,
    170–71
  expertise 87
  of research 10, 12, 84, 91, 92n3, 93n8
  and scientific quality 86
  in the university 82–84, 89–90
ethnographer 2, 4–9, 11–13, 16–25,
  26n9, 44, 46, 48, 52, 64, 66,
  69, 81, 86, 95–99, 101, 103–6,
  113, 117, 132n7, 141–42, 152,

167n20, 169, 171–73, 180–82. *See
  also* anthropological fieldworker;
  anthropologist; ethnographic
  fieldworker
  and anthropologists 100, 104–5
ethnographic
  consciousness 181
  context 2–3, 5, 8–9, 11–13, 30, 36,
    59–60, 63–64, 66, 107–9, 113,
    115–18, 122, 125, 131, 137–38,
    143–44, 172–74, 178, 181
  depth 9, 13, 64, 72–73, 78, 108, 112,
    124–25, 174
  fact 47
  field 1, 5, 7–13, 28, 30–32, 34,
    38–39, 71–72, 139, 141–42, 146,
    149n10, 149n16
    critique of 7
    diary 19
    discontinuity 59, 64–65
    emergence of 111–13
    as an extended site 113
    long-term engagement with 8,
      10–11, 13, 35–36, 103, 108,
      114, 117, 153, 161–62. *See also*
      long-term research; temporal
      continuity
    in motion 173
    multisited 62–63. *See also*
      ethnographic field, translocal
    notes 5–6, 8, 13, 19–20, 39–40,
      47, 105, 169–70
    policy as 57, 61, 65–66
    practices 95, 98–100, 102–6
    revisiting 83. *See also* ethnographic
      field, long-term engagement
      with
    shifting 169, 172
    and time 124, 128, 132n2. *See also*
      time
    translocal 56, 58, 66. *See also*
      ethnographic field, multisited
  fieldwork. *See also* anthropological
    fieldwork
    by appointment 13